de Gruyter Studies in Organization 35

Ryan: Making Capital from Culture

# de Gruyter Studies in Organization

International Management, Organization and Policy Analysis

A new international and interdisciplinary book series from de Gruyter presenting comprehensive research on aspects of international management, organization studies and comparative public policy.
It will cover cross-cultural and cross-national studies of topics such as:
— management; organizations; public policy, and/or their inter-relation
— industry and regulatory policies
— business-government relations
— international organizations
— comparative institutional frameworks.

While each book in the series ideally will have a comparative empirical focus, specific national studies of a general theoretical, substantive or regional interest which relate to the development of cross-cultural and comparative theory will also be encouraged.
The series is designed to stimulate and encourage the exchange of ideas across linguistic, national and cultural traditions of analysis, between academic researchers, practitioners and policy makers, and between disciplinary specialisms.
The volume will present theoretical work, empirical studies, translations and 'state-of-the art' surveys. The *international* aspects of the series will be uppermost: there will be a strong commitment to work which crosses and opens boundaries.

**Editor:**

Prof. Stewart R. Clegg, University of St. Andrews, Dept. of Management, St. Andrews, Scotland, U.K.

**Advisory Board:**

Prof. Nancy J. Adler, McGill University, Dept. of Management, Montreal, Quebec, Canada
Prof. Richard Hall, State University of New York at Albany, Dept. of Sociology, Albany, New York, USA
Prof. Gary Hamilton, University of California, Dept. of Sociology, Davis, California, USA
Prof. Geert Hofstede, University of Limburg, Maastricht, The Netherlands
Prof. Pradip N. Khandwalla, Indian Institute of Management, Vastrapur, Ahmedabad, India
Prof. Surenda Munshi, Sociology Group, Indian Institute of Management, Calcutta, India
Prof. Gordon Redding, University of Hong Kong, Dept. of Management Studies, Hong Kong

Bill Ryan

# Making Capital from Culture

## The Corporate Form of Capitalist Cultural Production

Walter de Gruyter · Berlin · New York 1992

Dr. *Bill Ryan*
Lecturer in Politics and Public Policy, and Sociology at Griffith University,
Brisbane, Australia

⊗ Printed on acid-free paper which falls within the guidelines
of the ANSI to ensure permanence and durability

*Library of Congress Cataloging-in-Publication Data*

> Ryan, Bill, 1946—
>    Making capital from culture : the corporate form of
> capitalist cultural production / Bill Ryan. — (De Gruyter
> studies in organization ; 35)
>    Includes bibliographical references and index.
>    1. Mass media — Social aspects.  2. Mass media —
> Economic aspects.  3. Popular culture.  4. Arts and
> society. 5. Organizational sociology. I. Title. II. Series.
> HM258.R93    1991
> 302.23—dc20                                    91-31582
>                                                      CIP

*Die Deutsche Bibliothek — Cataloging-in-Publication Data*

> **Ryan, Bill:**
> Making capital from culture : the corporate form of
> capitalist cultural production / Bill Ryan. — Berlin ; New
> York : de Gruyter, 1991
>    (De Gruyter studies in organization ; 35 : International
>    management, organization and policy analysis)
>    ISBN 3-11-012548-X
> NE: GT

Typesetting: Knipp Textverarbeitungen, Wetter. — Printing: Gerike GmbH, Berlin. —
Binding: D. Mikolai, Berlin. — Cover Design: Johannes Rother, Berlin. —
Printed in Germany.

68051

To my son Paul.

# Acknowledgements

To the many individuals in the culture industry who contributed to my research: Some of you demanded anonymity and confidentiality, accordingly, the privilege has been extended to all. Thank you for the many hours you gave.

I owe a considerable debt to several colleagues in two of the Universities in Brisbane, Australia: the Department of Anthropology and Sociology at the University of Queensland and more recently at the Division of Commerce and Administration, Griffith University. Most of all, my thanks go to Mike Emmison. John Western and Stewart Clegg deserve special thanks, as do Constance Lever-Tracy, John Forster, Craig Littler, Kathy Turner and Stephen Bell. My thanks also to Nicolaus Garnham of the Polytechnic of Central London, and Graham Murdock of Leichester University. All have helped with various aspects of this project – although I am not certain how many of them would want to admit to it.

# Table of Contents

# List of Figures

# Chapter 1
# Towards a Sociology of Culture: The Corporations of Culture and the Production and Circulation of Cultural Commodities

## 1.1 Introduction

Some of the ideas canvassed in this book are not, in themselves, new. They can be found in the work of other media/cultural theory analysts, in works which in some cases have been around for some time. Here, I stitch them together, and in doing so, find that there is a structural coherence to the culture industry. This may surprise some. To me, the surprise is that this analysis has not been carried out earlier.

The motivations of this book are captured in two papers which have been seminal influences in its development. Nicholas Garnham, in his call for a political economy of culture, argues that:

the development of political economy in the cultural sphere is not a mere matter of theoretical interest but of urgent practical and political priority. So long as Marxist analysis concentrates on the ideological content of the mass media it will be difficult to develop coherent political strategies *for resisting the underlying dynamics of development in the cultural sphere in general which rest firmly and increasingly upon the logic of generalised commodity production* (1979: 145 – emphasis added).

In much the same manner, after reviewing Marxist analysis of the mass media and focusing especially on the post-Althusserian emphasis on semiotic analysis, Murdock and Golding comment that:

Stuart Hall has forcefully argued that the growth of the modern mass media coincides with and is decisively connected with everything that we now understand as characterising 'monopoly capitalism' and that in their latest phase of development the media have penetrated right into the heart of the modern labour and productive process itself. Nevertheless, he argues 'these aspects of the growth and expansion of the media historically have to be left to one side by the exclusive attention given here to media as ideological apparatuses'. We would argue to the contrary that the ways in which the mass media function as 'ideological apparatuses' can only be understood when *they are systematically related to their position as large scale commercial enterprises in a capitalist economic system, and if these relations are examined historically* (1977: 204-205 – emphasis added).

Neither of these authors wish to replace the ideology problematic in the sociology of culture, but argue for the urgent development of a complimentary political economy of culture, which should eventually be connected to text-based analyses and empirical studies of consumption (cf. also Williams 1981, Wolff 1981). I hold a similar view. This book sets out to make a contribution to the political economy of culture, although not to fulfil all the requirements set by Garnham and Murdock. Rather, it is less ambitious, dealing with a narrow but important niche within this approach; namely, the form of organisation under which cultural commodities are produced and circulated by the privately-owned corporations of culture which dominate the present-day culture industry. In short, the focus is *the corporate form of capitalist cultural commodity production*. It examines some of the most important structural conditions confronting these corporations, how production and circulation imperatives impel managers and workers towards specific forms of work organisation. The corporate form is an important object of analysis in itself, but additionally, with knowledge of its constituent conditions, more valid examination of the contents of the cultural commodities thereby produced is possible, hence presumably, their possible range of ideological effects – although I will not canvass these possibilities other than in a few brief remarks in the concluding chapter.

In this book I investigate the corporate form of capitalist cultural commodity production in a sociological way and within that, from a historical, political-economic perspective[1]. Its theoretical and methodological framework is more or less Marxist in that it shares its critical spirit and takes the basic social structures Marx identified as 'capitalist' for granted. Limitations within the theory, however, mean that I am not concerned to canonise Marxist analysis but to develop and extend critical and theoreti-

---

1    This work is sociological first, and Marxist second. I regard the Marxist paradigm as one of several within the broader discipline of sociology, but a most valued one: a critical paradigm, capable of generating powerful hypotheses concerning aspects of capitalist societies and centring sociology on key questions of structure and power (Bottomore 1978). While my approach to Marxism is entirely non-dogmatic, in fact, even instrumental (which makes me suspect that some Marxists will disapprove of aspects of this analysis), in contrast to modern intellectual trends predicated on the impossibility of speaking of a 'real' social world, and the uselessness of Marxism, I retain a 'realist' position (e.g. Keat and Urry 1975) regarding the value of social science and its relation to reality, and a continued belief in the paradigm's scientific and political value.

cal understandings of a particular social formation, by generating historically specific mid-level or institutional ideas and concepts in the hope that
it will lead to more detailed empirical investigation of the corporations of
culture, the culture industry, and the institutionalised sphere of culture
more generally.

## 1.1.1 Foundations of a Political Economy of Culture

Garnham's (1979) contribution establishes the foundations for a political
economy of culture. To begin, he conducts what is to my mind an
even-handed and pointed critique of various strands of Marxist thought,
including writers such as Miliband (1973), who accept an unproblematic
account of the base/superstructure model. Garnham recognises the seminal influence on Marxist cultural studies of the Frankfurt School writers
especially Adorno and Horkheimer (1979), and the decisiveness of their
work on 'the culture industry', but who see the industrialisation of culture
as unproblematic and irresistible and ignore the significance of its economic contradictions. Equally, though Garnham ignores these points,
their notion of ideology is undercut by a disabling elitism, and their work
lacks an appropriate theory of consumption. Notwithstanding, I retain a
considerable respect for their contribution. The more recent Althusserian
turn, as Garnham notes, rejected the economism which had overtaken
much Marxist analysis but made the opposite mistake of assuming the
relative autonomy of the superstructure including its ideological and
political levels. In the important contributions of Stuart Hall (e.g. 1977),
for example, media and other cultural institutions are treated solely as
ideological apparatuses, a form of analysis which Garnham argues must be
preceded with a political economy – precisely the point that Hall rejects.
The last strand Garnham discusses is the writings of Dallas Smythe (e.g.
1977) and his arguments concerning the media commodity as the audience, created to fulfil the needs of advertisers. Garnham's criticisms of his
economism and functionalism are, I believe, correct. What is more, as I
will point out in chapter 3, Smythe's analysis is simply wrong. In contrast
to these approaches, Garnham argues in relation to the media that we
need to:

distinguish between the media as processes of material production (whether
capitalist or not is precisely a question for analysis) on the one hand, and as sites of
ideological struggle on the other and *the relationship between those two levels or
instances* (1979: 133 – emphasis added).

In other words, while accepting the importance of the ideology/reproduction problematic in the sociological study of cultural institutions, Garnham asserts the prior necessity of a political economy of culture on two grounds: first, on historical materialist premises, that the material conditions of production have actual and hence analytical priority; and second, that this applies especially in an era of the pervasive industrialisation of culture.

He then identifies some of the most important issues around which a political economy should gravitate, using terms and problematics drawn from Marx' historical materialism. I doubt that many of the original terms which Garnham preserves such as base/superstructure, material and mental production, and so on, are actually worth keeping. Some reflect 19th century concerns, others historical conditions which have been superseded, others are simply too abstract, undeveloped and unwieldy to be useful. In the light of this, my inclination is to leave these societal concepts behind, and develop a collection of *institutional* concepts.

Overall, Garnham argues for the importance of recognising the extensive industrialisation of the sphere of culture and the historical and sociological significance of the culture industry. In advanced capitalist societies, superstructure and base have collapsed into one another. Processes of 'mental' production have been transformed to a greater or lesser degree into capitalist commodity production. He also correctly emphasises that the *extent* of capitalisation needs empirical investigation: as will be seen in chapter 3 and 4, this varies across different sectors of the industry and there are significant differences between the creative and reproduction stages of production. Under these conditions, what is nominally cultural interaction has become simultaneously economic and political; to illustrate the point, Garnham points out how the purchase and consumption of a newspaper locates the consumer at once in relation to the economy, politics and culture. Under these conditions, the logic of capital enters into the production of cultural commodities as part of the overdetermination which shapes their form and contents – although he does not specify how.

Throughout the paper, Garnham raises a number of points which seem worthwhile. He emphasises, for example, the importance of grasping the contradictions underlying the culture industry, arguing that "the contradictory nature of the process is in part intrinsic; i.e. the conflict between capital and labour" (1979: 140). Some are extrinsic, relating to the relationship between developing capitalist production and the non-capitalist regions of the social formation, and that there are various barriers to valorisation as a consequence. He argues, for example, that cultural and informational goods have almost limitless use value which makes them classic public goods, making it difficult to attach exchange value to them (1979: 140), thereby introducing problems of realisation. The general point is undeniable but I disagree on the detail of Garnham's argument. Since capital is never realised concretely in its pure form but always in the form of particular industries, its contradictions take forms specific to that industry and it is these which must be the centre of analysis. While the notion of contradiction is fundamental to this book, it is not the pure opposition of capitalist and wage labourer which needs to be examined but the specific contradiction of capitalist and artist. On the other side of the coin, the issue of use-value is indeed crucial to the contradictions of the cultural commodity, but not in terms of its 'limitless' use-value. The undermining of its use value as a cultural object by its exchange value form is what underpins the contradictions of the cultural commodity and many characteristic dynamics of the culture industry.

Other points Garnham raises in considering the industrialisation of culture relate to the importance of analysing the dynamics of the culture industry as functioning capital; how, for example, concentration and centralisation within the culture industry itself generates new problems of valorisation including a sharpening struggle over the labour process, and heightened competition between capitalists in opening up and dominating new consumer goods and equipment markets. Many of these points are specifically investigated throughout this work.

In summary, Garnham's contribution to a political economy of culture is immensely important. Given difficulties with many of the concepts bequeathed to the Marxist tradition, however, I have doubts about approaching the issue from a theoretical perspective. Their level of abstraction provides a barrier to moving analytically from a societal to an institutional level, in connecting macro structures and logics with empirical agents and activities. This is where the gap seems to exist. The approach I develop here takes Garnham's arguments for granted but attempts to realise them in more institutional kinds of ways, at a lower level of abstraction.

## 1.1.2 Foundations of an Institutional Analysis

At one point, Garnham (1979: 127) makes the comment that "the purpose of a political economy of culture is to elucidate what Marx and Engels meant by 'control of the means of mental production'". Graham Murdock (e.g. 1978, 1982), sometimes with Peter Golding (e.g. Murdock and Golding 1974, 1977, 1979), has also promoted the case for political economy and in doing so has contributed much to institutional and empirical understandings of the control exerted within the corporations of culture.

Murdock's work compliments Garnham's – although is more specifically focused on a sociology of 'communication' (I comment briefly on this under-theorised term in chapter 7) where the mass media are one amongst many types of cultural institutions. Like Garnham, he accepts the ideology problematic as an important part of the overall study of social cultural reproduction which has traditionally occupied the heartland of sociological analysis, and more specifically of stratification theory (Murdock and Golding 1977: 12, 13-14). Hence, in his important late-1970s paper with Peter Golding, he works outwards from *The German Ideology* (Marx and Engels 1976) and its well-known arguments concerning the class with control of the means of mental production, noting how this passage gives rise to three propositions; that ownership of the systems for production and distribution of social knowledge has been taken over by capitalists; that this allows them to regulate the contents of the objects produced by their firms; and third, that ideological domination plays a key role in maintaining class inequalities.

Each of these propositions in turn raises a series of key questions for empirical investigation: questions about the relations between communications entrepreneurs and the capitalist class, about the relations between ownership and control within the communications industries, about the processes through which the dominant ideology is translated into cultural commodities; and about the dynamics of reception and the extent to which members of subordinate groups adopt the dominant ideas as their own (1977: 15).

While not accepting all of this, for example, the notion of a 'dominant ideology' (cf. Abercrombie *et al.* 1980), Murdock's work indicates useful directions forward, in particular, how "an adequate analysis of cultural production needs to examine not only the class base of control, but also the general economic context within which this control is exercised" (1977: 16). In 'Capitalism, Communication and Class Relations', Murdock and Golding, like Garnham, critique various types of Marxist thinking on the subject (Adorno and Horkheimer, Williams and Hall, and Smythe), and emphasise the priority of examining the political-economic conditions of cultural production. They argue that this should entail working out "the complex connections *between* economics and intellectual production, between base and superstructure" (1977: 19), not in a reductionist way, but within the limits of economic determinism, showing the impact of economic on cultural relations. The real value of their work lies in their movement from the theoretical to the institutional level. In this paper, for example, they sketch out the shift from concentration to conglomeration

(1977: 23-28), looking at the present stage of the culture industry and the dominance of transnational, vertically and horizontally integrated and predominantly Anglo-American corporations. They turn to the issue of ownership and control in this context, concluding that because of cross-directorships, "control over the key processes of resource allocation is still significantly tied to ownership, but that the owning group continues to constitute an identifiable capitalist class with recognisable interests in common" (1977: 33), a point which Murdock elaborates further in a later paper (1982).

The question then becomes one of examining the mediation of cultural production by these structures. They critique simplistic deterministic accounts such as those of Miliband, and suggest that even Althusserian versions, for all their theoretical sophistication, tend to fall into the same trap by representing the mass media as ideological state apparatuses whose function is to act as the ideological partners to the repressive apparatuses of the state (1977: 33). They also reject approaches which examine critically the output of the mass media and infer back to the avowed intentions and deliberations of the producers. As they point out, the weakness of this work lies in the fact that "it is quite divorced from any investigation of the *actual institutional imperatives, organisational routines and working exigencies*" (1977: 34 – emphasis added) in which texts are created. The question, however, is what to investigate? They propose two levels for analysis: one, normative, which links the content of a culture to particular occupational practices; the second, a focus on the conditions *"linking work situation and market situation"* (1977: 35 – emphasis added); for example, how the need of the commercial media to maximise audiences drives them towards "concentrating on the familiar and formula which are as similar as possible to the tried and tested" (1977: 39). These are useful suggestions. Murdock's contribution to the development of a political economy of culture is a prescription for detailed empirical investigation of the institutional context in which cultural commodity production is carried out, for analysis which reflects its simultaneously economic, political and cultural complexities. In a nutshell, that is the focus of this book.

Accordingly, a sociology of culture must set out to reveal the mode of cultural interaction, the structures and principles, the embedded relations and mechanisms, through which situated agents produce and exchange cultural objects[2]. This requires an institutional analysis of the culture

---

2 Despite Murdock and Golding's arguments, I am not at all certain that this means beginning with class analysis, which seems to be their preferred approach. While I accept the importance of understanding cultural production in

industry; in Giddens' (1984: 375) terms, a form of social analysis "which places in suspension the skills and awareness of actors, treating institutions as chronically reproduced rules and resources". It should discard the common Marxist tendency to presume determinant conditions at a high level of abstraction, yet neither should it be 'empiricistic', based on naturalistic methodologies. It should be empirical, certainly, but from data, searching out the specific structures and mechanisms which generate them; as Marx did in *Capital* (Sayer 1984, also Keat and Urry 1975). This must entail an analytical focus on institutional form: elucidating the distinctive characteristics of a particular form of organisation, its constituent objects, and their logics, their rules of combination. The result will be an account of the historical and structural conditions under which situated agents can act, the possibilities which are available to them as they construct their individual and collective projects (Giddens 1984, also Wolff 1982). Such an analysis must be detailed and take complexity for granted. It should painstakingly build models which link macro-historical structures with particular practices in particular types of organisations such as advertising, journalism, creative production, promotion, and so on. This prescription corresponds to arguments presented by Williams:

A *sociology* of culture must concern itself with institutions and formations of cultural production...But then a sociology of *culture* must also concern itself with the social relations of its specific means of production...A sociology of culture must further and most obviously concern itself with specific artistic forms...[and] the processes of social and cultural 'reproduction'...Finally, a sociology of culture must concern itself with general and specific problems of cultural organisation (1981: 30-31).

---

the context of class domination and reproduction especially through the operations of ideology, consistent with the present-day thrust in sociology towards non-functionalist forms of analysis (e.g. Giddens 1979, 1984), class and ideology have to be understood as effects; as structured consequences of the operations of institutions – for example, in the way that ideology is an effect of the form of economic relations which constitute capitalism (cf. Mepham 1979, cf. also Hall 1977). There are dangers in starting analysis with, for example, the class positions of entrepreneurs and managers and/or cultural workers and examining how their ideas and values enter into the types and range of commodities produced and their contents – although doing so might certainly be interesting at times such as election campaigns, during periods of intense industrial activity or economic downturn. Instead, it seems more important to analyse the practices in which agents are engaged, the embedded rules of the particular form of social life, and the entire circuit of production and circulation and consumption of cultural commodities, eventually interpreting their effects in terms of class, of the relations of power.

My argument is concerned with the first, second and last of the points raised by Williams. The sociology of culture is still in its formative stages; but for the prevalence of textual analysis in media/cultural studies, and elsewhere, deductive and dogmatic Marxist analysis, it might be more developed than it is. Because of this, in *Culture,* Williams attempts to organise and classify theories, concepts and problematics across the arena – but the openness and incompleteness of this book is both its strength and its weakness. My analysis is more focused. It picks out one region of analysis within the sociology of culture, that of corporate cultural production, and identifies its constituent conditions. Even so, more research is needed to see how different groups of actors use these conditions to achieve their goals, how corporate conditions are intersected by other conditions identified by Williams. To that extent, like *Culture*, this work too, is theoretical housekeeping; but, so to speak, in one room of the house.

## 1.1.3 The Corporate Form of Capitalist Cultural Production

Throughout this book, I focus on the corporate conditions of capitalist cultural commodity production – i.e. the form of cultural production represented by the corporations of culture – and do so by focusing on the institutions and practices through which they produce and circulate cultural commodities, their form of labour organisation, and the kinds of work carried out inside them.

Problems with two terms used throughout this work need to be registered but without debating them substantively: these are the notions of 'culture' and 'art'. Following Williams (cf. 1963: 13-19, 1976a: 32-35, 76-82, 1981: 206-233), in their modern usage, neither has any precise, single meaning; as he comments, "The modern history of the concept of culture is in fact a history of the search for such a concept" (1981: 206). A sociology of culture must search for a meaning which understands the term as "a realised signifying system" (1981: 207). Even this has two possible senses: the first, too broad and inclusive, referencing the fact that all human activity has signifying components; and the second, a more sociological version, which recognises that as modern forms of human life developed, manifestly and specifically signifying practices became separated from others which were primarily economic and political. Over time, their characteristic objects, relations, and mechanisms of realisation, took the form of social institutions; mass communications systems are one example (Williams 1981: 207-212). My use of terms such as 'culture' and 'cultural' throughout this work is based on this second set of meanings.

The term 'art', itself related to the notion of 'culture', has similar problems. To put it too baldly, but in way which serves my practical purposes, institutionalisation of specifically cultural practices went hand in hand with their differentiation and specialisation. The sphere of 'art' as a secular and extraordinary realm of human expression was differentiated from religion, science, engineering, law and accounting, and schooling, especially under the impetus of the Renaissance, the Enlightenment and later, the Romantic movement (Williams 1981: 212-214). In that sense, 'art' is an epochal form of 'cultural' practice. I make the term refer in this analysis to institutions such as music, writing and theatre and the more specialised forms derived from them, including film, recordings, the media, as well as journalism, advertising and marketing. Each shares a complex genesis through the constitution of art, even though some of the most modern forms discussed here – journalism is a good example – seem to exist at considerable distance from more centrally and obviously artistic practices. I use the term 'the artist' in similar fashion, although the closer this analysis comes to the present, its applicability in some fields such as the media and advertising seems forced.

Following Garnham and Murdock, the primary assumption of this work is that in modern capitalist societies, cultural production covers an enormous array of social activities which are wholly or in part specifically signifying in character. Many of these are now organised along capitalist lines. Historically, and especially since the last decades of the 18th century, and in new and expanded ways from the early 20th century, we have seen the consolidation of what Adorno and Horkheimer called the culture industry, where large and powerful systems of cultural commodity production and circulation have been constructed and dominated by large transnational corporations. These I will refer to as the 'corporations of culture'.

Using the figure 'the corporations of culture' creates a problem of boundaries in marking out the unit of analysis. As my argument unfolds, I consider various conditions 'within' these corporations. In reality, they are not definitively enclosed. There are many connections 'outwards'. Some are given by the general conditions of profitability which impact upon all companies, cultural and otherwise; others operate through trading or ownership linkages to major corporations in other spheres of industry; other links reach out into the periphery of the culture industry, in direct and short-term sub-contracting relations with independents and individuals in creative projects, and indirectly through licensing and distribution agreements, and into the amateur sphere which provides an ongoing pool of talent. 'Corporations', therefore, is used in this analysis as an institutional term which has empirical referents only as the complex of corporate offices, subsidiaries and divisions articulated through various transactions, sub-contracts and engagements to other sectors of the economy. Furthermore, the 'corporate' form of cultural practice instituted 'inside' the corporations of culture, in some cases, flows over into non-corporate spheres, variously and in different ways and with different effects. Nonetheless, I make the simplifying assumption that it is possible to bound the corporations of culture, to speak of work and organisation within them, identify its characteristics, and build a model of the corporations of culture in an *institutional* as opposed to a naturalistic, *organisational* sense, and work out its logic.

The problem of boundaries occurs in another, more crucial sense. In examining the corporate model of capitalist cultural commodity production, this work assumes that the causes of its conditions lie within the objects and relations which constitute the industry. Capitalist cultural production is presumed to be a closed system. While this analysis demonstrates that it is possible to talk meaningfully in these terms, there are also important determinants flowing from outside the industry but which play only minimal part in this analysis. By far the most important are linkages to the broader economy of which the culture industry is itself only a part; Garnham is correct to emphasise this. The conditions which allowed the development, expansion and continuation of the corporations of culture are also tied to macro-economic conditions and the dynamics of modern capitalist economies. The liberal democratic state is another important external influence, especially as a patron of many forms of cultural production such as the provision of funds for cultural organisations such as opera and ballet companies, regional and national orchestras and national broadcasting organisations, all of which influence not only the cultural labour market but just as directly, the cultural forms upon which corporate creative policies are built. As macro-economic manager and regulator of industry generally, the state sets many of the conditions which shape profitability and the conduct of business and the manufacturing and marketing strategies adopted by the corporations of culture. Technology and the capital goods industry are other major influences. Changes in cultural practice can follow technical innovations; the invention of television itself is a good example, as are recent shifts towards computerisation of creative and transcription equipment (some aspects of which are dealt with in chapter 3). So are information technologies, which, in the last decades of the 20th century, are set to transform the public goods sector. Further, some of the most important transnational corporations such as RCA and Philips, are manufacturers of consumer goods and have equipment divisions linked through ownership to manufacturing firms in the capital goods sector generally. Audiences too can generate effects. Taste changes are shaped by many factors and feed back to the corporations through product sales. Part of this flows from the struggle over meaning taking place through consumption, which many textual analysts talk about but few investigate empirically. Other shifts are triggered by changes in the larger society, such as reorganisation of workplaces and consumer markets which fragment and realign groups in new ways, laying the foundations for emergent taste communities. Even more problematic, partly because it cuts into the culture industry (an articulation which is inadequately dealt with in this work), is the issue of aesthetics and its institutionalisation in the academy. Assessments of cultural value by artists, the academy, and audiences, are shaped in part by metaphysical elements of creativity and talent which are sometimes beyond discourse let alone control by the corporations of culture. In this sense, aesthetics represents an external social formation which is real in its effects on corporate cultural production (Williams 1981, Wolff 1983).

Nonetheless, I intend proceeding on the assumption that it is possible to delineate the corporations of culture and discuss their functioning without reference to external conditions. Despite the apparent dangers of this approach, it is possible to identify internal dynamics founded upon what I refer to as 'the contradictions of art and capital'. I have deliberately blinkered this analysis in order to retain a clear focus on these; in that sense, it is most open to criticism for what it does not take into account.

## 1.1.4 The Organisation of Specifically Cultural Production

Throughout this work I adopt a Marxist-type approach to investigation of the corporate organisation of cultural production. While the term 'production' is often used within Marxism in the broad sense of production as opposed to consumption, the process itself involves two circuits, one of commodity production proper, the other, the circulation and exchange of value forms. While analytically separable, in 20th century capitalism and especially with the advent of marketing, they are fundamentally connected, more so than some analysts in this tradition seem to credit. The centrality of marketing is particularly important in understanding the operations of the culture industry. In fact, this analysis suggests that their interrelation partly shapes the corporate form of cultural organisation.

The organisation of corporate capitalist production is given by more than juridical relations of ownership. These are certainly important, but analysis needs to go deeper. There are many variants of capitalist relations in production and their specific relationships between ownership and control, productivity and output, need to be investigated at the detailed level of work and organisation, with the purpose of building abstract models of a particular form of social organisation of labour (Clegg and Dunkerley 1980: 469). Accordingly, I look at the different conditions of cultural practice in both production and circulation, and do so from a labour process perspective. This approach provides insights into the historical structures of power which underlie corporate work and organisation, in contrast to the naturalistic empiricism marking some attempts at a sociology of cultural production (e.g. Moran 1984, Tunstall 1971, cf. the stronger sociological imagination evident in the work of Elliott 1972, 1977, and Gallagher 1982). Having said that, labour process theory, like Marxism in general, is hampered by the heaviness and inflexibility of many of its concepts. Accordingly, like other analysts of the capitalist labour process such as Edwards (1979) and Littler (1982), whilst retaining its basic conceptual framework, I have developed its vocabulary of concepts outwards as necessary.

In this regard, Williams has done useful work in his book, *Culture*. This much under-rated work, a collection of theoretical identifications and classifications, has been a seminal influence on my own analysis and I would like to see more research develop out of it, if only as an appropriate epitaph to Williams' extraordinary contribution to the study of society and culture. While presuming many points he raises in the final chapter (in some ways, the least satisfactory) such as 'culture as a signifying system', 'the sociology of intellectuals', and 'historical changes', I build up a model of the corporate form of production by developing points Williams raises in earlier chapters, especially 'institutions', 'formations', and 'means of production'. Particularly important is his discussion of the changing production relations in which artists have been constituted, shifting from their initial constitution within new social divisions of labour in tribal and community forms of life, to patronage then market relations, as new kinds of society emerged. His discussion of modern forms of labour such as 'artisanal', 'post-artisanal', 'market professional' and 'corporate professional' relations (1981: 44-55) is particularly important, but while I follow the spirit of his analysis, I adopt a narrower focus and create a more specific vocabulary to draw out the features of modern capitalist/artistic relations. The same applies to his discussion of the means of production and the systems of control which are made to envelop artists in modern times (especially 1981: 90-97, 99-118).

In doing so, it seems fundamental to recognise the distinctiveness of the culture industry. This is not simply capitalist production. It is cultural production organised along capitalist lines. It *combines* the structures of capital and art; i.e. the activities subsumed under corporate production are derived in one form or another from art, a separate and specialised arena of society's culture which developed through complex forms of societal organisation, an historically specific institutional framework with constituent structures of objects and their relations. The culture industry is explicable not as purely capitalist but only in its combination with art.

## 1.2 Methodological Considerations

### 1.2.1 The Researcher as Insider

It is impossible to divorce this research project from my biography. Before turning to an academic career, I had spent many years in the periphery and core of the culture industry in New Zealand and Australia during a period when major shifts in organisational conditions were occurring. It included many years in both so-called serious and popular forms of music as both singer and instrumentalist, and several years in live theatre. In the second half of this period I joined the radio industry where, for 15 years, I worked in both state and commercial radio, first in programming and announcing and later in senior management, mostly in large media corporations. There were periods of heavy involvement in marketing and advertising, recording production and concert promotion, and more occasional single-project forays into television production and newspaper journalism. This career gave me an abiding concern with the conditions under which cultural workers are employed, the pressures operating on them, and the directions in which they were being pushed in their work. These are some of the problematics around which this analysis is constructed.

More importantly, in analysing the culture industry, my work experience gave me the status of an 'insider', particularly since my earlier career included periods as both worker and manager. Because I had left the industry some years before taking on this project, I attempted to bracket my own experiences during the course of field work and data analysis, but was intrigued to find I had retained what Giddens refers to as a 'practical consciousness' of industry conditions; as he describes it, "What actors know (believe) about social conditions, including especially the conditions of their own action, but cannot express discursively; no bar of repression, however, protects practical consciousness as is the case with the unconscious" (1984: 375). As such, it became a useful research tool. It helped me interpret the empirical materials I collected in the course of field work; it positioned me as a long-term participant observer, able to draw upon knowledges acquired while located within the community under study (Burgess 1984, Lofland 1971, Madge 1953). On the one hand, my grasp of the usual ways of doing things and the vocabularies and grammars of 'show business', seemed to give me a legitimacy which opened doors to workplaces and encouraged interview subjects to talk freely. It sensitised me to the practical and sometimes discursive knowledges held by subjects of the rules of the corporate cultural game, as revealed in my observations of their work, the informal discussions we held as they were doing it, and the responses they gave to more formal interviews. Most important, it provided me with a detailed background knowledge about the conditions of present-day cultural production upon which I could draw in abstracting its underlying structures.

## 1.2.2 Field Work and Data Sources

The primary empirical sources for this study were derived from a formal programme of field work based on interviews and observations within selected corporations of culture, and published materials collected from various sources.

Field work was built around organisations based in the Australian mainland capital cities of Brisbane, Sydney and Melbourne. Because a range of published academic and industry material was available on the recording, film and publishing industries, and partly because formal field work was restricted to Australia where there are only a few major companies in these arenas, interviews and observations were restricted to the media and marketing/advertising sectors. These were conducted at 3 radio stations, 3 television channels, 2 newspapers companies, 2 advertising agencies, 1 news agency and 1 production house. Media outlets were selected so as to represent each of the three major corporate grouping in Australia (details of each are provided chapter by chapter with each model constructed to demonstrate their operation). In each case, observations and formal and informal interviews were conducted with managers and workers, with questions eliciting accounts of the usual expectations operating on people working in the position. A small number of background interviews were conducted with personnel from publishing and recording companies.

Primary sources also included clippings from industry journals and periodicals and the daily consumer media including press, radio and television. Any project of this type collects an enormous range of news items, interviews and features from such sources, and this one has been no exception. There is a methodological problem here in relation to the culture industry. As later analysis will show, the media play a crucial publicity role in relation to the objects of the culture industry. It has been necessary, therefore, when using such sources, to read through these purposes, wherever possible using only those media conventionally regarded as authoritative, and using only the 'facts' they offered. Also available were several secondary sources, mainly books written by practitioners and insiders (e.g. Chapple and Garofalo 1977; Dessauer 1974). These amass the collective knowledge of particular fields within the culture industry in considerable detail and became a valuable resource in supplementing the primary data gathered during fieldwork.

A number of points are worthy of mention. The culture industry, especially the media, are notorious for being suspicious of academic researchers. Despite gaining easy access to some of these organisations by virtue of my insider status, many respondents, especially media managers, were willing to talk only with written guarantees of confidentiality. Accordingly, from an early stage of field work and to ease the process of negotiating entry, I decided to offer a blanket promise of anonymity to all respondents. As anticipated, this disadvantaged the study little. My concerns from the outset were structural and institutional, such that my analysis was oriented towards the construction of composite structural models, hence not dependent upon naming particular companies or individuals.

Actually, as the form of corporate production took clearer shape in the course of drafting, much of the on-the-ground data disappeared – or rather, was relegated to the role of an ever-present background chorus. Secondary analysis became more important as it developed. A number of data-rich studies of film, recording, publishing and media production were available which provided a useful foundation for my institutional analysis. Allowing these to carry much of the empirical load has the added advantage that others have access to their data in order to evaluate my critique. The fact that most of these studies were derived from empirical fields in the United States, Britain and Western Europe, brought another advantage: with largely Australasian data, this work could have been criticised on the grounds that its findings were not applicable to forms of cultural production on either side of the Atlantic. As it turned out, the similarities were more notable than the differences. My focus from the outset was on the cardinal conditions of corporate cultural commodity production which, barring some regional and national contingencies appearing at the surface, empirical level but not at the institutional level, apply wherever there are corporations of culture. Most of what I argue here is applicable to situations in the United States, Britain, Australia, New Zealand and Canada, and probably – although I am less sure of this because of a shortage of adequate comparative literature – West Germany, Holland, France, Italy, and other nations where capitalist cultural production dominates.

It could be argued that since this book is founded upon historical understandings of changes in forms of cultural production, a history of the culture industry should have comprised one of the chapters. In fact, that was my original intention. An adequate history, however, rather than a simplistic tale which simply indicated key turning points as stages in an apparently linear progression towards increasing capitalisation, would be detailed and complex, pointing up discontinuities as well as continuities, tracing its hesitant beginnings, its variant rhythms, and criss-crossing patterns of development. It would have to elaborate the conditions which enabled, for example, the commercialisation of printing and its rapid advancement with technological development throughout the 15th and 16th centuries; the initial commercialisation of non-guild theatrical and music performances in the 16th and 17th centuries; the advent of speculative partnerships and syndicates from the late 17th-early 18th century, coupled with the rise of the artist-manager and the possibility of professional employment; by the 19th century, the regularisation of production in music and theatre based upon repeated performances and tours/seasons, more specifically in the United States than elsewhere; the concentration of venue ownership and the advent of industrialised transcription technologies in the performing arts in the late-19th century, and so on. Such an account would require more than a single chapter in this book. Instead, I have included brief historical segments at those points where it seems appropriate. The absence, however, has confirmed in my mind the need for a specifically sociological history of the culture industry which conveys something of the long (and complex) revolution it represents (cf. Williams 1965) – and which compliments Hauser's magnificent social history of art (e.g. 1962a, 1962b).

## 1.2.3 Analysis: Theoretical and Methodological Aspects

There are various conceptual and methodological issues associated with the strategies employed in abstracting out the corporate form of cultural production, which warrant discussion. The principles adopted here are an amalgam of a simplified version of Marx' materialist/realist method (Sayer

1979, 1983)[3], the work of Stewart Clegg in the sociology of organisation and Anthony Giddens in the field of social theory.

As already indicated, this study identifies the organisational form through which cultural production is carried out in the capitalist corporations of culture. To analyse organisational form in this context, in effect, is to examine the issue of power and domination as it affects artists employed in the corporate workplace, by identifying the embedded practices which constitute corporate cultural relations in production and through which artists, if they are to be successful, must work. In that regard, this study is heavily influenced by the work of Stewart Clegg (1975; Clegg and Dunkerley 1980). Clegg's general argument is that the study of organisation and hence of domination has to move beyond naturalistic accounts of the surface level of power and the diversity of objects and issues experienced in the everyday workplace, to the structure of domination within which power is or can be exercised. Analysis should search out the rules which link power and domination. In fact, he argues, the three concepts of power, rule and domination provide the key to understanding an organisation's mode of rationality and the structure of relations which constitute it. The essential points of his arguments are summarised in Figure 1.1. From Weberian premises, Clegg argues that individual social actions are motivated by collectively recognised and publicly available social rules which orient individual social actions in rationally structured ways, where the rules themselves are profoundly influenced by the underlying structures of domination. The exercise of power, therefore, is constructed and acted out by individuals as ruled enactment. Individuals or members of an organisational stratum as social beings should be regarded as bearers of the particular rationality associated with an organisation or type of organisation, within which an objective principle is regarded as a concrete object which governs the domination. In particular, economic power in business organisations is embedded, displayed and

---

3    It may also be that Marx' method is founded on a transcendental realism, a
     label which might also apply to this work. Since it has a substantive and not
     methodological focus, I do not wish to contribute to the debate over a realist
     philosophy of science – even though I regard it as particularly interesting –
     preferring instead to adopt a conventional materialist methodology and allow-
     ing the results to stand for themselves. Sayer (e.g. 1979, 1983) has made impor-
     tant contributions on Marx' method (see also Mepham 1979, Nicolaus 1973).
     Bhaskar's work on realism (e.g. 1978, 1979) is particularly important; see also
     Keat and Urry (1975). Andrew Sayer (1984) takes a realist approach to
     method in social science; Erik Olin Wright (e.g. 1985, 1987) explicitly attempts
     to resuscitate a scientific Marxism using realist assumptions but based on a
     more positivist methodology than that used here.

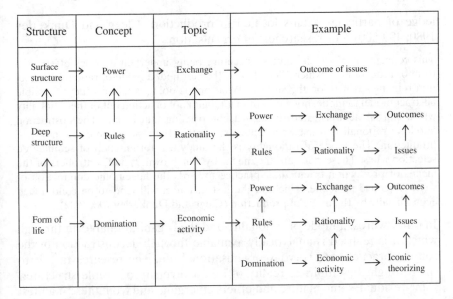

Source: Clegg (1975 : 78)

Figure 1.1  The Structure Of Power In Organisations

articulated through different types of rules which constitute the day-to-day realities of the capitalist labour process and which mediate and enable the range of strategies from which actors may select (Clegg and Dunkerley 1980: 444-456, for an extended discussion of the embeddedness of economic action and social structure see also Granovetter 1985).

Organisations, accordingly, need to be conceptualised as political units of structured selectivity rules organised around issues which are crucial or significant for the modes of rationality through which the organisation operates (Clegg and Dunkerley 1980: 480-481). Moreover, rule combinations are shaped by the one or several hegemonic forms of life which underpin an organisation. Each form of life represents deeply embedded, specific, historical human practices, reproduced through the dominance of unreflected, reified conventions. Combined, they make up a specific, situated mode of production. The theorising power of a hegemonic form of life (expressed through the organisation's 'organic intellectuals', the administrative and managerial strata), reflexively reconstitutes the mode of production of its own practice independently of the conscious knowledge of particular agents located in production (Clegg and Dunkerley 1980: 499-500). For researchers of organisation:

This conception of visible, diverse structure being underlain by rules offers us a form of reductionism which Clegg (1975) [has termed] a mode of rationality...Action remains, as it is, on the surface. What one is doing is to construct a possible abstract model (a mode, not a determinant logic) not of action but of the rationality which can be demonstrated through deconstructing that action. The abstraction 'mode of rationality' is itself conceptualised within the abstraction of the mode of production. The mode of rationality is the analytical formulation of sedimented selection rules. These rules are the means by which owners and controllers of the means of production orient their practice towards the hegemonic domination of some objective principle, which, in the last instance, will tend to be conditioned economically by the mode of production (Clegg and Dunkerley 1980: 502).

In other words, a mode of rationality and the organisational form through which it is realised is analytically available through deconstruction of the routine practices of everyday organisational life. The research task is to sift through the empirical reality of a vast diversity of visible structures, some residual, some mature and others emerging, and from these manifest contents and patterns, work out the inherent conditions which would make them possible. This can be achieved, in Sayer's terms, via critique: beginning with empirical data taken from the phenomenal forms of social life, retroductively formulating an abstract account of the underlying real relations and the mechanisms of their realisation, their institutional orders and their dynamics, and elucidating the underlying forms of life: "postulating mechanisms which should they exist would explain how the phenomena under investigation come to assume the forms in which they are experienced" (Sayer 1983: 40). From this perspective, the focus of enquiry must be the sets of embedded selection rules which constitute a particular form of organisation. This is its enacted environment, its mode of rationality, the constituent elements of which can be identified and modelled.

In this study, I take art and capital to be the forms of life which underpin the corporations of culture, and the art/capital relation as the foundation of the culture industry. I show progressively how its particular forms of expression – for example, in the contradictions of the artist/capitalist relation – generate particular logics which incline development in particular directions (this is the tendential sense in which the notion of necessity is employed throughout this analysis). In their modern, complex, capitalist form, the mechanisms for realising the fundamental relations of artist and capitalist under present-day conditions of capital accumulation appear as corporate conditions of production; in particular, they take the form of the project team and its characteristic structure of relations, formatting as a system of control, the necessity of publicity relations and the associated orientations of professionalism and commercialism, and so on. These provide structural explanations for the apparent multiplicity of stars and styles which comprise the myriad surfaces of the cultural marketplace and the tendency towards formula and cliché which marks so much cultural production.

Not that this analytical approach entails simply making deductions from the fundamental relations underpining the culture industry. Data and concepts are brought together in the gradual delineation of the historical forms through which the industry is constituted. Facts relating to organisations, activities and individuals are analysed by bringing macro-historical, epochal categories to bear. These include those devised by Marx in his critique of capital, and some from within the world of art (art, artist, artistry, creativity, originality) which I use in the same abstract sense as capitalist, wage-labour, use-value, exchange-value, and so on. Throughout the analysis, as the interplay of data and concepts proceeds, I gradually construct a set of historical categories including the project team, producer, director, executants, stars, styles, creatives, formatting, commercialism, professionalism, the publicity complex and so on. These specify the principal characteristics of the corporate form of capitalist cultural commodity production. In doing so, my argument constantly shifts from the empirical level to its structuring principles and back again. Other movements also enter the analysis. On the one hand, it moves progressively from the general, the abstract and the epochal (chapter 2 and 3) to the particular, the historical, the concrete (chapter 4 to 8) – so to speak, from far to near. Simultaneously, it moves laterally from production to circulation (as one would expect from an historical materialist analysis) and back again (which one might not), gradually broadening the field of vision to show how the rules which constitute the creative stage of production are mediated not only by the rules of value production but also by the demands of market realisation. These movements give the analysis an unfolding character. The early chapters construct a series of concepts which are examined initially from a production perspective and later from a circulation perspective. A good example is 'the star', discussed in different contexts as 'the contracted artist', 'leading executant', 'an artist of significant reputation', and 'an artist subject to commercialism'. None of these are equivalent representations of the same object but more like synonyms highlighting different dimensions of a multi-faceted object, each taking the specificity of their meaning from the context in which each is discussed. The shape of the corporate form is progressively delineated in its full complexity: though not as a complete and comprehensive unity, for social life is not that ordered (which is why I avoid offering a consolidated model in the final chapter), but more like a symphony which develops themes through different moods, tempos and instrumentation.

Before moving on, an associated device employed in the analysis should be briefly noted. In constructing a model of the corporate form, I piece together the fundamental structure of relations if which it is comprised, by identifying its constituent positions (my structure of relations provides some specific contents of Clegg's forms of life). As Marx developed his analysis outwards from the core capitalist/wage labourer relation, this analysis does much the same. The corporations of culture, however, cannot be reduced to unmediated figures such as capitalist and worker. Corporate capital is intersected by institutions such as management as distinct from ownership, marketing as distinct from financial and general management, as so on. Most importantly, the worker in the creative stage of production is a particular form of labour: the artist. Rather than focusing on the diverse and highly specialised technical division of labour found in the corporations of culture, I deal with various organisational or occupational strata as given by a common historical function, employment and authority relations (see also Clegg and Dunkerley 1980: 470-475, Crompton and Gubbay 1977: 94), defining each as a specific position in the corporate structure of relations. Hence, for example, within the creative stage of production, the artist (epochal category), when understood as the collective labourer, appears as the project team (historical category), comprising a producer, director, leading and supporting executant, and so on. The project team as an historically specific form of organisational life in the culture industry becomes the leading edge of my ongoing analysis.

To return to conceptual and methodological issues raised by Clegg and Dunkerley's approach to the study of organisation, they note that:

This model of organisation derives from an earlier analysis of language-in-use which treated conversational materials collected in an organisation as the surface manifestation of a deeper underlying mode of rationality (see Clegg 1975). In the context being developed here, the organisation structures can be conceived in terms of the selection rules which can be analytically constructed as an explanation of its social and practice (its surface detail, what it does). These rules, collected together, may be conceived of as a mode of rationality (1980: 504).

In his earlier study, Clegg had investigated the social structures operating in a construction site by prising open the talk between members of different organisational strata and the accounts they gave of their actions, to reveal the conditions which made them possible. In doing so, he was able to reveal the contextual, operative face of power, to demonstrate how relations of power, rule and domination constituted the workplace and relations within and between workers and managers. I have used this approach in this study, although across a wider range of empirical materials. Underlying structures can be inferred retroductively through deconstruction of surface appearances which, if they exist in the form postulated, would explain their form of appearance. Form can be abstracted from empirical materials such as actors talk and actions, accounts of their actions, spatial and cultural aspects of the setting, the iconisised objects which regulate issues within the labour process, and so on.

This approach raises certain methodological issues concerning the validity of using actors themselves to gain insight into the institutional orders within which and through which they work, and the analytical methods to be employed in prising open empirical materials such as actors' accounts.

In the final chapter of Giddens' *The Constitution of Society* (1984), he discusses 'Structuration Theory, Empirical Research and Social Critique' by comparing the demands of structuration theory with examples of already-existing research. His focus is the two polarities of research: the analysis of strategic conduct through hermeneutic elucidation of frames of meaning, and the examination and specification of institutional orders, where, among other points, he challenges the conventional view that the former demands so-called qualitative methodologies and quantitative methodologies for the latter. These claims derive from arguments sustained throughout all his recent works on the nature of society and hence sociology: in particular, his understanding of structure and its duality and the relationship between structure and agency. At one point he quotes from the transcript of a moment of interaction in a courtroom, where a judge, a public defender (PD) and a district attorney (DA) are bargaining over the sentence for a prisoner who has pleaded guilty to a second-degree burglary charge:

*PD*: Your Honour, we request immediate sentencing and waive the probation report.

*Judge*: What's his record?

*PD*: He has a prior drunk and a GTA [grand theft, auto]. Nothing serious. This is just a shoplifting case. He did enter the K-Mart with intent to steal. But really all we have here is petty theft.

*Judge*: What do the people have?

*DA*: Nothing either way.

*Judge*: Any objection to immediate sentencing?

*DA*: No.

*Judge*: How long has he been in?

*PD*: Eighty-three days.

*Judge*: I make this a misdemeanour by PC article 17 and sentence you to ninety days in County Jail, with credit for time served (Giddens 1984: 330).

Giddens makes a series of observations on this exchange which provide a concise account of the method of analysis employed in this study (Clegg 1975: 101-124, makes similar remarks). Because of their relevance here they are worth quoting at length:

Such a situated strip of interaction, like any other, can readily be prised open to indicate how what seems to be a trivial interchange is profoundly implicated in the reproduction of social institutions. Each turn in the talk exchanged between participants is grasped as meaningful by them (and by the reader) only in the tacit invocation of institutional features of the system of criminal justice. These are drawn upon by each speaker, who (rightly) assumes them to be mutual knowledge also held by the others. Note that the content of such mutual knowledge presumes vastly more than just awareness of the tactics of 'proper procedure' in such cases, although that is also involved. Each participant knows a vast amount about what a 'legal system' is, about normative procedures of law, about what prisoners, advocates, judges do, etc. In order to 'bring off' the interaction, the participants make use of their knowledge of the institutional order in which they are involved in such a way as to render their interchange 'meaningful'. However, by invoking the institutional order in this way – and *there is no other way* for participants in interaction to render what they do intelligible and coherent to one another – they thereby contribute to reproducing it. Moreover, it is essential to see that in reproducing it they also reproduce its 'facticity' as a source of structural constraint (upon themselves and upon others). They treat the system of justice as a 'real' order of relationships within which their own interaction is situated and which it expresses. And it is a 'real' (i.e. structurally stable) order of relationships precisely because they and others like them in connected and similar contexts, accept it as such – not necessarily in their discursive consciousness but in the practical consciousness incorporated in what they do...The 'facticity' of structural properties [is] is contained in the duality of structure. The point is a subtle and profound one, linking the very possibility of the mutual intelligibility and coherence of situated interaction to 'facticity' on a broadly based institutional level (1984: 330-331).

Of the points raised by Giddens, two have methodological implications worth highlighting. The first is that notwithstanding the possibility that there may be conditions of action of which they are unaware and consequences of their actions they are unable to control, since actors are bearers of detailed practical and discursive consciousness of the conditions under which they act in their everyday lives, actors themselves – or rather, the contents of their consciousness – are a valid and reliable resource to researchers concerning the institutional orders under investigation. This is particularly so if the researcher has acquired an insider's understanding of the terms through which those knowledges are sustained; if the researcher is able to share, in other words, in the mutual knowledges and collectively recognised and available social rules which link them and through which they act. The second major point is that the objective outcomes (discourse, objects) of relations between situated actors, contain within them mediated traces of the rules which constitute the positions in the first place. As Giddens has demonstrated, these surface phenomena can be unpacked to reveal the facticity of their underlying structures and the mechanisms through which they are realised; that is, the form and content of the rules which instantiate the institutional orders – or in Clegg's terms, the forms of life and modes of rationality – in which situated actors are embedded and through which they must act. For these reasons, the conventional practices and issues which arise in the corporations of culture became the empirical focus of this study, from which I have abstracted their underlying groups of structural principles which are crucial for the modes of rationality through which the organisation operates.

The study had begun from the recognition that the corporations of culture were capitalist organisations geared to profit via the production of cultural commodities but that they were underpined by two distinct modes of rationality – one art and the other capital – and that one contradicted the other. This meant that fundamentally, the sets of selective rules underlying organisations in the sphere of commercial culture would be related to those associated with the capitalist labour process. Two fundamental issues for the culture industry became, from the outset, the principle themes of the study. The first was that the production process inside these major business units is separated into a creative stage and a reproduction and distribution stage and that the former, as a workplace, is organised along lines quite unlike the industrial processes which mark the latter. I knew before the commencement of this project that creation of the original is a highly structured process but not in commonplace ways, because of the unusual characteristics of artistic or creative work and the personality and talents of the individuals employed there: the artist, in other words, represents a valorisation problem in the capitalist labour process. Equally, I was aware that another of the main problems of the culture industry is the truncated product life cycle of cultural commodities: that the work of art represents an enormous problem in achieving the full realisation of value for the corporations of culture. Before beginning the fieldwork, therefore, and with the assistance of ethnographies and studies conducted by writers such as Powdermaker (1950), Moran (e.g. 1982) and Coser et al. (1982), I had already begun formulating the framework of the ideas which are presented in chapter 2 and 3 (although, because the logic of research differs from the logic of presentation, their elaboration had to wait for the deeper understanding of the labour process that came with the final stage of fieldwork).

The first stage of fieldwork began as an exploration intended to gain a feel for the cultural workplace. Almost 40 days were spent in various Brisbane newspapers, radio and television stations, advertising agencies and recording studios, with operational managers and workers, observing as they did their work and discussing the process with them. This stage served to sensitise me to the fundamental issues and objects which constituted their everyday routines and conventions, and the everyday realities of their workplace (given my past, in effect, an opportunity to refresh my insider knowledge of the setting). It was during this period that I first started to develop the notion of the project team as the foundation of the creative stage of production with its constituent strata or positions, based on a specific structure of employment and authority relations and a division of labour. Guided by Clegg's notion as to the salience of organisational issues, I became more conscious of the significance, ubiquity and origins of formatting (under an organisational logo such as a masthead or call sign) as the principle mechanism of bureaucratic control within the labour process, and the complex and contradictory character of commercialism and professionalism as normative orientations binding the members of the team across the demands of production and circulation. These matters became the primary focus of the next, more systematic, wide-ranging stage of the research program: detailed interviews conducted in various types of cultural organisation in the major Australian State capitals.

Since my concern was to track down the specific embedded rule sets which constituted corporate cultural production and the mechanisms through which they were realised, I spoke with actors as bearers of the rationalities which underpined their organisations. These could be trapped by getting individuals to speak of their work routines not as individual artists, managers and impresarios, but of the conventions under which they worked, to theorise about the logics of their occupations, the institutional connections they would have to make and the things that they would have to do if they wanted to be successful in the industry (many questions were phrased along the lines of "What does a person in your position usually have to do...?"). I asked each individual, sometimes singly, sometimes in small groups, to speak of the characteristics of their position or organisational stratum in the labour process, their functions and tasks in commodity production, employment and authority relations, and the responsibilities and expectations associated with it, especially in relation to positions above and below them or prior to or following their position in the labour process. Initially, I attempted to cover all departments and sections across the organisation, but as the parameters of the project team and the limits of my study became clearer, interviews were restricted to actors in key organisational positions in and around the creative stage of production: the management stratum (owners and executive management), the marketing stratum (marketing, promotional and public relations personnel), operational creative management (producers and directors) and performers (leading and supporting executants). The collective industry knowledge thus acquired also allowed me to reinterpret the data provided in other academic accounts of parts of the culture industry (e.g. the studies by Moran), journalistic reports in media of various kinds (ranging from newspaper interviews to industry periodicals), and to grasp the production logics behind the outcomes achieved in the production and circulation of cultural commodities (e.g. the signs of creativity in packaging).

These empirical objects were deconstructed in precisely the matter proposed by both Clegg and Giddens. My concern was to penetrate beyond their surface appearances to the underlying structures which made them possible. As both had demonstrated, this was not as mysterious as it sounded. The political-economic practices which underpin the corporate cultural workplace are embedded in the conventions which make up its day-to-day reality. To a remarkable degree, their outlines were clearly visible in the manifest content of talk, objects, icons, and the surface patterns of the workplace. Moreover, as is clear in the many interview extracts used throughout the analysis, the actors themselves were frequently capable of providing clear theoretical guides to grasping the underlying realities of the form of domination to which they were subject. Not that any one individual would necessarily provide a comprehensive picture: fragments found here and there had to be pieced together to complete the outline of the deep structure which I hoped to find. Most of all, I had to be sensitive to recurrent themes and conceptions, to take them as important signs of rules and their mechanisms of realisation, to gradually fit them together into a structural framework and forms of life which would have to apply for the outcomes to take the form of appearance as experienced.

# 1.3 The Corporate Form of Capitalist Cultural Commodity Production

As a contribution to the political economy of culture, this book examines the organisational and workplace conditions under which the corporations of culture produce and circulate cultural commodities. More specifically, it is an institutional analysis of the structures under which cultural workers engaged throughout the corporate core of the present-day culture industry, create originals intended for reproduction and large-scale manufacture. Each chapter progressively elaborates further dimensions of the corporate form of cultural production. There are three themes running through the analysis:

1. the contradictions of the art/capital relation and their consequences in production and circulation;
2. rationalisation of the production and circulation of cultural commodities as an effect of attempts to confront these contradictions;
3. the corporate conditions of work for various types of artists engaged as cultural workers by the corporations of culture.

Chapter 2 considers the foundations of the culture industry: its constituent relation of art and capital. When combined, these two historically specific structures give rise to sets of contradictions, its two primary manifestations being the contradiction of the artist and capitalist and the contradictions of the cultural commodity. Capitalist relations are partly defined by their distinctive form of labour; the labourer is employed by the capitalist as an anonymous production factor, as labour power. As historically constituted, however, the artist is a named individual with unboundable creativity and talent. As a social object, therefore, artists exist in opposition to capital and present capitalists with major difficulties in incorporating them in the production process as labour power. The cultural object, the original artwork, as constituted through the structures of art, is valued for its originality and uniqueness. Widespread consumption under conditions of commoditisation brings familiarity with its contents, thereby undermining the characteristics which made it attractive to potential consumers in the first place. Successful exchange serves to devalue the market value of the cultural commodity and attenuate its market life. These contradictions are the epochal oppositions constituting the art/capital relation; they are crucial to understanding the shape and dynamics of the culture industry and the particularities of the corporate form of production.

Chapter 3 examines the division of labour which underlies the culture industry. A sectoral framework is created, based on the different types of cultural commodities, private and quasi-private goods (recordings, publications and films respectively), and quasi-public goods (the media), and the manner in which the companies which produce them realise their profits. The public goods sector is particularly interesting since problems in realising the value of their commodities force these firms to generate income via the advertising relation. This takes on considerable importance in later analysis.

Chapters 4 and 5 consider the production of cultural commodities. They examine the immediate consequences in production of the artist/capitalist contradiction and the form around which this relation is realised in the corporations of culture. Marx' model of capitalist production is the point of departure of the analysis. The artist, however, cannot be incorporated as wage-labour in degraded conditions of industrial production via traditional technical and bureaucratic forms of control. The corporate organisation of cultural production takes a specific and complex form.

Chapter 4 examines the organisational characteristics of the corporate form of cultural production, beginning with its division of labour. It is built around a division between the creative stage of production (production of the original) and the reproduction stage (transcription of the original and duplication in commodity form). Artistic work is carried out in the former (from this point on, the creative stage becomes the focus of analysis and reproduction plays no further role). A characteristic structure of positions lies behind the technical division of labour found in the creative stage. In the corporate form, the artist appears historically as the project team, comprising the positions of producer and director (creative management) and leading and supporting executants. Intersecting the project team are the production relations under which members are engaged, the two principal forms being contracted artists (a sub-contracting relation) and professional creatives (an employment relation).

Since artists cannot be reduced to simple labour-power, the creative stage of production in the corporations of culture is unlike industrialised, Fordist production systems, but organised along lines similar to a capitalist workshop. Within this structure, some of the traditional freedoms accorded artists are preserved whereby executants can countermand the organisational power of creative management. The character of creative management too, is unusual. Reflecting their history, creative managers are less authoritarian than other forms of industry management. They are more inclined to negotiate with executants – although as the producer position is incorporated into corporate executive structures and made subject to professional managerialism, the lines and manner of authority are hardening.

Chapter 5, however, suggests a more disciplined workplace than at first seems to be the case. It deals with a specifically corporate form of creative control: formatting. Creative management, as both experienced artists and the agents of capital in production, have acquired the right to imagine. They create a plan for an original based on conventional cultural forms and present it to executants as a set of rules, although leading and supporting executants differ in their degree of subjectivity to the format. Formatting builds a degree of rationality into creation under the corporate system. Other industry-wide forms of control cut across the project team and provide its members with institutional motives for their subjection: creative management, especially producers, are subject to professional managerialism (including commercialism), leading executants (contracted artists) are subject to commercialism, and supporting executants (professional creatives directed by the format) are subject to professionalism. Even so, artists can mobilise these normative orientations to their own advantage; by building reputations built on commercialism and professionalism, they can win back some of the freedoms and autonomies traditionally associated with the status of the artist. Creation in a corporate context represents a complex grid of systems of control and avenues of freedom.

The remainder of the book focuses upon the circulation of cultural commodities and draws out the implications its constituent practices have for the production process as a whole. The market behaviour of cultural commodities is qualitatively different from that of other types of commodities. Because of the contradictions of the cultural commodity, they evidence a truncated product life cycle, even those which become best sellers. Manufacturers, therefore, have to put much work into marketing their products. The institutionalisation of the marketer within the corporate structure of cultural relations signifies another aspect of its historical and structural specificity.

The marketing effort is part of a corporate attempt to make the cultural marketplace more predictable; in that sense it is an expression of the rationality of modern capitalism but applied in the circuit of circulation. This is the focus of chapter 6. The principal strategy is the making of stars and styles, intended to generate a constant flow of best and steady sellers to the market. To attract the attention of potential purchasers, some products are packaged in the signs of creativity which signify the claim of their creator to stardom. Similar processes construct styles by surrounding them in signs of conventionality. If successful, stars and styles come to function as brand names, maintaining a flow of sales and freezing audience tastes into relatively stable categories, against which appropriate creative policies can be constructed.

To create an impact upon release, cultural commodities have to be publicised. In chapter 7 we come across one of the most interesting aspects of the culture industry, the systematic publicity relations which underlie it. Public goods producers, especially the media, use the products of the manufacturing sector in making their own commodities. The effect of this is to give free advertising to the stars/styles which manufacturers are marketing. The publicist displays their features publicly, and promotes them to a superior position in the hierarchy of value which stretches across the cultural marketplace – an objective order which is a necessary condition of exchange. Publicised stars and styles appear to consumers as cultural objects of considerable significance, hence definitely worth purchasing. This symbiosis between the manufacturing sector and the publicity complex in easing the difficulties of circulation is of the utmost importance in understanding the culture industry. Historical advantage has become structural necessity. It gives both sectors their present-day shape and logics, especially the duality of the public goods sector/publicity sector, and has institutionalised the publicist as a further position within the structure of relations which constitute the corporate form of production. However, predictability in the market is short-lived. The continued operations of the public goods sector necessarily upsets the patterns established in the market, creating cycles of fashion which undermine the order of cultural things they have previously put in place and forcing manufacturers to create new ones as their existing stars and styles go into decline. In other words, the playing out of the manufacturer/publicist relation reintroduces irrationalities into the system: where marketing and publicity sought to overcome the contradictions of the cultural commodity, they transform them into a more complex form.

Marketing and publicity have had determinant effects back in the creative stage of production by creating demands for commercial originals. The embedding of marketing and publicity as corporate strategies in circulation and the integration of production and circulation systems for cultural commodities, underpins the form of labour organisation in the corporations of culture, its structure of work, authority relations and systems of control – and its dynamics of change. It is a fundamental condition of the corporate form of cultural commodity production. On the one hand, it is driving creation towards deeper subsumption under the capital relation, yet on the other, creates conditions – not unlike those traditionally associated with artistic work – which major stars, directors, and small independents are able to exploit to their own advantage. The art/capital contradiction remains, but in new and specific forms.

# Chapter 2
# The Contradictions
# of the Art-Capital Relation

## 2.1 Introduction

After her year-long foray into Hollywood, anthropologist Hortense Powdermaker (1950) criticised what she referred to as the corruption of the artists employed there, how the "human properties of the artist, his (sic) sensitivity, his imagination, his ability to create" are destroyed by subjection to the values of commerce, to the demands of the "front-office" (1950: 286). Whilst generally appreciative of Powdermaker's study, Tudor (1974: 46), however, makes the point that:

So much that is written about Hollywood shares this distaste for the commercial strictures placed on the artistic spirit...this is a reflection of the traditional view that art should be free of such constraints: the artist should create in solitary splendour.

The modern epoch has constituted 'art' and 'the artist'[1] as social objects with specific and unique characteristics – this is the traditional view of art Tudor refers to and a set of values which Powdermaker has obviously internalised[2]. As socially constituted, both art and capital are real forms of

---

1    In the following discussion the terms 'art' and the 'artist' are used merely in the descriptive, transhistorical (Sayer 1984) – or rather, epochal – sense to designate institutionalised signifying practices wherein various types of symbolic goods are created and disseminated within a technical division of labour.

2    Despite Wolff's (1982) injunction, I take an aesthetically neutral position throughout this book, regarding aesthetics (broadly defined) and the art academy as objects of sociological analysis. While recognising the reality and hence effectivity of these definitions within the world of art, especially when combined with the structures of capital, I am unhappy about importing an aesthetic or Leavisite critique into historical or sociological analysis. It tends to reify judgements concerning particular artistic objects and accord them something of an eschatological status, resulting in a profound elitism which is oblivious to its own historical specificity, and derogates the output of the culture industry and especially its audiences. Two of the more important writers of this

social existence which clash when combined; this I refer to as 'the art-capital contradiction', an historically-determined opposition which is the subject of this chapter. It is the source of the conflicts and tensions which emerge when culture is transformed into capital, when capitalist companies organise the production and circulation of cultural objects as exchange-values. As such, this contradiction is the motive force which underlies the development and accumulation of private capital invested in the sphere of culture.

The arguments presented in this chapter are the nub of the analysis which follows. These ideas are invoked and developed in different ways as various institutional characteristics of the industry become the focus of attention throughout following chapters. By identifying and analysing the various dimensions of the art-capital contradiction, this chapter uncovers the general conditions, the structural relations and their logics of realisation, underlying all forms of capitalist cultural production. By looking at the form in which art and artists have been historically and structurally constructed and by comparing them to the types of social objects presumed by the capital relation, we can begin to see why and how art is incompatible with the imperatives of accumulation. We come to see that generally – although not always directly, since contradictions are frequently significantly mediated in their realisation by other more contingent conditions – the contradiction of art and capital is played out in various ways. On the one hand, we see it as the contradiction of artist and capitalist in the production process, as conflict within capitalist relations of cultural or signifying production. On the other, its appears as contradictions which lie submerged within the cultural commodity itself and which surface in its circulation. Hence we find that in the production process, capitalists cannot manage artists like they can other categories of worker; the social existence of artists as a form of labour makes them less amenable than other forms to incorporation as abstract labour-power to be employed in the process of valorisation. As far as cultural commodities themselves are concerned, once manufactured and released onto the

---

type include Gombrich (1975) and Leavis (1979). It even enters into the otherwise brilliant work of art historian Arnold Hauser (especially 1982). Within Marxism, this applies also to the Frankfurt school writers such as Adorno (1978a, 1978b), Adorno and Horkheimer (1979) and Marcuse (1972). Swingewood (1977) offers a somewhat simplistic, even prejudiced counter to their approach. Frith (1978), Hall (1981) and Tudor (1974) offer selected comments in line with my own. Hadjinicolaou (1978) and Laing (1978) attempt substantive critiques but both are ultimately inconclusive. Williams (1965, 1981) and Eagleton (1976, 1983) offer useful points albeit from differing positions. Wolff (1982; 1983) probably remains the most important writer on this difficult issue.

market, their circulation pattern differs from that of most other commodities. Each production cycle creates a new product, each of which has a relatively brief market career. These conditions mean that generally, companies face difficulties realising the value of the capital invested in production and that cultural commodities test their ingenuity in achieving the goal of expansion.

## 2.2 Contradiction and the Culture Industry

This analysis relies heavily on Marx' notion of 'contradiction' as both a principle which guides enquiry and as a framework for explanation. Like many of his concepts, contradiction has had a difficult career, especially in so far as it reflects something of the influence of Hegel which, depending on one's point of view, either strengthens or weakens his analysis (e.g. Althusser 1979, Colletti 1977, Nicolaus 1973). As far as this work is concerned, these debates are of little interest in themselves. I simply want to align myself with those who accept that Marx, the materialist, successfully inverted Hegel's otherwise idealist dialectic, that it is important to grasp the reality of contradictions in social life, and the methodological validity of identifying ruptures in the social fabric as an entry point for analysis. To that end, rather than working from some of the more important recent contributions from within Marxism such as Althusser's essay 'Contradiction and Overdetermination' (1979: chapter 3) and Godelier's (1972) 'Structure and Contradiction in *Capital*', I want to draw on selected aspects of Giddens' account of the concept (1979: 131-164, 1981: 230-247). Whatever other difficulties there may be with his work, I agree with his view that the term has been used too liberally, that his exegesis is consistent with the general thrust of Marx' use, and that he achieves his declared aim of clarification (cf. also Keat and Urry 1975: 96-118).

Giddens (1979: 134-135) argues that despite a certain diversity in Marx' use of the notion of contradiction, it is possible to identify two main contexts in which it appears. The first, typified by the often-quoted section of the 'Preface' to *A Contribution to the Critique of Political Economy*, is in relation to the general portrayal of historical materialism as an approach to the explanation of social change. The second context and the more important in relation to this analysis, is one wherein Marx is concerned to examine the specific character of the contradictions of capitalist production. Here is found, according to Giddens (1979: 135-136), over and above the canonical formula of the contradiction of the forces

and relations of production which underlies all societies, those contradictions specific to capitalist societies. From the most fundamental, the
contradiction between private appropriation and socialised production,
emerges also:

1. The relation of capital and wage-labour, as a class relation;
2. The connection between use-value and exchange-value...of commodities;
3. The circumstances involved in the generation of surplus-value, especially as
   involving the tendency of the profit-rate to fall;
4. The nature of the labour-process, as expressed in the alienation of the worker set
   by the side of the wealth created by capitalism (Giddens 1979: 136).

Giddens emphasises, correctly I think, that contradiction is not synony-
mous with conflict, and has to be understood as "the *opposition or
disjunction of structural principles* of systems where those principles
operate *in terms of each other* but at the same time *contravene one
another*" (1979: 141), a point he develops further in his critique of
historical materialism:

I mean by 'contradiction' the existence of two structural principles within a societal
system, whereby each depends upon the other but at the same time negates it...its
implication is that societal totalities are *structured in contradiction*, involving the
fusion and exclusion of opposites. In other words, the operation of one structural
principle in the reproduction of a societal system presumes that of another which
tends to undermine it (1981: 231-232).

Like Godelier and Althusser, Giddens also discriminates between what he
calls primary and secondary contradictions:

By primary contradictions I mean those which can be identified as fundamentally
and inextricably involved in the system reproduction of a society or a type of
society – not on a functional basis, but because they enter into the very structuring
of what that system *is*. By secondary contradictions I mean those which are brought
about through the existence of primary contradictions and which are in some sense
a result of them (1979: 143).

In this manner, capitalism multiplies contradiction upon contradiction,
piling source of conflict upon source of conflict such that new institutional
forms constantly emerge and consolidate, forming layers of higher level
contradictions. This approach, as Giddens points out (1979: 137), allowed
Marx to see the determinate historical and structural connections between
private appropriation and socialised production as the fundamental
conditions giving rise to competition and co-ordination between different
masses and units of capital, the antagonism of private and class interests,

the centralisation of capital, and so on. Similarly, he was able to discern how private exchange necessarily leads, for example, to extension of the system of trade and eventual dependence on world trade, and how fragmented acts of exchange make a system of banks and credit necessary (cf. Marx 1973: 159).

These ideas and the methodology they imply, play a pivotal role in this analysis. The primary contradictions of the art-capital relation have generated a complex system for the production and circulation of value within the culture industry, itself containing many secondary contradictions, each of which sets limits to expansion of capital in the sphere of culture and mediates the path of its development. Accordingly, the contradictions of the art-capital relation are the fundamental conditions constituting the culture industry and give it its internal logic[3]. They are the source of antimonies between artists and capitalists in the production process, complications confronting the realisation of cultural commodities, the dynamism of the industry's growth, and the struggles engaged in by different forms of capital operating within its systems of production and circulation. Some of the secondary contradictions they give rise to are identified and elaborated in later chapters.

## 2.3 The Social Constitution of Art and the Artist and Residues in the Culture Industry

Art and the artist were constituted through a social and then technical division of labour in the cultural sphere, becoming fundamental objects in the new structures of signifying relations being erected within modernising societies in Europe. In order to grasp the oppositions generated when art and capital confront each other in their historical forms of existence, their historically constituted characteristics need to be briefly outlined.

Whilst this work is not concerned with tracing the historical genesis of

---

3  As indicated in chapter 1, for pragmatic reasons associated with space and manageability, this work concentrates on the art/capital contradictions, emphasising its cultural outcomes. A more comprehensive work would also need to investigate the form in which other secondary contradictions appear in this industry as a consequence of the operation of the law of value, such as the tendency towards overproduction, the rising organic composition of capital and the decline in the average rate of profit, and so on, as outlined by Marx.

modern artistic practice[4], in simple terms it can be said that its formation was one of the many causes and effects of the breakup of feudalism and the construction of capitalism throughout what is now understood as the Western world. As the city replaced the court as the site of cultural production, regal and aristocratic patronage gave way first to private patronage and then market relations organised by entrepreneurs, and as the rising middle class became the cultured class, a differentiated and specialised realm of 'art' emerged. It existed tangentially to the society to which it referred and was instituted around relations between a group of expert practitioners (artists) and non-expert, non-participants (audiences), mediated by the exchange of objects (works of art). Equally, under the influence of Renaissance humanism from the 15th century onwards and most crucially that of Romanticism in the 18th and 19th centuries, the cultural practices and institutions which developed positioned 'the artist' at the centre of the world of art, inscribing these individuals as the source of cultural value (e.g. Hauser 1982: 242-307, cf. also Garnham 1987).

Williams notes (1976a: 33) that by the 17th century, the artist was socially recognised as the practitioner of a group of activities presided over by the seven muses: history, poetry, comedy, tragedy, music, dancing and astronomy, which were progressively overlaid by the more specialised sense of painting, drawing, engraving and sculpture. As the new social structures and intellectual movements of Europe consolidated throughout the 18th and 19th centuries, artists acquired a specified social status. Differentiated from artisans, especially in the sense of skilled manual workers, and scientists, with whom they shared intellect but put to different purposes and using different methods[5], they came to occupy a

---

4    Fragments of this can be found in several works. Arnold Hauser's four volume *The Social History of Art* (1962) remains the most important; see also his *The Sociology of Art* (1982). For the social history of music see Raynor's excellent *A Social History of Music* (1972); for theatre, despite being short, Hartnoll (1968) is valuable, especially if supplemented by Hartnoll (1967) and Freedley and Reeves (1968); for literature, see Febvre and Martin (1976), Steinberg (1955) and especially Laurenson and Swingewood (1971), particularly Diana Laurenson's contributions (Pt II), and, of course, Williams (1981).

5    It could be argued that this analysis should define 'cultural' work sufficiently broadly to include scientific workers such as chemists, physicists, and engineers, perhaps even doctors, in the sense that these occupations emerged out of specialisation in the signifying division of labour when intersected by the structures of science (Hobsbawm 1962: 327-348; Rose and Rose 1963: 1-36). The same argument can be applied to accountants, lawyers and educationalists. For pragmatic reasons I have chosen a narrower focus. However, I am intrigued by how many of the points raised in this analysis concerning the corpo-

specialised position in the social division of labour, with a monopoly over the expressive use of signifying skills (Williams 1976a: 34).

This technical differentiation was connected to a unique, instituted form of practice. Troubled by the utilitarian, rationalist, industrial world developing around them and to which, in varying degrees, they existed in opposition, artists demanded the freedom to work according to what was constituted as the unpredictable inspiration of the muse and outside of discipline and expectation. Generally, their adoring 18th and 19th century publics came to concede these conditions. In gaining this social space, artists constructed around themselves a spectacular persona; the creative personality came to be associated with the ideal of artistic genius with its originality and subjectivism (Hauser 1962a: 49). Under the impact of Romanticism, and in contrast to the earlier forms of intellectual activity in earlier periods based on explicable and learnable rules of taste, creativity appeared as:

a mysterious process derived from such unfathomable sources as divine inspiration, blind intuition and incalculable moods...The genius...lives not merely free from the fetters of reason, but in possession of mystic powers which enable him (sic) to dispense with ordinary sense experience. 'The genius has presentiments, that is to say, his feelings outrun his powers of observation. The genius does not observe. He *sees*, he feels' – says Lavater...[The artist now appears as] the guardian of a mysterious wisdom, the 'speaker of unspeakable things' and the law-giver of a world of his own, with laws of his own (Hauser 1962a: 111).

The work of these extraordinary individuals was constituted as 'art'. More than anything, it represented human expression, the product of genius, and hence by definition, original and innovative. Surrounding each work was a new kind of aura (cf. Benjamin 1973: 219-253), an aura of uniqueness which gave art its cultural value, regarded in some sense as significant by virtue of its originality, and authentic as distinct from a copy. The internal properties of each proclaimed its difference and distinction through its unprecedented form and/or content, making it appear as the bearer of an exclusive expressive or aesthetic as opposed to practical truth, from which its audience might derive insight and delight. These properties were taken as signs of the talents of its creator, against whom the object had to stand; a crucial element of its legitimacy stemmed from the imprint it carried of an identifiable artist (Williams 1976a: 72-74, 192-193).

The status of the artist as talented, creative genius, and the work of art

---

rate conditions of artistic practice are applicable in the present day to these professions. It may be that this conceptual and methodological framework might be usefully employed as a starting point in investigating their organisational and workplace conditions.

as unique and original expression, were the essential elements of artistic practice as instituted in the early period of the modern epoch, notions which, to a significant extent, remain embedded in modern cultural practice. Hauser, for example, argues that the whole of modern art is the result of this romantic fight for freedom. The aloneness, the solitary talent of the genius, and the seminal character of artistic inspiration, remains the vital principle of modern art. He declares that:

However enthusiastically the artist of our time acknowledges the authority of schools, groups, movements, and professes faith in his (sic) companions in arms, as soon as he begins to paint, to compose, or to write, he is and feels alone. Modern art is the expression of the lonely human being, of the individual who feels himself to be different...from his fellows. The Revolution and the romantic movement mark the end of a cultural epoch in which the artist appealed to a 'society', to a more or less homogeneous group, to a public whose authority he acknowledged in principle absolutely. Art...becomes an activity of self-expression creating its own standards...the medium through which single individuals speak to single individuals...and their work brings them into a constant state of tension and opposition towards the public (1962a: 144).

This continues in the present, even in the most capitalised regions of the culture industry. According to Becker, for example, in his symbolic interactionist examination of 'art worlds':

Both participants in the creation of art works and members of society generally believe that the making of art requires special talents, gifts or abilities, which few have. Some have more than others, and a very few are gifted enough to merit the honorific title of 'artist'...The myth [of the artist] suggests that in return society receives work of unique character and invaluable quality. Such a belief does not appear in all, or even most, societies: it may be unique to Western European societies, and those influenced by them since the Renaissance (1982: 14-15).

While these realities remain at the core of art, since the constitution of social objects is an ongoing historical process, artistic practice has been overlaid especially throughout the 19th and 20th centuries, with new sets of conditions. As the culture industry emerged and consolidated and expanded within existing conventions of art, it adapted and modified them. Like other forms of capitalist industry, it reconstructed the original artistic division of labour around new technological forms and reconstituted the artist as an enormous variety of specialised occupations ranging from novelists to cartoonists, from chamber musicians to rock groups, from dancers to copywriters, from composers to graphic designers, from actors to radio announcers, and so on, but retained residues of its origins within each. To a greater or lesser extent, cultural workers employed in the creative phase of production[6] are treated by employers, managers, their co-workers and publics – and most of all by themselves – as artists, as talented individuals with rare expressive skills and unconventional personalities. In the course of my fieldwork I heard respondents at all organisational levels and in all cultural forms, time and again, referring to the work of producing originals as 'artistic' or 'creative'. This practical consciousness is strongest in cultural forms based on the performing arts such as theatre, music and dance, and in the general area of literature. In industrialised forms of cultural practice, their artistic content has been overlaid by layers of occupational conventions expressed through professional and technical discourses and peopled by individuals possessing artistic personalities and talents albeit of less spectacular kinds. The most significant index of this genesis is found in the special status of the artist in the production process (to be detailed in chapter 4): the explicit separation and preservation of the creative phase of production from the reproduction phase. This is fundamental to the organisation of cultural commodity production whether in theatre or musical companies, film or recording studios, media companies, advertising or news agencies.

These residues of the romantic constitution of art and artists are still present in the modern era and underpin the art-capital contradiction. This epochal antimony is realised in two primary historical forms, the contradictions of the artist-capitalist relation and the contradictions of the cultural commodity, both of which need to be examined separately.

## 2.4 The Contradictions of the Artist-Capitalist Relation

Unlike many other types of workers, capital is unable to make the artist completely subservient to its drive for accumulation. The reason is simple. Since art is centred upon the expressive, individual artist, artistic objects

---

6   This refers to a distinction made in chapter 4 between the creative and reproduction stages of the production process. Cultural workers create the original which is then reproduced by other workers; some transcribe it onto a master, others make duplicates, the commodities proper. My argument here applies to employees engaged in the creative stage but not to those in the reproduction stage, although as will be seen later, some transcription workers are frequently called upon to demonstrate a creative flair in their work (e.g. lighting and camera operators).

must appear as the product of recognisable persons; the *concrete and named* labour of the artist is always paramount and must be preserved. As socially constituted, artists appear to capital as the antithesis of labour-power, antagonistic to incorporation in the capitalist labour process as *abstract* labour. A brief summary of Marx' discussion of the conditions of wage-labour will help to indicate why.

## 2.4.1 The Capitalist Labour Process: Concrete and Abstract Labour

At various points throughout Volume I of *Capital* (1954: Part III), Marx deals at length with how the capital relation transforms free labourers into a generalised capacity to work – what he refers to as 'labour-power' – and how their employment in the labour process creates and conserves value which is embedded in the commodities they produce in the course of production. The unpaid portion of their labour, the surplus labour value component of the commodity's total value, is realised when the commodity is sold, and returned as the capitalist's profit.

In Marx' analysis, labour-power has two dimensions. When people work, they do two things simultaneously: first, they work at a definite craft or trade, as, say, a carpenter making chairs, a printer producing newspapers, or a potter making dining utensils; and second, they are part of the social labour force which supplies society with the goods it needs for its accustomed standard of living. In other words, as carpenters and potters and printers, workers perform *concrete* labour, a specific kind of work, in the production of particular use-values. As part of the labour force as a whole, their labour is also labour-in-general, socially necessary labour, *abstract* labour, of which a certain quantity is embedded in each commodity in its making (Marx 1954: 56-57).

The amount of abstract labour in a commodity is what establishes its exchange-value. When placed on the market, goods are exchanged according to ratios of their common attribute, the amount of labour socially necessary for production (Marx 1954: 47). The exchange-value of a particular commodity is larger or smaller depending on the magnitude of abstract labour embedded in it; i.e. the total number of units of simple labour-power (where skilled labour-power represents multiple units of simple labour-power), by the time over which they were employed. Abstract and not concrete labour is therefore capitalists' prime concern (1954: 48-53). Competition demands they organise production so that the minimum quantity of abstract labour appears in each individual commodity. The smaller that quantity, the more competitive the commodity seems when compared to others produced within that industry, yet the greater the potential surplus it might realise, the greater the potential profits flowing from sale (1954: 173-204). Accordingly, the capitalist lengthens the working day or intensifies the work process to achieve an absolute or relative increase in the unpaid component of abstract value, surplus value, in each commodity (Marx 1954: Parts III and IV).

Abstract and concrete labour are in contradiction. A greater abstract content in a task presumes reducing its concrete content to average levels. Historically, the usual capitalist strategy is to break up and fragment workers' craft and trades skills, thereby reducing the necessary work to that of a generalised type which can be performed by average workers of few specific skills and in the shortest possible time. Under these circumstances, workers appear in the labour process as a generalised capacity to work at any one of a number of unskilled tasks, as personifications of abstract labour, as anonymous production factors, as labour power. Old skills are incorporated into progressively more productive apparatuses of various types and the labour process reconstituted around a reconstructed technical division of labour. Each stage in the process is gradually converted into simple, repetitive tasks which can be performed by an operator with average levels of intelligence, education and dexterity (or better still, lower than average levels, because labour costs will be less and the potential surplus greater). What is embedded in the manufactured commodities is units of average labour-value, which creates the possibility of realising an ever-greater surplus at the moment of exchange, while returning relatively less to workers in the form of wages. Expressed in its simplest form, this has been the historical tendency of the capitalist labour process organised according to the logic of accumulation[7] (Marx 1954: Part VII, see also Braverman 1974: 45-58, Littler 1982: 20-25). This movement is based on the practical premise that technological substitution of labour generalises the concrete labour content of tasks in the work process. This has been the path of development of many industries especially during the 20th century. The history of the labour process in the culture industry, however, has been quite different.

---

7　The summary provided here deals only with the essential tendencies of the capitalist labour process. Empirically, the process is much more complex. Amongst others, Littler's (1982) contribution to the post-Braverman debate makes this point effectively.

## 2.4.2 The Artist in the Capitalist Labour Process

The key to understanding the artist-capitalist contradiction lies in grasping the fact that as historically and ideologically constituted, the artist represents a special case of concrete labour which is ultimately irreducible to abstract value. This is because the structures of art make artists incompatible with the structures of capital. The employment of artists in whatever technical form necessitates recognising and preserving their named, concrete labour. They cannot be employed as labour-power, as anonymous production factors functioning under the sway of capital. Why is this the case?

Objects which are defined as artistic objects do not, indeed could not, appear as generalised art, as an undifferentiated collection of more-or-less similar paintings, writings or music. As historically constituted, a work of art must always appear as a unique and original object of a particular kind, a particular poem or choreography, a painting, or piece of music or writing, and imprinted with a mark identifying its human creator, so that audiences can recognise it as such. Equally, as constituted, artists are said to possess outstanding gifts for a particular type of art; an exceptional capacity possessed by an individual to write in a particular form, perhaps play a given musical instrument or paint a picture of a certain type. Artistic workers, therefore, cannot be made to appear in the labour process as generalised, undifferentiated artists. Invariably, theirs is a specified kind of work which depends on them bringing distinct capacities and high levels of innate and/or acquired skill to the task, whether as a journalist, poet or author, orchestral, rock or jazz musician, or film, drama or television comedy series actor. They must appear in the commodity production process, in other words, as specialised and singular concrete labour, as a particular type of worker.

More than that, artistic labour demands an even more identifiable specificity. Attributes conventionally ascribed to artists, the innate talents and acquired skills which are the necessary means of artistic production, are defined as personal and idiomatic qualities, as characteristics belonging on to particular human beings. Kiri Te Kanawa, Stanley Kubrick, Mikail Barishnikov, Doris Lessing, John Cleese, Bob Dylan, Alfred Brendel, Anthony Burgess, Laurence Olivier, Jackson Pollock to name a few, as well as the multitude of first and second rank talents working in all areas of cultural production, are regarded as artists precisely because of the identifiable, expressive abilities attributable to and inseparable from each and each alone. Each has a monopoly over the specific talents ascribed by their name. These are inimitable capacities regarded as fundamental means of production which cannot be alienated and instilled in an apparatus or organised out of the creative labour process. Certainly capital may attempt to reorganise the conditions of artistic work by reconstituting some means of production in new technological forms, hence circumscribing artists within a framework of industrial technique, but the act of creation, as socially constituted, is crucially dependent on the exercise of talents which are indivisible from the particular individuals who personify them. This runs counter to the demands of accumulation, the usual path of development of capitalist commodity production and the real subsumption of labour under capital (Marx 1976, see also Campbell 1986, Mandel 1976). Every book must has an author, every score a composer, every film a writer, director and cast of actors[8], unlike cans of peaches, lines of cars and shirts on a shop rack where the direct producers of these commodities are entirely unknown to their purchasers. Artists must be engaged as *named, concrete labour*. This is the core and consequence of the artist-capitalist contradiction when artists are introduced as variable capital into the capitalist cultural commodity production process.

## 2.4.3 The Immediate Consequences in Production of the Artist-Capitalist Contradiction

The characteristics of the artist-capitalist relation leads immediately to several conditions which, seen from the point of view of capitalist firms, complicate the process of production considerably. The first of these is the necessary structural independence accorded the artist within the valorisa-

---

8    As later chapters will show, some forms of cultural production have been extensively capitalised. There, commodities appear under a generic name representing the company (e.g. a newspaper masthead or radio station call sign) which stands for the collective artist. Teamed production (such as film production) is signified by individual names, whether representing particular persons or appearing as a convenient fiction – *auteur* theory seems blind to present-day political economic conditions (see also Becker 1982: 21, Frith 1978:201). Works which appear unsigned or with false human accreditation have difficulty being accepted as works of art. In this sense the debates over computer-composed music, the validation of signatures on paintings, and the confirmation of authorship of plays and poems, are instructive (see, also the Australian case of the anti-modernist Ern Malley hoax, discussed in McQueen 1979: 88-89).

tion[9] process; what I will refer to as *the relative autonomy of artists in the capitalist labour process.*

Whilst approaching cultural production from a different paradigm from that employed here, Becker captures the relative autonomy enjoyed by artists when he notes that conventionally:

We think it important to know who has the gift and who does not because we accord people who have it special rights and privileges. At an extreme, the romantic myth of the artist suggests that people with such gifts cannot be subjected to the constraints imposed on other members of society; we must allow them to violate rules of decorum, propriety, and common sense everyone else must follow or risk being punished. The myth suggests that in return society receives work of unique character and invaluable quality (1982: 14-15).

This immunity from social regulation has particular consequences in production. Art, it is said, can only spring from a social context wherein artists are accorded freedom from discipline and expectation, especially relief from commercial pressures; it is generally considered that they need social space to exercise their individual talents, to let their imaginations run freely in the search for expressive truth. This represents a considerable organisational difficulty for capitalists. As employers, they seek to control the work process, directing artistic workers towards types and rates of work which constantly expand their investment. Artists confront them as an recalcitrant form of labour, a form doubly so, over and above the indeterminacy usually associated with employed labour-power. As constituted, artists necessarily occupy a position of structural independence within the capitalist commodity producing process which places them beyond the organisational disciplines to which waged labour is normally subjected: they are assigned creative licence in the very heart of production itself. This imperative applies even to cultural practices which operate

---

9    The precise meaning of this term seems unclear. Mandel (1978b: 598) defines it
     as "the process whereby capital increases its own value by the production of
     surplus value", that aspect of the production process wherein "labour power
     produces additional value over and above its own value". However, as Harvey
     (1982: 84 fn 7) points out, "While this has the virtue of making a clear distinc-
     tion between processes of realisation in production and processes of realisation
     in the market...it has the disadvantage of diverting attention away from the
     necessary continuity in the flow of capital through the different spheres of pro-
     duction and exchange". He elects to use the term realisation to refer to the
     perpetual motion and self-expansion of capital. Valorisation is used to refer to
     realisation through the labour process. Since I too am concerned to emphasise
     the essential unity between production and circulation in capital's expansion, I
     will follow Harvey's lead.

at the industrial extremities of the signifying division of labour such as radio announcing, as illustrated by a radio station manager who, when interviewed, spoke of the relationship between the organisational rules of creative production (the station format) and the necessary freedom given what he called 'creative personalities'. He expressed the view that:

> You can't employ an announcer who's a creative personality and then put a narrow band of restrictions around them: 'You'll talk two minutes every twenty minutes'. Put super-restrictions around them and that stops the flow of creative juices. What you've got to do is say 'Here are the guidelines that we work within. Should we walk outside of those guidelines then obviously we need to discuss it'. And by feeding them creative ideas and by them expanding their creative thoughts, at times right to the border of those guidelines, there's no denying that brings out the best in them.

Of all cultural workers, stars enjoy the most open employment conditions[10]; successful authors are a case in point. They are generally permitted to prepare their manuscripts outside systematic control by the publishing house. Within certain limits they are free to set the rate and intensity of their work and create according to the demands of their imagination. Generally, contact with the publisher is restricted to occasional consultative meetings (Lane 1980: 59-72, Laurenson and Swingewood 1971: 117-139)[11]. Even artists employed as full-time professionals in the more industrialised forms of production in the corporations of culture enjoy conditions quite unlike those usually associated with modern workplaces. The organisational form tends to be more 'organic', there are few direct organisational controls, and there is an ethos that creative work should be done independently (Elliott 1972: 128-129, Tunstall 1971: 24-42). These conditions differ markedly from the 'mechanical' system of organisation imposed upon the reproduction stage of the production process which is more typical of work organised by capital; it is subject to a technical division of labour, routinisation, and the strictures of management (Elliott 1972: 129-131). The status and character of creative occupations, the capacities ascribed the individuals who people them, the organisational space they are accorded, and the general conditions of their labour – in short, the relative autonomy granted artistic labour in the labour process – originates in the genesis of each form of work and bears residues of their romantic constitution. To capital, the artist represents an organisa-

---

10  I am ignoring amateur and artisanal creative production here (e.g. amateur singers and actors, potters and painters directly supplying a localised market) since by definition they are not involved in capitalist forms of production.

11  For parallels in music see Frith (1978), and Powdermaker (1950) for the movie industry.

tional problem of significant proportions; it is a form of labour structurally incompatible with yet fundamental to the process which creates cultural commodities.

The artist-capitalist contradiction also produces a set of specifically economic consequences in production, which I want to refer to as *the economic irrationality of the creative process*. It is conventionally held that artists necessarily work long and hard in creating their works of art. The aura of originality and uniqueness associated with a work of art is generally held to flow in part from its lengthy and frequently painful gestation (Throsby and Withers 1979: 14-15). The laborious task of artistic creativity, the dialectic of the aesthetic, demands that artists sharpen and evaluate their perceptions and techniques, that they work and rework their ideas in the struggle to realise the truth of their insights through the medium they are working with, and be intensely preoccupied until the object comes close to the ideal of perfection they seek (Hauser 1982: 397-404, also Sontag 1979: 115-149). To complicate the process further, artists may be blocked for substantial periods of time and unable to find the creative spark, until eventually, it is claimed, under the capricious inspiration of the muse, they return to their work full of ideas and possibilities, again able to create.

From the point of view of capital, this is a hopelessly irrational process. On the one hand, the finished original which companies need for commoditisation contains a considerable labour content as a result of the artist's exertions. This makes profitable reproduction uncertain. On the other hand, capitalist production is premised on regular cycles of ever-expanding production relying on the scheduled and interlocking supply of raw materials. The unreliability of the creative process is problematic for capitalists if machinery and a labour force are left standing idle while artists struggle to find the inspiration to perfect their works. The contradiction of art and capital generates situations wherein capital is confronted with the need to rationalise (Weber 1976)[12] the process of creativity and the supply of originals in order to expand and accumulate.

There is another dimension of economic irrationality in the high value of the original which derives from *the high value of artistic labour itself,*

---

12  I use this term in sense in which Weber (1976) spoke of the rationality of modern capitalism; how its calculative, measuring thrust acts to impose goal-oriented bureaucratic controls over forms of social life. Further, it is a special type of rationalisation; one which can increase value production and which operates in and through the everyday routines and rules of production within organisations (Clegg and Dunkerley 1980: 499; on the rationality of organisations, see Clegg 1975).

itself a direct consequence of the necessity to preserve the named, concrete labour of the artist in the capitalist labour process. Artists must spend many years developing their talents and perceptions, learning the codes and conventions of their art and honing their expressive techniques, and maintaining them at a high pitch of performance (e.g. Stanislavski's (1967) account of life as an actor, cf. also Becker 1982: 40-67). This raises the reproduction costs of artistic labour, giving it a higher economic value in production and a high value content to the originals they create. Furthermore, the monopoly artists hold over their rare talents allows them to invoke the laws of supply and demand when it comes time to negotiate fees or sale of the works (e.g. the advertising agency managing director who complained in the course of fieldwork interviews that "the high salaries we pay copywriters are a function of demand"). These conditions apply upwards pressures on both the value and cost of artistic labour[13]. For capital, artists represent a significant and necessary investment in variable capital at a level which constantly threatens to undermine profitability[14].

---

13  Whether the actual monetary value of wages, fees and royalties rises is another matter (cf. the transformation problem of the relation between value and money in the labour theory of value; e.g. Harvey 1982: 61-68). Whilst payments made to an artist for an *individual* work or period of employment whether in the form of royalties, fees or wages, may represent adequate hourly or weekly earnings according to the conventions of the time, they do not represent adequate compensation for the many years of training and experience necessary in order to be able to create that work (e.g. The Australia Council 1983).

14  The economics of publishing illustrates the point. Dessauer (1974: 190-196) sets up a hypothetical model based on publication of a history title designed for both the general and academic markets, and provides a profit and loss analysis for three different marketing and retailing arrangements. By combining his figures for author's payments and editorial costs it is possible to get a broad indication of the costs associated with producing the original manuscript. In all three cases royalties totalled between 12.5 and 16.4% of nett sales revenue, and editorial salaries between 7.0 and 8.2%; in total, around one fifth to one quarter of nett sales revenue. By way of comparison, the production and general and administration salaries paid to presumably a much greater number of employees totalled no more than 12% (see also Gedin 1977: 154-177). Sterling and Haight (1979) provide voluminous statistics on a variety of media industries including (pp.111-218) operating figures for book publishing, newspapers, film production companies, the recording industry and commercial radio and television. Again, their figures are suggestive. To take a few examples: a 'typical' unidentified 250,000-circulation 7-day newspaper in the United States between 1950 and 1976, spent 15-16% of its direct production expenses on editorial salaries (1979: 166, see also Brown (1986: 3) on newspaper first copy costs and economies of scale). Recording companies too, face considerable costs

Consequently, capital in the culture industry has developed in such a way as to rationalise the value of artistic labour engaged in the production of originals.

Immediate consequences in production flowing from the artist/capitalist contradiction include the relative autonomy of the artists and the organisational and economic irrationality of creativity. This is not to say that capital is powerless when confronted by the artist. Grappling with these conditions and finding ways of ameliorating the effects of their functioning has occupied capitalists since they began organising forms of cultural production since the early 15th century. How those strategies have been realised in the 20th century in the corporate era of the culture industry, and how they have rationalised the creative stage of production, will be discussed in later chapters.

## 2.5 The Contradictions of the Cultural Commodity

As artists were socially constituted as the expressive genius, so their works must express their seminal insights. A work of art, according to its epochal conventions, is defined by its aura of uniqueness: it must carry a significance stemming from its *originality*. These qualities and properties give it its utility as a cultural object; they constitute its use value. It must appear to audiences as a novel object which promises to satisfy their needs for knowledge, meaning and pleasure by virtue of the new meanings it bears and which it alone possesses. The problem for capital is that *commoditisation of cultural objects erodes the qualities and properties which constitute them as cultural objects, as use-values, in the first place*. This is the primary contradiction of cultural commodities. To grasp how and why it operates necessitates returning briefly to Marx' discussion of the commodity form.

---

obtaining an original which can be reproduced. 1976 figures for Warner Communications production of long-playing records indicate that artist royalties (the right to reproduce the original) cost the company from 5 to 15% of the retail price (Sterling and Haight 1978: 192, also Chapple and Garofalo 1977: 173). The same authors note that the increasing proportion of wage costs in total production expenditures in the film industry in the first half of the 20th century (up to 60% by 1947) was due mainly to the rising salaries paid to top stars (1979: 181, also Powdermaker 1950: 209-220).

## 2.5.1 Use and Exchange-Value in the Commodity Form

In what is probably one of the most widely-read sections of *Capital*, Part I of Volume 1 (1954), Marx launches into the results of his research with a complex set of arguments about the apparently trivial thing, the commodity, as produced within the capitalist mode of production.

Value in commodity form, as produced within capitalist relations of production, is a combination of use-value and exchange-value; this is its two-fold character, flowing from the dual aspects of the labour expended in its manufacture (1954: 78). An object has use-value if it satisfies human wants – remembering that wants are socially constructed in relations of exchange, and it matters not, as Marx says, "whether...they spring from the stomach or from fancy" (1954: 43). Use-value refers to the socially constituted characteristics and capacities of an object. Since a useless object is unlikely to attract buyers, use value is a necessary attribute of every commodity[15]. Commodities are also goods produced by human labour for the express purpose of exchange. In exchange, commodities confront each other in quantitative not qualitative relations, as equivalents, as relative measures of abstract labour, of the socially necessary labour time which went into their making. This determines the ratios by which commodities exchange. The value at which the commodity exchanges is its value as indicated by its price, the given amount of money, the universal and abstract measure of exchange, which the consumer pays at the time of purchase (Marx 1954: 43-75, see also Harvey 1982: 1-38).

Use and exchange value are opposites, combined in the form assumed by the commodity. As such, argues Marx, they are in contradiction. Objects which are patently different when considered as objects designed to meet human wants and needs are treated on the market as relative equivalents. More than that, the ratios of their equivalence are expressed in terms of a third commodity, money, which has become simultaneously the store of value and the universal equivalent by which all commodities exchange (Marx 1954: 54-75, see also 1973: 266-273). The motivations associated with human desires and the formal equalities of modern societies which declare that all individuals have equal rights to satisfaction of their preferences, are negated by the cold, hard fact of economic inequality in the marketplace. Without the appropriate quantity of money, individuals cannot satisfy their needs and wants. The insertion of exchange transforms a socially useful relation into an impersonal economic one, a

---

15  Few Marxists acknowledge this, but use-value should be expressed in the plural form since the same object may have different or multiple uses to different consumers.

qualitative human relation into a quantitative relation apparently operating beyond the immediate control of the participants, in and through the interplay of unequally distributed things (1954: 76-96, cf. also Harvey 1982: 16-20).

The act of exchange also transforms the form of labour which went into the production of the commodities presented to the market. Since products cannot be compared and contrasted on the basis of their differences as created by the various forms of concrete labour, the logic of exchange backgrounds these differences and foregrounds their similarities. When buyers and sellers treat commodities as equivalents of each other, in effect, they deal with them as relative containers of a common denominator; in Marx' terms, as repositories of abstract labour, of comparable quantities of socially necessary labour time (1954: 61-68). Like use and exchange-value, concrete and abstract labour are in contradiction. Particular labours expended in the manufacturing process clash with and are subordinated to the logic of abstract labour, labour-in-general, in the process of exchange. The result in production is the intensification of alienation; workers are hired for their generalised capacity to labour rather than for the particular forms of work they can undertake. As exchange becomes the principal form of relation, value is institutionalised as the primary mediator of social life. Society comes to regard all labours as the equivalents of each other, without regard for the social usefulness or otherwise of each type. In other words, the fetishism of commodities measures the historical transformation of socially useful relations between people, the ways in which they work together and the objects which they produce, into a contradictory form of social existence, one which appears in objective opposition to their *praxis*. In Marx' often-cited words:

the existence of things *qua* commodities, and the value-relation between the products of labour which stamps them as commodities, have absolutely no connexion with their physical properties and with the material relations arising therefrom. There it is a definite social relation between men (sic), that assumes, in their eyes, the fantastic form of a relation between things (1954: 77).

In that sense the contradiction between use and exchange-value in commodities is a microcosm of capitalist relations generally, one of the principal and specific expressions of the general contradiction between labour and capital which underlies the character and development of the capitalist mode of production.

## 2.5.2 Contradiction of Use and Exchange-Value in the Cultural Commodity

The contradiction of use and exchange-value represents a substantial problem for capital in the culture industry, perhaps more so than in other industries. We have already noted that the use value of a work of art lies in its originality, an effect of the particular significance ascribed to it by its creator, the artist. Commoditisation of artistic objects, on the other hand, undermines the utility upon which their circulation depends; in the words of Walter Benjamin in an analysis which touches on issues raised here, "that which withers in the age of mechanical reproduction is the aura of the work of art" (1973: 223). In other words, *the production of artistic objects as exchange-value erodes their use-value*. This is the essence of the contradiction of the cultural commodity.

When manufactured as an exchange value, a cultural commodity is designed to be compared and contrasted with other types of commercial objects: a quantity of money, and indirectly, a quantity of carrots, or shirts, or building materials, or cars, or anything else which can be bought on the market. According to the conventions of its constitution, however, art is supposed to transcend the earthly, utilitarian realm. Its expression in the practical and economic language of the marketplace undermines its socially constituted use-value as an aesthetic object. It offends the supposedly finely-tuned sensibilities of artists, critics, collectors and audiences to speak of their subject in the same breath as they speak of money. Art which has 'sold out', gone 'commercial', is regarded as inauthentic, as lightweight and insubstantial and by definition, not worth serious consideration. Similar judgements are made of the artist or artists who created it. Hauser, from a sophisticated neo-Leavisite position, for example, sees popular art as ranging from the pleasant and agreeable to non-committal sentimentality and crass sensation, but that:

The inadequacy of popular art does not merely stem from the fact that it is entertaining, amusing, and lighthearted...The evil does not stem from the intention of creating attractive, appealing, effortless works, but from the readiness of the artist to make compromises unhesitatingly and to sink below his (sic) own level in order to achieve success (1982: 580-581).

Equally, by appearing as equivalents of other commodities, cultural commodities lose something of the uniqueness whereby they exist as individual artistic objects. By virtue of this comparison, they appear to audiences whose purchase is dependent on the promise of their originality, as objects defined in relation to the everyday, the typical and conventional, rather than as innovative and original, thereby losing something of the lustre and mystique which otherwise might make them attractive. They appear instead as objects of no particular uniqueness and of relatively little artistic significance.

Benjamin (1973) applauds this development in that it reduces the social distance between object and audience, making it more accessible, but there are also other economic consequences which are important to the corporations of culture. Under the capitalist form of cultural production the commodity appears on the market as a 're-production' of the original (cf. Collins *et al.* 1988: 9). Production in volume, and its later development, mass industrial production, entails constructing a master from an original, and manufacturing large numbers of copies taken from the master. The logic of reproduction, of copying, of imitating, of transcribing, directly contradicts the aura of originality and uniqueness within which the cultural object conventionally exists. Moreover, with mass production comes extensive publicity and mass sales. These erode the artistic value of the cultural commodity. When a company makes commodities of a work and successfully sells them, it exploits the market to the fullest while its product is new and attracting attention. Retail outlets are kept fully stocked and the commodity is extensively promoted. Success, however, hastens the work's demise as a commodity. The more units are sold, the more its audience becomes familiar with the work, so its novelty wears off. The element of surprise and freshness it relies upon for sales is diminished. Audiences begin to tire of the work, and regard it as out of date, old, valueless, worn out, and no longer worth purchasing. Under the logic of repetition underlying publicity and popularity, the special characteristics the cultural object initially possessed are systematically undermined by its very success in exchange.

These are the conditions which can be spoken of as the contradictions of the cultural commodity. Its exchange value form undermines its use value. Its uniqueness and originality are undone by reproduction, familiarity and over-exposure. It is the primary expression in circulation of the general contradictions of art and capital with underlie the culture industry.

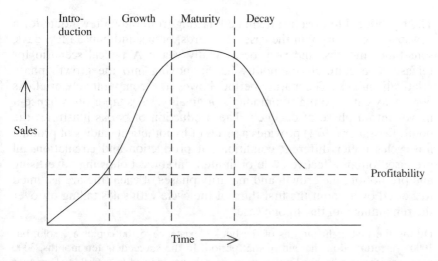

(Adapted from Baker, 1986 : 206)

Figure 2.1  Stages in the Product Life Cycle

## 2.5.3 The Immediate Consequences in Production and Circulation of the Contradictions of the Cultural Commodity

The contradictions inherent to the cultural commodity give rise to immediate consequences in both circulation and production which have historically confronted the manufacturers of cultural commodities. The erosion of use-value by exchange-value results in each cultural commodity having only a brief life on the market; this can be referred to as *the truncated product cycle of cultural commodities.*

Using the terminology of modern marketing, most commodities have a 'product life cycle' (Baker 1985a: 204-207) which approximates to an inverted 'U' curve, as shown in Figure 2.1. The sales, marketing and promotion efforts of manufacturers are oriented towards stretching out the mature phase of the cycle, giving most successful products an effective life of anything from two to fifteen or more years (Clifford 1981). Because of the primary contradiction operating within cultural commodities, elongation of profitable market life on this scale is rarely possible. As their attractiveness to the audience as use-values diminishes, sales decline.

Their product life cycle is attenuated, lasting from only a few hours for a newspaper edition to, in the case of records, books and films, a few days, sometimes months, and very occasionally years. A typical scenario for release of a cultural commodity has it moving into the growth phase relatively quickly. The mature period, however, is comparatively brief. As popularity cuts into the commodity's originality, sales taper off, whence it moves into a phase of decline[16]. The production of books illustrates the point. Dessauer (1974) provides a series of hypothetical studies of product life cycles under different conditions of production and circulation, all premised on an effective cycle of limited duration. Following advertising and promotion, the growth and maturity phases of each title are assumed to extend over about the first third of the cycle with sales tailing off over the remaining months. In one case:

During the first eight months of the book's existence, 5,100 copies are sold, but 1000 are returned at the end of that period. In the succeeding ten months, 3000 more copies are sold but by that time the sale has slowed to a trickle (Dessauer 1974: 191).

However, the precise shape of the sales curve, the amplitude of the growth and maturity phases of the product cycle, depend on the value of the work as represented in its socially recognised qualities, its originality, and its subsequent popularity. This can be expressed in terms of two polar types of product life cycle, distinguished within the culture industry variously as the differences between 'best-sellers' and 'steady-sellers', as typified in Figure 2.2. According to Steinberg, best-sellers quickly reach a high peak of sales and dominate the market for a period of time, after which their sales rapidly decline. An example is:

a book which immediately on, or shortly after its first publication, far outruns the demand of what at the time are considered good or even large sales; which thereafter sometimes lapses into obscurity making people wonder why it ever came

---

16  There are, of course, exceptions in all categories. Some products, in the language of the music industry, are 'sleepers', lying dormant on the market for weeks, sometimes months before taking off. Some become 'cross-overs', achieving popularity progressively across a range of audience segments, hence achieving viable sales for a significant period. Like some major 'hits', they occasionally metamorphose into steady sellers.

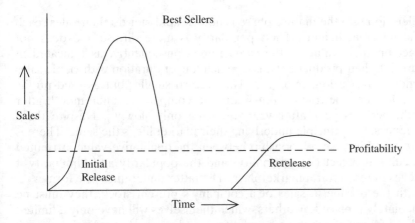

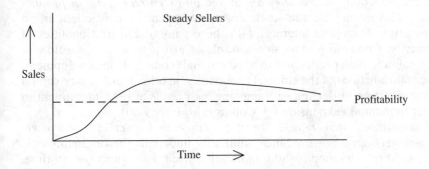

Figure 2.2  Cultural Commodity Product Life Cycles

to the front but which sometimes graduates into the ranks of steady sellers (1955: 237)[17].

Best-sellers, in other words, are works whose popularity grows quickly and to enormous heights, but where their success rapidly undermines their use-value. Steady-sellers have a less spectacular sales history. Their

17  Best-sellers are frequently redefined later as classics, as standards. When placed on the company's backlist, medium or long-term sales may settle at a level which provides small but assured profits and do so for months or even years. At a certain point, however, sales decline below a level which justifies continued production, whence it will be dropped. If demand continues to accumulate, it may be later repackaged and re-released as a standard, as indicated in Figure 2.2.

acceleration into the mature phase is not as rapid, nor do their sales reach the same great heights. Their popularity is more diffuse and does not impact on their value at the same rate. Consequently, as indicated in Figure 2.2, their product cycle is of much longer duration with viable sales extending over a longer period. They return smaller but assured profits over a longer time-frame, contributing to company revenue month after month, perhaps year after year, reducing only slowly[18]. Despite these differences, the principle underlying their market life is the same. There is a direct and inverse relationship between the qualitative value attributed to a cultural object (its originality) and the popularity and familiarity it achieves in the cultural marketplace. The latter undermines the former.

With the decline in sales of a company's present stock, they must be immediately replaced by others, which themselves will have only a limited market life and which must be replaced, and so on. Accordingly, companies must organise production to generate a constant flow of originals to the reproduction process: *they are locked into recurrent cycles of production*[19]. This means constant cycles of reinvestment in artistic labour, an imperative which also interacts with the organisational irrationalities of creativity. Companies must sign a stable of artists to maintain a flow of originals and plan production to have originals constantly in development. The contradictions of the cultural commodity, in other words, place capital in the situation of dealing with ongoing high levels of risky investment in order to maintain expansion (cf. Collins *et al.* 1988: 7-10).

Furthermore, *new releases must be made to impact on the market immediately upon release.* Since familiarity undercuts the originality of a new cultural commodity and familiarity itself is a function of time, manufacturers must attempt to make the immediate rate of sales growth accelerate as fast as possible following product launch. All other things being equal, the faster the rate, the higher the peak before the inevitable downturn. Accordingly, success of the release depends on urgent and extensive marketing and promotion, itself an expensive exercise, which subtracts from the potential profits attracted by the release.

Because of the uncertainty of the cultural marketplace, companies tend to overcompensate by *the overproduction of new releases*. This appears as

---

18   See also Lane (1980: 35) who provides life cycle charts for best-sellers by little-known and well-known authors, and typical backlist books.

19   Not all 'originals' need be new. Cultural producers have learnt from their counterparts in other industries how to repackage goods (e.g. Lilien and Kotler 1983: 608-613). Cross-marketing to other target audiences is one example; another is the repackaging of standards and classics.

the 'throw it up against the wall and see if it sticks' or the 'buckshot' philosophy of product release (Denisoff 1975: 98). The difficulty confronting all cultural commodity producers is that popularity is difficult to predict: cultural commodities are caught in the ebb and flow of fashion, with market demand constantly shifting under the impact of competition and the flood of new releases it generates. To stay ahead, companies are forced to release a range of releases covering several genres and/or stars in the hope that one will become a best seller. Few do: hence the volume of unsold stock which is periodically dumped or remaindered. Thus, while companies attempt to make careful judgements about the commercial potential of each release, they confront difficulties in rationalising their new release patterns.

In short, the contradictions of the cultural commodity generate a number of production and circulation pressures which bear constantly on producers. The truncated product cycles demonstrated by cultural commodities mean that historically, producers have been driven towards forms of organisation which guarantee a constant flow of originals to the reproduction stage of production, usually too many for effective demand, which means that some of their investment is wasted. Furthermore, once commoditised, their new releases demand expensive work in circulation to realise their investment before time and familiarity undercut its value.

## 2.6 Conclusion

This chapter has identified the fundamental disjunctions created when the structures of capital are combined with the structures of art. Out of these we have been able to grasp the principal contradictions of the artist-capitalist relation and the contradictions of the cultural commodity. From these conflicts and tensions, and given a general knowledge of typical capitalist development, it has been possible to identify structural tendencies in production and circulation which are major obstacles to the expansion of capital invested in the sphere of culture. From these, several questions emerge which warrant further investigation in order to grasp the specificities of the capitalist production and circulation of cultural commodities:

1. Given the socially constituted status of the artist hence the high cost of artistic labour and the indeterminacy of the creative process, to what extent has the capital relation rationalised the creative stage of production?

2. Given the truncated product cycle of cultural commodities hence the need for a regular supply of new artists and works which must be transformed into commodities, to what extent has capital rationalised the creative stage of production?
3. Given the truncated product cycle of cultural commodities hence the difficulties of creating product lines, priming demand and maintaining long-term accumulation, to what extent has capital rationalised the process of circulation?
4. Given these conditions, what if any are the reciprocal determinations operating between the production and circulation circuits of cultural commodities ?

The following chapters of this work take each of these questions as a basis for focusing on the specific institutional forms constructed around the corporations of culture. Ultimately, these flow from the contradictions of the art-capital relation, but not as direct realisations or instantiations. Structural tendencies represent imperatives, the conditions impinging upon capitalists and workers as they go about their work, the historical conditions they inherit and under which they conduct their agency. What can be achieved is given not only by their general content but also by the mediations of the present, by the myriad other tendencies and contingencies under which cultural life in modern societies is constructed and reconstructed. What follows is an account of the historically and structurally specific tendencies which characterise the production and circulation of cultural commodities in the corporate era of the culture industry, an institutional analysis of the corporate form of capitalist cultural commodity production.

# Chapter 3
# The Production and Circulation of Cultural Commodities: A Sectoral Analysis of the Culture Industry

## 3.1 Introduction

The moment we begin to examine the culture industry in detail, it becomes clear that much of the sorting and classifying work necessary for a political economy of culture is yet to be done. Even the industry itself *as an industry* is little understood. From a media/cultural studies perspective, analysts are used to speaking of the specificities of the film, publishing and recording industries and the press, radio and television, but it is easy to forget that together these comprise a *single* industry producing a single type of commodity: the *cultural* commodity. Looking behind the obviousness of descriptive terms like 'films', 'newspapers', 'books' and so on, and classifying these objects in terms of the *types* of cultural commodities each represents, we can characterise the elements of this industry and its constituent *sectors*. It is these that this chapter sets out to reveal.

By focusing on the production and circulation of cultural commodities and by building outwards from Marx' analysis of capital, a specific set of sectoral relations representing the political economic foundations of the culture industry can be modelled. The major points of my argument are that:

1. understood in political-economic terms, there are different types of cultural commodities, each requiring specific systems of circulation;
2. the problems of realisation confronted by these different types have generated a complex set of sectoral relations between cultural producers and the providers of circulation services.

We need to begin by recognising that the term 'cultural commodities' is an abstraction which camouflages important differences. As entrepreneurs began commoditising cultural objects in the search for profits, only some have been transformable into fully *private* goods. As a result, the culture industry produces and circulates various types of cultural commodities, which I will refer to as *private goods, quasi-private goods, and quasi-public goods* (sometimes abbreviated in the following discussion to private and public goods). While their systems of production are similar, each requires different approaches to circulation. Looking specifically at what must be done in each case to realise the value created in a production cycle, we find a particularly interesting and complex set of relations which emerged first as a matter of historical advantage but are now embedded as structural necessity. It centres around the producers of public goods (the media) who, in producing their own commodity form, use goods manufactured by the private goods (manufacturing) sector. In doing so, they assist in the circulation of private goods by providing publicity. This duality of the public goods sector/the publicity sector becomes particularly important later in this book.

Unfortunately, the path towards a sectoral analysis of the culture industry is not straightforward, because of gaps in Marxist theory when considering the interrelation of the circuits wherein commodities are produced and circulated. In particular, there is a significant gap in the literature on the emergence and function of marketing, a practice which has become immensely important to corporate accumulation strategies and in which the public goods sector of the culture industry is intimately involved in producing and circulating its own commodities. In order to build a sectoral analysis of the culture industry and in later chapters, give detailed consideration to the work of marketing in this industry, we must first consider recent developments in the process of circulation.

# 3.2 Commodities, Realisation, Marketing and Publicity

According to Marx (1954, 1956, 1959, see also Harvey 1982, Mandel 1968), capitalism is a mode of production predicated on accumulation via the production and circulation of commodities. Accumulation occurs through recurring cycles of investment, wherein machinery, raw materials and labour-power are purchased and combined in the capitalist's workshop or factory, with labour-power set to work producing a particular type of commodity, overseen by management. The result is a quantity of finished commodities ready for sale, containing more value than that of the workers' wages. When sold, this surplus-value is realised in money form which is claimed by the capitalist as profit and reinvested in more or better productive capacity in order to make even greater profits.

In traditional Marxist terms, competition demands that capitalists seize every opportunity to expand profits; not doing so carries the risk that competitors will gain a market advantage. Each strives to constantly increase the rate of exploitation in production, organising the labour process to increase the absolute and relative surplus labour value produced by workers, usually by extending the working day, reducing wages (without a corresponding decrease in working hours), or by purchasing more sophisticated machinery which increases labour productivity – in short, by 'degrading' the conditions of production (Braverman 1974). Despite these efforts to increase the rate of exploitation, the increase in surplus-value will only be realised as profits if capitalists compete on the market to ensure that the goods that they have produced and not those of their competitors' are actually purchased. Accordingly, each employs a sales team to sell their products into retail outlets ready for potential customers, and engages in publicity and promotional strategies to induce them to purchase. The point is that capitalist expansion presumes completion of *both* the production and circulation circuits; there is, therefore, an indissoluble unity between the spheres of production and circulation in the capital relation – in the language of the market, a fundamental and necessary link between production and sales and marketing.

## 3.2.1 The Development of 'The Sales Effort'

Since the circulation of cultural commodities becomes a major focus later in this chapter, and because few Marxists have paid much attention to the operation of this sphere much less its enlargement in corporate capitalism, a lengthy deviation is necessary to outline aspects of the operation of marketing and advertising.

Marx' arguments offer a beginning point. In chapter V and VI in Volume II of *Capital* (1956) and in Part IV of Volume III (1959, see also Mandel 1968: 182-203), he suggests that as the capitalist mode of production prospered and expanded, urban centres of commerce developed at some distance from the manufacturers' factories. Trading was carried out by merchants, the two principal forms being commercial and money-dealing (finance) capitalists. Their work significantly improved the efficiency of expansion as a whole. Commercial capital, wholesalers and retailers, attended to the business of exchange by employing labour-power to sell the factory output they had purchased at trade prices. Since this work involves no more than a change in value form, it creates no further value. Commercial profit flows from the difference between trade and retail prices, where a share of the surplus created in the labour process is conceded by manufacturers to wholesalers and retailers in return for their commercial services. The manufacturer's rate of profit on the completed production cycle is reduced, but because their original investment plus nett profits are available for reinvestment sooner than would otherwise be the case, they can reinvest quicker, hence (all other things being equal) they will increase their rate of production and annual rate of profit. In aggregate, while commercial capital participates in the share-out of surplus-value without producing any part of it, its exchanges with the manufacturing sector contribute indirectly to the expansion of capital, but only *indirectly*.

Nonetheless, Marx concedes that some commercial activities are technically indispensable for the conservation of use-value of commodities and are a pre-condition for realisation. Transportation of commodities from factory to market is one example (1956: 152-155). Whilst a cost of circulation to the manufacturer, the practical necessity of transport conserves use-value, thus its value enters into the total value of the consignment and a proportion is added to the value of each commodity. As such, it becomes "a separate sphere of investment of productive capital", its distinguishing feature being "that it appears as a continuation of a process of production *within* the process of circulation and *for* the process of circulation" (1956: 155). In other words, whilst it plays only a minor role in his analysis, partly because this development was only emerging while he was writing, Marx is ready to acknowledge the historical transformation of unproductive services into *productive* capital.

Since the 19th century, the business of circulation has expanded immensely. What Mandel (1978b) calls 'late capitalism' and Baran and Sweezy (1966) 'monopoly capitalism' but I prefer to call 'corporate capitalism', is characterised by concentrated, centralised and complex masses of capital, appearing empirically as national and transnational corporations of enormous size and value, built around complex and costly production technologies which have dramatically raised labour output, and the organisation of domestic and global markets for its immense diversity of products. With these developments, the internal contradictions of this economic system have driven the capitalist world economy into periods of chronic stagnation. Attempts to mitigate these tendencies have included an increase in state expenditure on public works and armaments (Harvey 1982, Mandel 1978b), but most crucially for the purposes of this study, what Baran and Sweezy (1966: 117-144) have referred to as 'the sales effort'[1]. Difficulties confronting the expansion of capital have led corporations to develop specialised marketing, merchandising and publicity divisions, and enabled the emergence of independent agencies providing specialised goods and services to these corporations. Baran and Sweezy observe that:

Conceptually [the sales effort] is identical with Marx expenses of circulation. But in the epoch of monopoly capitalism it has come to play a role both quantitatively and qualitatively beyond anything Marx ever dreamed of (1966: 119).

Since, according to the Marxist model, corporate accumulation generates a tendency towards overproduction relative to effective demand, corporations compete to ensure that their products capture the largest possible market share of sales, thereby realising a disproportionately large share of the total mass of surplus-value circulating in the market, and enabling them to sustain long-term viability. The most important of these marketing techniques are product differentiation and market segmentation, the targeting of specialised product lines to carefully delineated consumer segments; and brand competition, the inclusion of a range of product lines or models under the rubric of a brand which is then extensively promoted. Not only do the massive financial and human resources of the major corporations enable them to undertake these competitive strategies, but they are indispensable tools for protecting oligopolistic position. If successful, market share can be maintained, commodity prices raised in line with production cost increases and profit margins preserved (Baran and Sweezy 1966: 117-135)[2].

---

1    Their otherwise useful analysis I think is weakened significantly because, as Harvey (1982: 141-142) argues, they prematurely abandon the competitive model of capital which is so fundamental to Marx' analysis. I would add to this the importance of grasping the form of competition which underlies 'monopoly capitalism' rather than presuming its elimination. Consequently, they mistake the political-economic character and function of the sales effort. Arriaga (1984) also criticises their assumptions but like many Marxists, presumes that marketing and advertising is *a priori* unproductive.

2    The extent to which the expansion of marketing, merchandising and publicity are a necessary consequence of the crisis tendencies of the advanced capitalist mode of production, much less the reciprocal determinations they create in mitigating a decline in the average rate of profit (Marx 1959, see also Harvey 1982, Mandel 1978b), are beyond the concerns of this work, but would make a valuable and interesting area of research.

## 3.2.2 Marketing and Publicity: The Creation and Allocation of the 'Publicity Surplus'

To ask a classic question within Marxist political economy, do marketing and publicity in their modern forms represent the unproductive creation of saleable appearances, or, as Marx noted in the case of transport, are they constitutive investment in the production of use-values, adding to the sum total of capital in the process of self-expansion? Or to put the same question another way, is the investment tied up in marketing and publicity – in circulation – *productive* capital, capital *proper*?

The general tendency amongst Marxists is to assume that it is not; Baran and Sweezy (1966) are a case in point (see also Arriaga 1984). Mandel seems to believe differently when, in a passing comment, he argues that:

[creative] wage-labour employed in making advertisement films is productive, whereas the cajoling of potential clients [by account executives] to purchase or order such films is as unproductive as the labour of commercial representatives in general (1978b: 45).

He dissects Marx' arguments on this contentious issue noting discrepancies between *Theories of Surplus-Value* and the later version in *Capital*, concluding eventually that the latter is the more considered position. He argues therefore that:

The frontier between productive capital and circulation capital thus runs between wage-labour which [creates,] increases, changes, or preserves a use-value, or is indispensable for its realisation – and wage-labour which makes no difference to a use-value (1978a: 405, see also 1978b: 45).

Use-value is the key category. If a labour process is productive in any of the above senses, it adds to the total amount of abstract labour-value embedded in that commodity. Unproductive labour, on the other hand, is "wage-labour which is indifferent to the specific use-value of a commodity" (1978b: 46). Mandel notes further (1978a: 406), I think correctly, that at the very least, so-called 'service' capital in modern political economies, usually said to include marketing and advertising firms, like merchant capital, indirectly increases the sum total of value by accelerating the turnover time of invested capital. Additionally, as a general rule, once services are commercialised, corporate capitalism tends to convert them into commodity-producing processes which directly increases aggregate private and social capital. In other words, Mandel presumes a historical dimension to the productive-unproductive boundary which depends on the stage of development of the form of capital under examination. This point is important.

Whether or not the business of marketing and advertising in the present day has become productive of value can be examined via a case study; a suitable example is the Australian launch of Agree Creme Rinse and Conditioners by the U.S.-based manufacturer S.C. Johnson and Sons Pty. Ltd. (the company marketing report is reprinted in Layton 1980: 108-136, cf. also Baker 1985: 292-350)[3].

When commissioned by a manufacturer to prepare publicity materials – in the Agree case, brand logos, label, packaging and sample layouts, a print and television advertising campaign, and shelf-tray and free-standing bins layouts – an advertising agency employs in-house or sub-contracted labour-power in the form of copywriters, graphic artists, performers and directors, and combines them with means of cultural production such as concepts, advertising conventions, writing and graphic techniques, typewriters, processors and film, photographic and audio recording equipment, in the production of tape recordings, audio-visuals, films, camera-ready artwork, and other cultural objects. Once finished and approved, the originals, the 'masters', belong to the advertiser. The agency negotiates with the selected medium in drawing up a campaign schedule which determines where and when their messages are delivered to the audience. Advertisements, posters, labelling and other publicity materials are obviously produced as material objects; as films, tapes, artwork, and so on. They have a sensual, physical, as well as cultural existence; but they

---

3   From evidence collected in the course of field work, it is more usual to find a multiplicity of firms and commissions involved in marketing and launching a product. Packaging and logos, for example, are sometimes designed by specialist agencies, sometimes by the corporation's marketing division, sometimes by the agency contracted to handle the advertising campaign. Some major or specialist firms may set up an advertising section within their marketing division but advertising is generally handled by independent specialist agencies. 'The agency' in the above discussion represents a function rather than a firm; one or several may be commissioned, whether substantial companies or small independents. Depending on the state of competition, packaging design, advertisement production and the booking of media campaigns may be handled by one or several agencies who may themselves sub-contract aspects of their work. 'The medium' too, refers to a function: multi-media campaigns are more usual than single-medium campaigns. The following discussion focuses on the advertising campaign, but the operation and social effects of package design, labelling and point-of-sale advertising are identical. Baker (1985a) offers a useful and comprehensive overview of the operation of marketing and advertising. Other works drawn on here include: Baker (1985b), Baker et al. (1983), Wilmhurst (1984). For marketing case studies see Layton (1973, 1980) and McCarthy et al. (1987). For advertising see Fowles and Mills (1981), Rossiter and Percy (1987). For the history of advertising see Fox (1984), Turner (1965).

are also *commodities*, objects produced for sale, although monetary exchange transpires not with their *cultural* consumers, the intended audiences, but with their *economic* consumer, the advertiser, to whom they become assets, part of the company's capital stock. In other words, *publicity commodities are produced as intermediate goods and enter into the advertiser's constant capital.* To advertisers, they have a use-value as signifying objects which publicise the characteristics of their own products, and their exchange-value is underlaid by the value of the cultural labour expended in their production. Hence, *publicity commodities represent value in the process of expansion and add to the sum total of value in circulation.*

Embedded in publicity commodities is the surplus-value extracted by the employing agency from creative staff in the course of their production, which is realised when paid for[4]. Does this labour value enter into the exchange-value of the commodity being advertised? To the manufacturer, advertisements and packaging represent circulation costs which are added to overall production costs and becomes part of the unit cost of each commodity. Is this simply a redistribution of costs on to the consumer or, given Mandel's definition of productive labour, do they add to, increase or conserve the advertised commodity's use-value? Deciding this *economic* question necessitates examining the realisation of the *cultural* value of publicity commodities.

Advertising and packaging are designed to "position a product or a brand in relation to other brands" (Fowles and Mills 1981: 13), in other words, to proposition customers on behalf of the commodity, to enunciate its potential uses relative to consumer desires and preferences and assert its worth in order to attract sales. Product differentiation and brand competition are corporate marketing strategies which attempt to exploit not only consumers' subsistence needs but also their desires for pleasure and enjoyment, sociability, affiliation and their insecurities. Artists of various types are employed to create the signifying objects which play on the commodity's surfaces and project its claims into the public sphere. Their rhetoric attempts to provide a material guarantee for the commodity's promised use-value and upon which the potential customer, the

---

4    This discussion is focussed primarily on the cultural dimensions of marketing and publicising, hence this remark emphasises the surplus-value generated by cultural labour-power in creating the original. Labour-power in the form of camera operators, sound recordists, make-up artists, editors and dubbing suite operators and so on, is also employed in transcribing and copying the original. They too create a surplus for their employer but I am ignoring these physical aspects of this cultural labour process.

addressee, can imagine its worth as a private possession. Brand names, logos and slogans draw and articulate a plausible collection of possible satisfactions around a commodity and promise that these will be realised in its consumption. The print advertisement for Agree ("Helps stop the greasies"), for example, headlined a question from the young female spokesperson fronting the campaign: "Dry, Normal or Oily hair, you need a hair conditioner that doesn't make your hair greasy. Agree ?". The body copy continued with extensive explanation of the product's consumer benefits claiming that "Agree is 99.75% oil free", "Agree is pH balanced", and includes a picture of the cosmetic pack designed to emphasise the personal care orientation of the product (Layton 1980: 115-117). The potential of advertising to make assertions appear as facts and the commodity as both use and exchange value, flows from *the constitutive capacities of language*[5]. Its signs bear a semiotic power which capital grasps and uses to mobilise human desires to meet the demands of accumulation. The work of positioning a brand or product pre-emptively attributes a complex of uses[6] to the objects represented, in a manner appropriate to the targeted consumer segment and their assumed context of consumption[7].

---

5    The term 'constitute' here points to the determinate and situated relations between reality and the languages which agents create in its construction. Signification is part of the making of what is real, "and a grasping of this reality through language...And since this grasping is social and continuous...it occurs within an active and changing society.... Signification...is a specific form of the practical consciousness which is inseparable from all social material activity" (Williams 1977: 37-38). For a useful discussion of these issues see Williams (1977: 21-44). Seminal contributions to recent debates on the nature of languages which underlie the above discussion, in addition to Williams, include Barthes (1967), Eco (1976), Hall (1977) and Volosinov (1973).

6    There is a misleading tendency amongst Marxists to treat use-value as a unitary property possessed by the commodity and which pre-exists consumption. In fact, it is constituted in relations of exchange and consumption. Marketing constitutes possible uses to potential consumers and identical goods may have various uses to different people – and I use the plural form deliberately. Uses are realised in the course of consumption, in conditions under which consumption must be understood as a mode of agency in the production of a life(style). I would argue that Marxism badly needs a theory of consumption-as-agency, and, as I comment at various points throughout the following chapters, nowhere is this more necessary than in the sociology of culture.

7    In constituting use-value, of course, advertisements also construct the human subject of consumption. A number of recent studies have examined the relationship between subjectivity and consumption of publicity texts and the mechanisms which produce such effects, from perspectives which combine structural-

There seem to be two processes in play here: publicity *displays* these characteristics so as to signify an explicit, identifiable and unmistakable brand or product image, and simultaneously *promotes* it against its competitors. Projected uses are located implicitly or explicitly on a scale of value, of relative worth to the consumer, measured as value for money. The makers of Agree, for example, compared its performance against its (unnamed) competitors. In the television advertisement the female spokesperson (a typical consumer figure) asked: "Would somebody please explain? No matter what kind of hair you have, dry, oily or normal, why does it sometimes get greasy, stringy and sticky *after using a conditioner?*" (emphasis added). After the male expert (a hairdresser figure) explained the properties of Agree and how it solves the problem of greasy hair, he evaluated its claims and affirmed their veracity by commenting over a shot of the product pack "No wonder it's America's No 1 Creme Rinse and Conditioner" (Layton 1980: 118). Public display and promotion are the two mechanisms of publicity; an advertisement objectifies the subject of its discourse and differentiates it from its competitors in terms of the satisfactions it promises, then locates it in a superior position within a status hierarchy of utility. The question is, why should companies set out to achieve this?

Display and promotion are a necessary condition of the price mechanism in a competitive, impersonal market. Since price-tags signify relative claims to exchange-value represented in money form, they must be underpined by a guarantee of the good's relative utility. The commodity is made to appear as the bearer of relative market value. If the good seems as good as its promise – all other things being equal, and ignoring the fact that some campaigns do not work – then it will be more likely to sell than its competitors. It seems then that marketing and advertising do, in Mandel's terms, add to, increase or conserve use-value, but in a much stronger sense than even he seems to realise. We can say that it is *the signifying capacity of publicity commodities created by cultural workers has the effect of constituting use-value prior to consumption, and as such underlies a proportion of the increased exchange-value carried by the marketed commodities.*

What work underlies the rest of the increase? In short, that of the media workers who make the distribution vehicle, the media content into which the advertisement is inserted. As a signifying object, the advertisement is of no use to the advertiser unless it is transmitted into the public arena, its

---

ist and psychoanalytic insights. Useful examples include Bonney and Wilson (1983: chapter 6-8), Haug (1986: chapter 2-3), and Judith Williamson's seminal *Decoding Advertisements* (1978: especially chapter 2).

message made public via the media. Advertising agency staff plan a campaign on behalf of their client and buy the necessary time or space depending whether they are using broadcast or print media, to achieve reach and frequency; i.e. they schedule insertions of the advertisement so that its message reaches audiences of preferred size, demographic and socio-economic characteristics, and often enough for them to remember its propositions. In the Agree case, a budget of $700,000 (1979 prices) was allocated for a campaign using prime night-time television and national women's magazines as the "optimum vehicles to reach the target group identified as women aged 14-24 years". Six different publications were used in order to "get coverage of 90% of Australian women who would be exposed to the advertisements on average nine times throughout the year" (Layton 1980: 117, 119). The selected medium and the agency draw up a contract whereby the medium agrees to transmit or publish the advertisements as specified in the schedule[8].

Programmers, announcers, journalists, continuity writers, directors and other cultural workers of various kinds employed by the medium, prepare and present programmes or editions. Curiously, for reasons to be detailed shortly, media either do not or cannot sell their products to consumers at full value, if at all. Yet media production is organised as commodity production; media produce a 'quasi-public good' (see later discussion), and its free consumption by readers, listeners and viewers provides a possible pool of addressees for advertisements. Their capacity to speak to extensive and widespread audiences which flows from consumption of their commodity form, is a useful effect which can be 'sold' by media organisations to those seeking audiences for their messages.

As part of the advertising process, media firms commission research agencies to produce circulation reports, ratings books, and so on (e.g. Fowles and Mills 1981: 85-94)[9], which provide detailed sociological and

---

8　For the operations of media planning and buying departments in agencies and their relations with media sales departments see Baker (1985a), Fowles and Mills (1981), Rossiter and Percy (1987) and Wilmshurst (1985). For case studies as part of the overall marketing process see, for example, Layton (1973, 1980).

9　Again, I am referring here to a function rather than a firm. Some media, especially media conglomerates, have their own research departments. Specialist firms such as AGB-McNair, Morgan-Gallop Polls, and Australian National Opinion Polls to name a few Australian examples, carry out the bulk of research. For details on the commissioning of research, the types and value of different forms of data analysis and presentation, the transformation of this information by media into rate cards and packages and subsequent relations

psychological information on different groups within the aggregate audience, and their regular patterns of media use. In Australia, *The Age Lifestyle Study* (Melbourne Age 1982), for example, used factor analysis to identify 15 lifestyles (e.g. Average Successful Dad, Urbane Sophisticate, Career Mother, Aussie Chauvinist, Doting Grandmother), the consumption patterns of each across a variety of product categories (e.g. clothes, beverages, holiday and travel, finance) and their media exposure (e.g. press, radio and television preferences and use). McNair-Anderson radio surveys, on the other hand, provide aggregate figures such as the numbers of cumulative (unduplicated) and consecutive quarter-hour (duplicated) listeners for each quarter-hour of transmission across all stations in a market. Using this and other market information, each company produces a rate card, a list of charges for carrying advertisements. Rate cards are set at a level which offers advertisers the lowest possible cost per thousand impacts; i.e. the unit charge made for delivering a message of given size or duration to an audience of specified size and composition. The base advertising rate is established by pricing the relative audience size and type attracted by their product with the costs of its production, varied for different pages or time zones according to their popularity (for examples, see *b&t yearbook* 1984). In other words, *advertising rates reflect the distributive efficiency of the medium mediated by the cost of producing its content, and media attract income by renting their capacity to deliver advertisements to the specific audiences consuming their products* (for a contrasting view, see Smythe 1977[10]).

With publication of the campaign, the use and exchange-value of the brand or product are objectified in the public realm. This is the effect of cultural work performed in marketing and advertising agencies and the media. The value of these labours also enters into the commodity, pre-emptively constituting its use and exchange value prior to consump-

---

with agencies in campaign planning and signing, see especially Baker (1985a, 1985b) and Fowles and Mills (1981).

10   This is the correct formulation of the political-economic operation of the media. In an influential paper, Dallas Smythe (1977) argued that audiences and readerships are the commodity form produced by mass-produced, advertiser-supported communications under monopoly capitalism (1977: 3), a conclusion reproduced by Bonney and Wilson (1981) and McQueen (1977). But Smythe is incorrect. Advertisers do not 'buy' audiences: they rent the access media offer to their practical and discursive consciousness. Media have an effective monopoly on the cultural and technical means (content, equipment) of delivering messages to the habituated audiences each attracts. To advertisers, this is the use-value of media operations, and the useful effect they are willing to employ.

tion. Brands and products which sell in quantity as a result of marketing and publicity attract a substantial market share, those selling most realising a larger-than-average slice of the sum total of value created in manufacturing output, a share which considerably exceeds the quantity of surplus-value carried by their own commodities. In other words, *they appropriate a share of the surplus-value created by the employees of competing firms*. Marketplace competition through marketing and publicity serves to distribute and allocate the value in circulation, while adding to it itself. It enables powerful firms to realise what I want to call a *publicity surplus*, or in its monetary expression, *publicity profit*, which is *the end result of the cultural labour which creates a relative increase in marketability for the advertiser's goods*.

The exchanges which underpin marketing and publicity bring significant benefits to the manufacturing corporations which can afford it, while simultaneously creating the conditions of expansion for publicity capital. There are at least three identifiable flows of surplus-value:

1. that created in making publicity materials and vehicle, returned to the agency and the medium;
2. that created in the manufacturing process, returned to the manufacturer;
3. that created by competing manufacturers and appropriated as publicity surplus, shared between advertiser, agency and medium.

Of course, agency, medium and client struggle over apportionment of these additional appropriated profits. Most is claimed by the advertiser, the manufacturer of the advertised commodities. In the course of 'pitching the account' and deciding the size of the agency fee relative to total budget, and pre-campaign rate negotiations between agency and medium over the rate to be charged[11], both medium and agency publicise their *own* products and set a price upon them which maximises their individual shares. In other words, their capacity to negotiate, to battle over the terms of apportionment, is determined by their market reputations, the signs of the exchange-values of agency and medium in their own spheres of competition.

---

11    Judging by interviewees' comments, media and agencies engage in much heavy warfare over this. The distribution mechanism operates through agency commissions, a deduction from the campaign cost they pay to the medium which, while set at an industry standard in most countries, can be surrounded by invisibles (additional or preferred placements, promotional support, and so on). Equally, the agency service fee paid by their client generally includes all production charges and some creative costs, with shortfalls made up out of media commission.

To sum up: by examining the advertising process and the interplay of its cultural and economic aspects, we begin to see that publicity capital is a historically new and complex capital generated by the difficulties confronting the accumulation of corporate capital, representing the articulation of forms of economic and cultural practice, and appearing as media, marketing and advertising organisations. Publicity capital expands by assisting in the circulation of commodities produced by manufacturers, by producing and circulating additional specialised goods. The surplus-value embedded in them is realised when sold to advertisers, and their circulation enables publicists to share in the division of publicity surpluses realised by advertisers. This system of realisation distinguishes publicity capital from merchant capital out of which it grew in the late-19th to the early-20th centuries, where publicity capital evolved as a form of productive capital operating in circulation by creating the publicity process as the mode of realisation underlying its accumulation. Its expansion indicates influential structural changes within capitalist economies built upon the new relationship forged between the 'productive' sphere of production and 'unproductive' circulation that began, as Marx observed, with transport. What were once services have been capitalised. Cultural workers in the publicity sector create an independent source of profits for their employers by creating signifying objects which materialise the propositions of marketability borne by competing commodities. This costly prerogative can only be mobilised with the massive resources of the major corporations, thus consolidating their industrial dominance and long-term profitability. It is clear that publicity profits are a significant site of conflict between competing corporate capitals and that publicity is a circulation strategy which is fundamental to the ongoing accumulation and concentration of capital in modern economies – a point which , as we will see shortly, is particularly germane to understanding the operation of the culture industry.

# 3.3 Types of Cultural Commodities, Their Systems of Circulation and Relations of Distribution

With a clearer understanding of the functioning of the marketing process, we can now return to an examination of the culture industry as an industry.

Bonney and Wilson, amongst others (e.g. Garnham 1979, Hall 1977,

Murdock and Golding 1977, Wolff 1981), emphasise the political and analytic importance of investigating modern commercial cultural institutions:

as organisations operating within a certain kind of social, political and economic structure, and engaged in a certain kind of business for profit. They are engaged, like other businesses, in the production of *commodities* - production of output for *sale* or *exchange* (1983: 23-24).

However, capitalisation progresses under specific technical and cultural conditions and not all non-commoditised cultural forms are equally amenable to transformation. For viable capitalist investment, a technical form must be available for producing and exchanging the object as a commodity, and a controllable system of realisation must be available. From a sociological perspective, the distinction made by economists between 'private' and 'public' goods (e.g. Bannock *et al.* 1984: 361) can be usefully employed to develop this point. Private goods have a form which excludes potential customers from access to their use-value prior to or outside of exchange. Their sale can therefore be controlled. Because of this, they can be designed for private, domestic consumption, produced as discrete, mass-produced items manufactured, and sold at relatively low unit costs. On the other hand, the use-value of public goods is readily and freely accessible and consumption by one individual does not exclude that of another. Private capital can profit little from investment in public goods unless they can be transformed into private form: since there is no moment of exchange, any surplus-value created in their production cannot be realised.

## 3.3.1 Private Goods

Books, magazines, and musical recordings are all produced as private goods and represent the culture industry's most mature commodity forms. Periodicals and newspapers are an ambiguous case; they have the *technical* form of private goods, but in so far as their contents such as political and economic news are regarded in liberal democracies as information to which citizens have a right, they represent public goods. In other words, in contrast to their technical form, they have the *cultural* form of public goods[12]. For the sake of simplicity, I treat newspapers and periodicals in this analysis as public goods.

Private goods in the culture industry are manufactured and distributed in a system which conforms with the basic model of capitalist commodity production. Publishers and recording companies invest in labour-power and means of cultural production. Two types of labour-power are employed; cultural workers to create an original work and manual workers who reproduce it by transcribing the original on to a master and mass-producing copies, the commodities proper. Both types of workers create surplus-value which is realised when the resulting commodities are sold to consumers. To realise these profits, manufacturers supply their products to retailers such as book and record stores who merchandise them by creating an appropriate layout in their shops and publicising their stock. The manufacturer-retailer relation, therefore, is the fundamental institutional relation realising the production and circulation of private goods. As the scale of the culture industry expanded, as manufacturers grew, so did retailers, drawing their income from the value produced in the manufacturing sector.

As argued in the previous chapter, however, concealed within all cultural commodities are the contradictions of the art-capital relation. These generate immediate complications in production and circulation, the most important of which, from the point of view of manufacturers, are the truncated product cycle, the necessity for recurrent production, and the tendency towards overproduction of originals. Consequently, each of the new releases flooding onto the market needs extensive marketing and publicity. Historically, this has given rise to a complex set of institutional arrangements operating across the production and circulation of private cultural goods.

Because of overproduction and the intensity of marketplace competition, a merchandising approach where commodities are simply placed on display in retail outlets, is, from the manufacturer's point of view, insufficient to guarantee sales. Accordingly, the firm's marketing division packages the commodities to make them stand out from their competitors

---

12  This contradiction exerts downwards pressures on cover-prices and many newspapers sell at a price well below their costs of production. Subsequent cost pressures have led newspaper companies to carry advertising, which inevitably locks them into a logic which intersects with that of their existence as private goods. Their functioning as manufacturing capital frequently conflicts with their functioning as publicity capital, a dualism which underlies the contradictions of journalism and commerce which are part of the everyday world of newspaper editorial staff.

in the retail setting. The firm's marketing division packages the commodity; this involves providing covers for books and recordings, trade advertisements, and merchandising aids such as posters, stickers and point-of-sale materials, and publicity and promotional activities and tie-ins (Grannis 1957: 177-186, Frith 1978: 75-86)[13]. In an era of impersonal, self-service retailing, most of the in-store selling work is done by the packaging; it is designed to attract the attention of potential purchasers and project the commodity's claims to use and exchange value (cf. Denisoff 1975: 172-176, Schmoller 1974: 317). We have already seen that packaging is produced as intermediate cultural goods and that the value of the labour consumed in their production is added to the value of the commodities being circulated, realised in exchange and returned to the manufacturer, whence it is distributed to each of the participating capitals. The production/circulation system of private goods which developed historically within the culture industry, therefore, inserts a marketer between the manufacturer and retailer – usually a division or department within the corporation but sometimes an independent company.

Packaging itself is generally insufficient to ensure realisation. The urgency of publicity confronting all types of cultural commodity usually requires additional signifying objects such as consumer advertisements, video clips, biographical information and publicity leaflets. These are prepared by the marketing division or subcontracted through specialist agencies, freelancers and independents, and designed for use through the publicity system (e.g. Grannis 1957: 144-147, 164-174, Frith 1978: 75-96, Stockbridge 1985: 29-36). These objects too are produced as intermediate publicity goods and their value enters into that of the finished commodity.

Accordingly, advertisements are circulated in the media to publicise the commodity, its value and its availability. Here we come across a significant institutional element of the culture industry which assumes considerable importance in later chapters. Generally, private cultural goods are not extensively advertised in the consumer media. This is obviated because of an additional set of publicity relations between manufacturers, the media

---

13 Dessauer (1974: 102-124) also looks at promotion and sales promotion in the book trade and also discusses alternative retailing systems such as book clubs, mail-order selling, wholesalers and jobbers. Hirsch (1970: 43-48) does the same for the popular music industry. For a discussion of the social and economic conditions which have transformed 'shopkeeping' into 'merchandising', see Jefferies (1954: 281-291 for newspaper and book selling and pp.405-410 for radio and electrical goods). Bluestone *et al.* (1981) look at recent developments in department store retailing, noting in particular (pp.27-35) the struggle between department and specialist stores, especially relevant to the book trade.

and their audiences, which is part of the institutionalised system whereby private goods are circulated. Its origins lie in the increasing use of all types of private goods in the preparation of media contents, especially since the 1950s (the genesis of this will be dealt with under 'quasi-public goods'). Some use is direct; for example, films are used in television programming, commercial recordings in radio programmes and their associated video clips in television music programmes. Indirect use includes press, radio and television news and reviews dealing with newly released books and recordings, publication of best-seller lists, interviews with artists, features and backgrounders dealing with types of works or artists, biographies, and so on. Manufacturers of private cultural goods permit the producers of quasi-public goods to use their commodities as intermediate goods in their own production for relatively small fees[14]. This seems contradictory. Given that it permits free or cheap access by audiences to the commodity's use-value which might adversely affect sales and hence the quantity of value realised, why do manufacturers allow it?

The reason is the *publicity effect* of media use, the *free advertising* it endows. Consumption by media in their own production has the effect of drawing attention to the commodity, a publicity effect which, in effect, provides unpaid assistance in the circulation of cultural commodities. It flows from the normal operations of the media in their own production and is vital to manufacturers in making their products competitive in the market. Because of the realisation problems confronting cultural commodi-

---

14  There is considerable struggle between manufacturers and media over this is-
    sue, although the outcomes have varied in different countries. In general, in so
    far as producers are able to charge fees for use, they realise a proportion of the
    labour-value embedded in the final commodity (if a charge is made for use of
    an intermediate good, its value is realised directly, reducing the need to raise
    the price of the final consumer good, which, when competition and cost pres-
    sures are mounting, as in the case of the recording industry, is advantageous).
    On the other hand, if fees are not charged, this represents a proportion of
    surplus-value forgone by the manufacturer in favour of long-term publicity
    profits flowing from the publicity effects of media use, as discussed shortly. In
    other words, this is another point of struggle between different forms of capital
    over the distribution of value. In Australia, for example, television channels
    pay fees for the use of films. Arguments have recently broken out over
    whether they should pay recording companies for the use of video clips (e.g.
    Stockbridge 1985: 30-31). Radio stations have traditionally been supplied with
    recordings free but have paid for ongoing rights of various kinds (e.g. mechani-
    cal, transmission rights) to manufacturers and publishers. The battle has re-
    cently hotted up with stations being forced to pay a wider range of fees and
    recording companies looking for more (ABT 1986: 119-122).

ties and the highly competitive nature of the cultural marketplace, media use of a new release is permitted – indeed sought – at certain points in the circulation phase, especially upon release (Chapple and Garofalo 1977: 69-122, Grannis 1957: 161-174)[15]. Manufacturers allocate considerable resources to gaining free publicity, for it is here that the battle of the marketplace is generally won or lost (Music Board of the Australia Council 1987: 207-213, Frith 1978: 89). Recording companies, for example, try to obtain radio airplay of selected tracks from the recording, and telecasts of the accompanying video clip. Equally, review copies are supplied to specialist magazines and the daily press for review, and artists make themselves available for interviews and appearances. The media attention attracted by the commodity raises its market profile above that of its competitors, legitimating its claims to use and exchange-value, hence making it more likely to sell. This manufacturer-publicist relation which has developed within the culture industry is no accident: it is a rudimentary principle of survival for the makers of private goods in the context of the modern culture industry.

The publicity effect on private cultural goods reveals the symbiosis between manufacturer and publicist on which both rely not only for short-term publicity profits but also long-term competitive advantage. For manufacturers, it maintains the superiority of their artists and keeps their back-catalogue alive which, with skilled marketing and merchandising, can be converted into long-run market share and sustained sales. For the part that they play, advertising agencies and the media also share in the glory. Each makes a claim on the publicity profits secured by the manufacturer as a result of their efforts. If a medium received no advertising income, a radio station for example, may otherwise acquire a reputation for broadcasting popular items, for 'making the hits', for being 'up with the play', a significant station in the market. This increases its audience and enables it to command higher advertising rates and hence demand a greater proportion of the publicity surpluses realised by all its advertisers. In other words, like its paid counterpart, the publicity effect of media consumption instigates flows of value which ultimately profit both manufacturer and

---

15  See also Dessauer (1974: 136-140) for the book trade, who notes that "the sheer volume of titles and authors and the limited available news, review and airspace make for a fiercely competitive situation" (p. 137). Lane (1970) also deals with promotion and publicity and deals in particular with the importance of subsidiary rights for publishers' profitability. Frith also deals with promotion in popular music (1978: 74-138); see also Denisoff (1975: 136-137). Hirsch (1971) sees this process as part of a pre-selection system which filters new releases.

publicist of private goods, and have underpined the growth of publicity capital[16].

These are structural relations whose roots lie in the internal contradictions of cultural commodities, even their most mature form, private goods. The secret to their successful circulation depends ultimately on the reproduction of exchange relations between different forms of capital operating in the culture industry, each serving a different purpose. If manufacturers of private goods are to expand their capital, competitive cooperation with retailers, marketers and the producers of quasi-public goods (i.e. the media – and promoters as producers of quasi-private goods) and marketers, is indispensable. Their reproduction creates the conditions which these other forms of capital require to expand.

## 3.3.2 Quasi-Private Goods

Films, plays, concerts, festivals, tours and live performances of various kinds all fit into this category, but since private capital has concentrated around film-making, I will focus on this. 'Quasi-private goods'[17] are produced as consumer goods, but in addition to the problems associated with cultural commodities generally, because of their technical form, they

---

16  Manufacturers also cooperate with the artist's personal management and promoters in organising 'gigs', concerts and tours. Again, the reason is publicity (e.g. Chapple and Garofalo 1977: 123-154). While recording companies commonly underwrite the cost of a tour, since promoters carry the costs of putting on the show, as exhibitor capitalists (to be dealt with the in the next section), nett profits after paying the performers flow principally to them. There are also sizeable long-term benefits to manufacturers; successful live performances maintain an artist's popularity which in turn creates the conditions for immediate and future publicity surpluses in the record market. Hence artists are pressured by their employers to make live appearances, especially while their work is newly released.

17  The label 'quasi-private' is used here since these goods are consumed in a theatre with a finite number of seats. One person's purchase of an admission ticket in effect excludes another from attending the same showing (cf. public goods). Also important is the fact that opera, concerts, plays and movie-going is a collective not communal activity engaged in simultaneously by an aggregate of individuals. Each sits in a darkened theatre acting as if it is their own private showing; others in the audience are treated as strangers and not permitted to intrude on their private space (cf. Goffman 1971). The same applies to galleries, concert halls, etc. This pattern of behaviour contrasts with the sociality of the public concert during the 16th to 19th centuries: for example, at opera and orchestral concerts (e.g. Raynor 1972: 155-179).

face particular difficulties in the circuit of circulation. Herein lies the seeds of their complex history (e.g. Cowie 1971, Kindem 1982a, for an Australian perspective see Dermody and Jacka 1987, Tulloch 1982).

Where quasi-private goods production is carried out in the performing arts, there are considerable problems in expanding the value of the original investment. The only method of reproducing the commodity is by repeating the performance, a costly, labour-intensive form of reproduction which attracts little capitalist investment. The conditions of quasi-private production changed in the late-19th and early-20th centuries with the invention of technologies capable of recording performances and creating reproductions which could be made widely available to attract large audiences. New cinematic technologies, for example, enabled transcription of theatrical performances, which encouraged a flow of investment from theatre into these new and profitable forms. Cinema capital too has faced hurdles in realising the value of the commodity. Despite its technological composition and the division of labour introduced via the studio system (Staiger 1982), films contain a high labour value which makes them too costly for individual purchase. Equally, replay technologies are costly, imperfect, complex and liable to damage, consequently movies are technically unsuitable for private, domestic modes of consumption. This necessitates consecutive showings or exhibitions in many different semi-private venues to which individuals are charged admission and which gradually return profits over time. The system of realisation for quasi-private goods, therefore, is predicated on producer-exhibitor relations and progressive realisation of the commodity's value.

The exhibitor, therefore, developed as the owner of the means of exhibition, theatres and replay equipment and employer of the staff to operate them. Copies of the film are hired from the producer and shown over a season. Door takings realise some or all of the surplus-value created in making the commodity, some of which is retained by the exhibitor to cover the cost of showing the film. The rest is returned to the producer. In other words, the exhibitor of quasi-private goods is essentially a form of merchant capital akin to the retailer of private cultural commodities, and functions as a technically necessary element in the circulation of quasi-private cultural commodities.

If the producer-exhibitor relation is the kernel of the circulation system, supplementary positions developed and became institutionalised as the quasi-private goods sector expanded. To realise the maximum proportion of the value produced in making the film, the production company needs to maintain tight control of copying and distribution at the regional level. Distributors became a significant part of the business, usually as part of the same corporate group as the production company or as independent agents. In passing, it is worth noting that there is a business logic in combining not only production and distribution but also production and exhibition; to maximise annual returns, integration provides guaranteed access to theatres, control over the length of a season and the turnover of films – hence the sweeping vertical integration which has characterised the operation of the movie industry virtually from its inception[18], and the growth of the massive Anglo-American combines which came to dominate the national and international flow of film throughout the modernising world (Cassady 1982, Cowie 1971, Gomery 1982a)[19]. The important political economic point is that distribution work involves simultaneously organising the hire and supply of copies to exhibitors and acting as a marketing agent in publicising the film's showing. This relation became an important part of the accumulation strategies adopted by cinema capital and remains in place today – giving rise, in fact, to a further position in the circulation system.

Since film production involves high labour costs which cannot easily be reduced, and because like all cultural commodities the film needs an immediate impact on the market to attract cinema-goers, producers concentrate instead on securing box-office success in a competitive market by mounting marketing and publicity campaigns. If superior marketing helps turn their film into the most popular of the season thereby excluding competing films from access to exhibition outlets, producers realise publicity profits, a disproportionate share of the total mass of surplus-value in circulation produced by industry workers in all competing firms.

18  Despite the extent of concentration and centralisation throughout the movie sector (figures on motion picture industry ownership concentration in the U.S. - are summarised in Sterling and Haight 1978: 87-89, see also Guback 1982), and the frequent interlocks between producers, distributors and exhibitors, each is dealt with in this analysis as a separate function within circulation. It is worth noting that in countries such as Australia where there is considerable indirect foreign control of film distribution, while distributor-exhibitors such as Hoyts Theatres and Village-Roadshow are formally independent companies, their links with the majors turn their independent distributor function effectively into an arm of the producer-distributor (e.g. Dermody and Jacka 1987: 108-134).

19  In addition, Boyd-Barrett (1977) and Tunstall (1977) locate the growth of the cinema within capitalist imperialism. Guback (1982) looks at the monopolising effects of American trans-nationals on the international film business. Dermody and Jacka (1987) and Tulloch (1982) examine the effects of this within the Australian context, with particular reference to the difficulties faced by the indigenous industry in getting a foothold. On this see also Pendakur (1982) for the Canadian case.

There are several keys to making marketing work. The first is the star system, borrowed from the theatre, where the reputations of well-known performers are exploited to boost the film's marketability and attract consumers (Kindem 1982b). Success depends on the efforts of the enormous marketing and publicity divisions set up by major film companies which organise posters, billboards, signs and stills around and inside theatres, advertising campaigns, promotional visits, personal appearances, interviews and reviews, stunts, first-night launches, and so on (Gomery 1982b, Tulloch 1982). The film marketer, however, is fundamentally dependent on the cooperation of the media, the quasi-public goods sector, which, in producing their own commodity, including news and reviews of the film and its stars, serves to publicise both. In other words,a quartet of producer-distributor-exhibitor-publicist relations is necessary in the circulation of quasi-private goods, with all activities geared towards making the film a long-run blockbuster which takes publicity profits out of the market.

What are the value flows under this system? How does each type of capital profit and hence expand? Production is financed by the producer (which may include an advance from the distributor). Exhibition costs including gross film rentals are deducted from gross takings and divided between exhibitor and distributor with the lion's share going to the latter. From the distributor's share, costs of prints and advertising organised are deducted, the remainder split between distributor and producer (Dermody and Jacka 1987: 161-166). Under this arrangement, the exhibitor operates as merchant capital sharing commercial profits with the distributor. The distributor also takes a share of commercial profits, but as the regional publicity agent for the producer, also makes a claim with the publicist on some of the publicity profits taken by the film. These flows were the foundations of their accumulation and expansion of each unit in the chain.

It is interesting to note that for a time, the simple exhibition model was, for a time, replaced by a second, more complex one. From merely showing a film, exhibitors began to assemble a show – the film combined with live performances – which was presented in palatial palaces and based on a revue/vaudeville formula. Exhibition capital, in other words, began to take the form of capital producing a further quasi-private good. Thus, from the 1920s, exhibition capital involved ownership of the means of exhibition, exhibition labour-power (e.g. attendants, projectionists) and artistic labour-power (e.g. incidental musicians, performers, actors). The show possessed a use-value over and above that of the film, although was partly constituted by it and to which it added, by exploiting the consumption-based leisure patterns being adopted by the urban working and especially middle classes; habits associated with 'going out' as a semi-private mode of consumption of capitalised 'entertainments' (Tulloch 1982: 19-22)[20]. From the middle decades of the century, however, the conditions of accumulation changed. Suburbanisation encouraged domestic modes of consumption. The cost and formality of going out seemed increasingly less attractive when compared to the convenience, comfort and cheapness of new forms of entertainment. Radio and record consumption had grown in the decades before, and television was dramatically restructuring the cultural marketplace (on television's challenge to film, see Stuart 1982). One of the most important changes, however, especially in the U.S., flowed from political action taken against the motion picture monopolies, which brought about significant although not complete divorce of producers from exhibitors (Whitney 1982, Gomery 1982a). In principle, exhibitors regained their independence, but producers still controlled supply and had the market power to impose conditions such as block-booking. The tightening cost-structures of exhibition demanded rationalisation. Interest in showmanship declined, and exhibition returned to the simple model of circulation required by quasi-private goods.

Two last points are worth noting. From a situation in the 1950s and 60s where film companies feared television, they have since discovered that surplus profits can be squeezed out of old movies by renting them to television stations for use in their own quasi-public forms of production; in fact, it is not uncommon now for television rights to have been pre-sold before film production is completed or for production to be partly financed by a station or network. Equally, film studios now additionally engage in television production, realising the surplus value produced in sales of rights to many stations for specified periods. While these are direct economic benefits, if shrewdly cast, marketed and merchandised, a television production can exploit the publicity effect this usage brings by maintaining the reputation of current movie stars, making their next film more likely to achieve blockbuster status. Another important recent development is the use of the film distribution system as an advertising medium. Exhibitors are increasingly renting their penetration into the movie-going audience on the same basis as the media. They calculate their venue's distributive efficiency, create a rate card, and circulate advertisers'

---

20  Cunningham (1980) and Walvin (1978) offer useful overviews of the emergence of 'leisure' from the Industrial Revolution to the present. See Wild (1979) for a complimentary localised study of the period 1900-1940. Dumazedier (1974) remains a seminal contribution, as does Paul Thompson (1975). Erenberg (1981) offers an interesting account which picks out how 'steppin' out' into the developing nightlife of a major city was increasingly defined as a significant if risky pleasure.

messages for a charge; in other words, exhibitors in recent times have begun to act as publicity capital.

The last point to note is that the advent of cable and satellite delivery and the video-cassette loom large as a major threat to future profitability of exhibitors. When dubbed onto videotape and released on video-cassette, filmed commodities are transformed into private goods, which eliminates the need for public exhibition and converts them into items suitable for domestic consumption[21]. It also gives producers the ability to realise profits for themselves, and makes it possible to diversify into cheaper but highly marketable productions such as musical concerts, sports events and so on. With this development, it is not difficult to imagine the eventual decline of exhibition capital as it has operated throughout most of the 20th century.

### 3.3.3 Quasi-Public Goods

These are the programmes transmitted by radio and television stations, and the items (intermediate cultural goods) produced for their use, such as serials, series, variety shows, musical features and concerts, documentaries, quizzes and game shows, news feeds and sporting broadcasts and so on. As noted earlier, newspapers and some periodicals have an ambiguous relation to these categories: they are partly private, partly quasi-public goods. Although the following discussion focuses on broadcasting, much of what is said also applies to print media.

Like all types of cultural commodities, radio and television stations employ labour power of various kinds, combining workers with means of cultural production to produce a specific type of commodity: a programme or edition. Quasi-public goods are unusual in two important respects in their production processes. First, much of the work performed in their creative stage of production uses both intermediate quasi-public goods (such as those created by radio and television production houses, and news agencies and syndicators), and existing private goods produced by the manufacturing sector (their commodities and the stars who created them) which they use under arrangement (fees, licenses). Second, in the

---

21   Australian motion-picture exhibitors at their 1988 conference were told of recent research which found that only 9% of the population were regular movie-goers, that most people found ticket prices (around $9 in the cities) too expensive, and that of the 58% of Australian homes with video recorders, most had switched to hiring movies as their major entertainment source with an average hire of 1.8 videos weekly (*The Courier Mail* 18 August 1988: 20).

case of broadcasting, there is not the extensive reproduction stage of
production (transcription, duplication) found in all other forms of cultural
production – the flow of pre-recorded/live programme items assembled in
the final stage of creation is simultaneously transformed into an electromagnetic signal and transmitted live (note that quasi-public goods producers also control the system of circulation for their products). The reasons
are linked to technical form of the good and their recent history.

Quasi-public goods are confronted by massive problems of realisation[22].
While produced in the form of commodities, for historical reasons, they
have no moment of exchange. While their technical and economic form is
that of public goods, as a *cultural* form, they are more akin to private
goods: evidence their design for individual consumption in domestic
settings such as home and car, and their mode of address within which the
audience appears as the singular 'you' (Higgins and Moss 1981: 31-70)[23].
Hence my use of the category *quasi*-public goods (cf. 'impure' public
goods). Companies producing quasi-public goods, therefore, are unable to
directly realise the value of their products in sales to those for whom the
commodity is intended: the audience. Instead, *indirect realisation via
publicity rents* is the primary accumulation strategy of this type of cultural
production.

Their mode of realisation is what underlies the duality of quasi-public

22   Brown (1986: 60-62) usefully discusses a number of economic aspects of broad-
     casting products as public goods, noting that few goods are either purely pri-
     vate or public in character, and concluding that because the cost of producing
     broadcasting programmes is independent of the numbers in its audience, they
     come very close to being pure public goods. As a sociologist, I feel compelled
     to emphasise the contradiction between the programme as an economic as op-
     posed to cultural entity – hence the label 'quasi-public' goods.
         Collins, Garnham and Locksley (1988: 7-9) do likewise, and further, connect
     the specific characteristics of this commodity form to the structure and opera-
     tion of the television industry in the U.K. I note, however, that there are many
     points where their *economic* analysis of television seem to intersect with my
     *sociological* analysis of corporate cultural production. To that extent, it would
     seem useful at some stage to elaborate any connections between these two
     different types of investigation.
23   Media programmes position the aggregate (economic) subject of their content
     as its individual (cultural) consumer; this is the contradiction of media at the
     level of consumption. Bonney and Wilson (1983) and Williamson (1978) are
     excellent studies revealing the possible individual subjectivities constructed in
     and through media texts. Note that the personal mode of address affected by
     media is determined by their publicity function. Since advertisements are ad-
     dressed to individuals as private consumers, the media product, an ostensible
     public good, must be culturally consumed as a private good.

goods – already touched upon in the discussion of private goods. Quasi-public goods production is a complex form: it involves producing a good whose consumption creates a useful effect and operates simultaneously within its own sphere of production and the circulation circuits of other commodities. Like all cultural commodities, quasi-public goods are intended to be consumed by audiences but in this case, an audience to whom the good cannot be sold. Through consumption, audience members become familiar with the different items and objects which comprise the media content; for example, television audiences come to know local drama series and their stars, the directors and stars of films used in movie slots and review programmes, visiting authors and their books through arts and entertainment news and magazine programmes, the current recordings available through music video shows, and so on. This is the publicity effect created for other cultural commodities, generated by the internal production processes of quasi-public goods production. Consequently, *publicity is an inevitable by-product of the consumption of this type of cultural commodity, and is why the quasi-public goods sector is simultaneously the publicity sector.* The realisation problems created by the technical form of these goods are resolved by producer companies turning this effect to commercial purposes. Manufacturers wishing to publicise their commodities can employ it, in an exchange which *indirectly* realises the value of the labour employed in making the media programme or edition in the first place; they rent the distributive capacities of the medium for the time or space it takes to speak their message. It is worth noting in passing that since distributive efficiency is dependent on the size of the audience (and the marginal costs of reaching increased audiences can be low), accumulation strategies have also pushed media corporations towards their characteristic horizontal integration and cross-media ownership.

The fundamental relation underlying capitalised quasi-public cultural commodity production and circulation, therefore, is a complex relation built upon intermediate goods producer-quasi-public goods producer/publicity medium-advertiser relations, with the duality of the producer/publicist at its centre. As seen in the earlier section on marketing, quasi-public goods producers accumulate by setting advertising rates which reflect their own competitive position, the costs of producing the programme or edition (some of which is returned to the intermediate goods producer in the form of fees), and a share of the publicity profits (and/or reputation) they generate for their advertisers and/or the private goods manufacturers for whom they act as publicists. In this way, quasi-public goods producers/-the publicity complex have become a central element of productive capital

within the culture industry, even though apparently located in the sphere
of commodity circulation.

Interestingly, there was no historical necessity to this. The economic
form of quasi-public goods is not inherent to their technical form but
followed from the political conditions of their introduction. From the
outset, it has been technically possible to transmit electromagnetic signals
to exclude access by consumers. There are two possibilities: the first is the
so-called 'sealed set' option where receivers are manufactured such that
they receive only a single frequency and their owners pay a subscription or
licence fee at regular intervals to the station; the second is to scramble or
encode transmissions so that individual listeners must buy or hire a
decoder from the station to hear or see the programme. Many governments throughout the Western world canvassed these options in the 1920s
and 1930s in relation to the introduction of radio (Barnard 1983: 99,
MacDonald 1979: 24). The struggles between different social groups,
different fractions of capital, and the state, over the form of the radio
system and for a controlling stake, was more or less duplicated with the
introduction of television in the middle of the century (Mundy 1982, see
also Barnouw 1966-1970, Briggs 1961-1971).

Furthermore, the producer/publicist-advertiser relation presently at the
centre of quasi-public goods production, has historically, not been the only
model. Differentiating them necessitates distinguishing between the *production* of items to be transmitted, and their *programming*, where the two
models differ in terms of the extent of control the station exerts over
production. When first introduced, commercial radio stations served to
distribute cultural objects prepared independently, whether talks, variety
shows, plays, musical recitals, gramophone records, or whatever. Stations
programmed but did not generally create items, an approach which
dominated both radio and television until about the 1940s (e.g. MacDonald 1979: 1-90). The essence of this first model was the sponsorship system;
where commercial sponsors (a modern form of patronage) or their agents
(in fact, advertising agencies tended to be the active entrepreneur in this
arrangement) contracted cultural producers such as individual artists or
established musical or theatrical companies to produce items. The sponsor
then rented a quantity of airtime to broadcast both item and the advertisements contained within it. In paying for production costs, sponsors had
effective ownership and control over the master and its content, and
exclusive naming and advertising rights. The station did little more than
organise various pre-recorded items into a programme and present it to

air[24] – as the mere medium, the station could make little claim on the profits being made by agency or sponsor.

Complex and multifarious conditions during the 1940s and into the 1950s led eventually to a modification of the model, which became the foundation first of television and later radio practice. Media companies were beginning to recognise the potential profits in being master of both programming and production, selling not exclusive but multiple advertisement around items; further, as they began to grasp the commercial potential of coupling tightly controlled demographic programming with audience research, they learnt to sell the idea of saturation campaigns to advertisers wanting market impact for their products, rather than single spots (e.g. Hall 1976: 48-61)[25]. As manufacturers scrambled to exploit the post-war fervour for families, suburban homes and new types of domestic commodities, they enlarged their marketing departments and increased

---

24  MacDonald (1979) provides a useful overview of radio, and Fox (1984: 173-217) a less-academic account of television's adoption of this first model during its first decades. Hall (1976), Kent (1983) and Walker (1973) are histories of Australian television or radio written for popular consumption but contain many details of the sponsors, agencies, artists and media involved. Williams (1981: 42-43) also discusses sponsorship but without much detail. My model represents the simplest form of media production in its early stage and necessarily ignores many variations and complexities. Some are worth noting. The artists and/or companies used in the earliest period were combined into a temporary production unit, usually identified by the sponsor's name, but these units later metamorphosed into independent production companies specialising in radio and television production. The medium usually provided the transcription facilities and staff for the unit (which would have marginally effected the value flows), ultimately deciding whether to broadcast the item and at what time. Stations did organise some production themselves, some, especially network head-offices, forming highly successful production units of their own. Most remarkable is the fact of advertising agency control, or rather, the lack of station power to control production. MacDonald (1979: 32) cites figures for one radio network in 1929 indicating that 33% of its programmes were produced by agencies, 28% by the network for its sponsors (which would have been mediated by agencies), 20% by the sponsors themselves and 19% by independent producers.

25  Hall (1976) deals with television in Australia, MacDonald (1979) and Walker (1973) examine radio in the U.S. and Australia respectively. Gitlin (1978) remains a highly suggestive account of the connections between the development of social science departments in American universities, the institutionalisation of particular types of commercially-funded media research, and the inhibiting effects of this combination on social scientific analysis of systems of mass communication.

advertising budgets, but as advertising rates increased, they demanded greater cost-effectiveness, encouraged by the increasingly influential market research agencies who were offering a more disciplined approach to advertising (e.g. Fox 1984: 172-217)[26]. This encouraged stations to adopt even tighter approaches to programming, an approach I refer to in later chapters as 'formatting'. In other words, a second model of quasi-public goods production was being erected during these decades: out of the basic sponsor-medium structure emerged the producer/publicist-advertiser model which exists today. For the media, this represents a more advanced and more profitable development of the first, although still retaining the basic system of indirect realisation inherent to the economic form of quasi-public goods.

There were other consequences. Because these goods are made by assembling pre-recorded or intermediate goods into a continuous flow, the growth of the media provided opportunities for further independent producers. Companies specialising in the production of items for incorporation within programmes and editions have become a specialised albeit dependent form of capital operating within the culture industry, as intermediate quasi-public goods producers who realise the value of their production by sale or lease to broadcasting capital (e.g. Boyd-Barrett 1980, Moran 1982; 1984). Quasi-public goods production also generates exchanges between broadcasting media and the manufacturers of private consumer goods, especially television stations with film companies and radio stations with record companies. These are immensely important aspects of the culture industry: in that sense, quasi-public goods production is fundamentally implicated in the circulation of private cultural goods and derives its profits from this position.

A last point should be made. In a situation which echoes the conditions of their initial introduction, the late 20th century is seeing the introduction of 'pay' television and radio. The delivery of media programmes via an encoded or cabled system whether originated locally or distributed via satellite, enables the insertion of a moment of exchange (Barr 1985, cf. also Collins et al. 1988: 4-5). This suggests the real reason why broadcasting capital is interested in participating in their development: they transform quasi-public into private goods, which offers broadcasting companies possibilities for expansion free of the dependence on publicity

---

26  Fox (1984) deals with the American case. Stephen (1981) provides an excellent account of the impact of these methods in Australia in the context of the expansion of suburbanisation and consumerism. Ewen (1976) examines some of the social and psychological aspects of this transformation of advertising practice.

rents. In that sense, they foreshadow, perhaps, a different future for capital invested in radio and television.

## 3.4 Conclusion

We have seen throughout this chapter that cultural commodity producers of various types must cooperate with other capitals in order to realise and expand their value. The imperatives of their accumulation thus provide the conditions for particular exchanges between specialised capitals where these relations have, over time, hardened into an industry division of labour. The linkages which constitute the sectors of the culture industry are represented diagrammatically as in Figure 3.1:

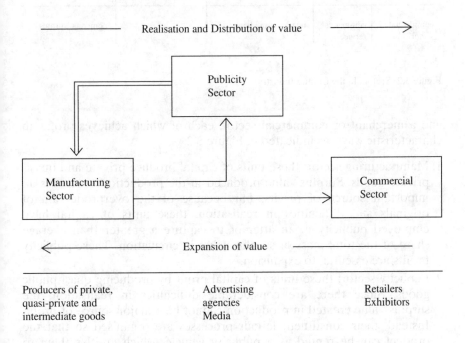

Figure 3.1 Division of Labour in the Culture Industry and Flows of Value

From this industry division of labour we can identify the three principal sectors in the culture industry: a manufacturing sector, a publicity sector

| Sector | Product | Production and Circulation Relations | Realisation | Source of Profits |
|---|---|---|---|---|
| manufacturing sector | private goods | producer - retailer (marketer, publicist) | direct & immediate via retail sales | labour surplus publicity surplus |
| | quasi-private goods | producer - exhibitor (marketer/distributor, publicist) | direct & progressive through box office | labour surplus publicity surplus |
| publicity sector | quasi-public goods | producer/publicist - advertiser (intermediate goods supplier) | direct through advertising | publicity rent labour surplus |
| commercial sector | commercial service | retailer - supplier | — | comercial surplus |

Figure 3.2  Sectors In the Culture Industry

and a merchant or commercial sector, each of which achieves profits in characteristic ways, as indicated in Figure 3.2:

1. Manufacturing sector: these units of capital produce private and quasi-private goods. Surplus-value produced in the production process is an important source of profits, but because of the overproduction of originals and difficulties in realisation, these units of capital have employed publicity in an attempt to capture a greater than average share of the total mass of surplus-value in circulation. These publicity profits are essential to expansion.

2. Publicity sector: these units of capital profit by producing quasi-public goods. Since there are considerable difficulties in realisation, the surplus-value created in production cannot be a major source of profit. Instead, their constituent labour processes are organised so that the product can be rented as a publicity vehicle, which entitles them to claim a share of the publicity profits appropriated by their clients.

3. Commercial sector: capital invested in this sector, like commercial capital in other industries, profits by taking a share of the surplus-value created in the production processes of the manufacturers whose goods they exchange. This applies both to both exhibitors and retailers.

Perhaps one of the most notable features of the culture industry suggested by the preceding analysis is the importance of the publicity sector within the culture industry. Not only does its operation act to increase the relative value of an advertiser's output and thus increase the likelihood of realisation, but the production and circulation of quasi-public goods also creates the conditions for expansion of the culture industry generally, then allocates particular capitals to beneficial positions. As the publicity sector plays a more and more significant and necessary role in expansion for the corporations of culture, so the accumulation strategies of this sector flow back into core areas of production. Private goods are increasingly produced in a form which makes them easily assimilated for transmission through the publicity system.

From knowledge of the structural underpinnings of each sector, its industry function and hence its primary source of profits, we can begin in following chapters to consider the forces operating in the labour processes which make up each sector and the diverse surface appearances of each. We can begin to identify why each labour process takes the form it does and which forces are pushing development in which directions. It begins to suggest, for example, why manufacturers search out artists and works which have potential for publicity, who possess mannerisms and styles which are a combination of conventional and consciously idiosyncratic features, an appearance, which can be marketed and publicised. Equally, we can see why production of intermediate publicity goods is organised around the display and promotion of another commodity, a task whose referent is not itself but the selling of another object. Why it is that to the workers employed to carry out this task, the purpose and referent of their work is given, as are the conventional languages and techniques to be used, as well as the audience their work is intended to attract – and why their art is to speak rhetorically of another. In the case of media production, the making of quasi-public goods, where the primary source of profits is publicity rent, we can see why media workers are organised to programme and present an object which is not only to be enjoyed in itself by the largest possible share of the targeted consumer segment, but which is designed to organise these individuals into preferred patterns and habits of use in their consumption of the programme. In this way, the results of their work are expected to increase the distributive efficiency of the station or publication on which they are employed.

By the same token, knowing the primary sources of profit of each sector, suggests the extent to which degradation of the conditions of labour is an issue. In the manufacturing sector, for example, we might expect to find that reducing the value of some forms of labour is important, but that ultimately, the work done in circulating commodities allows the continued employment of selected highly-paid stars. On the other hand, since the quasi-public goods sector has considerable difficulty realising surplus-value, we might expect to find that the value of the labour employed in these labour processes has been significantly reduced. Thus we will see in later chapters that the media have extensively 'formatted' production such that their programmes are presented by labour-power of relatively average characteristics.

# Chapter 4
# The Corporate Organisation of Cultural Production: The Creative Stage and the Project Team

## 4.1 Introduction

If, in abstract, epochal terms, the artist is an historically constituted form of labour which is incompatible with the capital relation, it raises empirical issues concerning the organisational conditions of artistic work in the culture industry. How has the capitalist production of cultural commodities been organised in the present era and especially in the corporations of culture?

There seem to be a variety of views on the matter. Theodor Adorno, writing in 1941 suggests that:

the production of popular music can be called 'industrial' only in its promotion and distribution, whereas the act of producing a song-hit still remains in a handicraft stage. The production of popular music is highly centralised in its economic organisation, but still 'individualistic' in its social mode of production. The division of labor among the composer, harmoniser, and arranger is not industrial but rather pretends industrialisation (1978a: 205).

In similar vein, Garnham (1979: 139) and Miège (1979: 301) have made more recent references to artisan forms of labour organisation within the culture industry. On the other hand, Bonney and Wilson have argued that throughout the Western world, media workers are employed as wage-labourers in an industrial, capitalist commodity production process (1983: 30-60). In a broader, more ambitious argument, Raymond Williams (1981) lists a selection of concepts he considers necessary for a sociology of culture, including various types of institutions (artists and patrons, artists and markets, post-market institutions), means of production (inherent resources, non-human, reproduction systems, and so on), and production relations (e.g. artisanal, post-artisanal, market professional, corporate professional).

From within non-Marxist paradigms, a small number of ethnographies have examined particular occupations and their organisation. Most popular have been studies of journalism (e.g. Gans 1979, Glasgow University Media Group 1976, 1980, Tuchman 1978, Tunstall 1971, Schlesinger 1978), film and television production (e.g. Elliott 1972, 1977, Moran 1982, 1984, Powdermaker 1950) and music recording (e.g. Chapple and Garofalo 1977, Denisoff 1975, Frith 1978). Most of these, however, are restricted to a single form of cultural practice, are based on naturalistic methodologies, and have little explanatory power. Their number and focus reflect the fact that as Wolff points out, there has been a remarkable lack of interest in the institutional context in which cultural production occurs (1981: 31). More specifically, *none of these examines cultural production as a labour process organised around the capital-labour relation or the embedded specifics of its constituent relations* (cf. Garnham 1979, Miège 1979, also Wolff 1981: 48). This is the focus of this chapter.

## 4.2 Accumulation and the Capitalist Labour Process

### 4.2.1 Marx and the Labour Process

Marx' analysis of the labour process was central to his account of the history and structure of the capitalist mode of production (see especially 1954: Parts III, IV and V, also 1976, see also Braverman 1974, Elger 1982, Harvey 1982, Littler 1982), which developed historically out of the practical and juridical dispossession of direct producers from their means of production and their subsequent employment by the emerging bourgeois class. Capitalist production is primarily exchange-value production undertaken to expand capital. This means that work expended in producing the capitalist commodity creates a surplus component of labour value which, when converted into money, becomes the profit returned to the capitalist after exchange. Profits enable expansion: the greater the overall surplus, the greater the rate of accumulation. Under pressures of competition, the immediate concern of capitalists is how to increase the rate of surplus-value production in the labour process itself, how to cheapen and reduce the value of the labour consumed in production relative to the total value of the output. Particular valorisation strategies available to capitalists depend on the conditions in which they are operating, but historically, the primary mechanisms have involved reconstructing the division of labour around technological innovations and the progressive separation of conception and execution, embodying the former in a management stratum. Under these conditions, workers are reduced to possessors only of their labour-power, a generalised capacity to labour.

Marx identified three 'stages of development' of the labour process within the capitalist mode of production[1]; simple cooperation, manufacture and modern industry (machinofacture), each based on a particular form of labour organisation. Since aspects of these models will be important later in this analysis, their central features need to be summarised.

Simple cooperation (Marx 1954: 305-317) is the most basic model, a form of capitalist production wherein in its earliest stages, "The workshop of the medieval master craftsman is simply enlarged" (1954: 305). Here, the labour process is inherited from a previous mode of production: the types of workers employed, the equipment, techniques and human skills set to work, are drawn from the handicraft system of production found in the guild workshop with its craft divisions of labour and hierarchical structure of masters, journeymen and apprentices. As the cooperation model develops, there are qualitative shifts in its constituent relations of production. Capitalists come to acquire ownership of the workshop, the materials and the equipment used, and employ otherwise independent craft workers as wage labour to perform the work of production. Retention of the craft division of labour mediates the capitalist authority relations in production; since workers retain control of the working methods and the knowledges these require, they are able to maintain a degree of control over the form and content of the labour process within the workshop.

---

1    Littler (1982: 21) raises the issue of whether Marx intended these as analytical or historical models, and if the former, the subsequent problem of periodisation. There is a tendency, partly due to Marx, to regard them as invariable and unilinear stages of capitalist development whose chronology can be identified (e.g. Braverman 1974). The work of Littler (1982), Edwards (1979), Stark (1980) and others suggests that there are several variant models of capitalist production, and that because of different conditions and rhythms – and reversals – of development in different industries, any number may coexist throughout production generally. Diversity amongst capitalist production systems derives from the specific forms of capital and labour which constitute them and their historical relations, especially through the mediation of the state (cf. also Edwards 1979: 21): in that sense, Littler (1982: 34-35) is justified in demanding more historical and industry-based studies. Marx' models, therefore, are best treated primarily as analytical types, with the question of their historicality being decided via empirical research – the strategy I follow in this work.

Nonetheless, capitalist proprietorship has transformed the general conditions of production. By concentrating workers and means of production within a single workshop, cooperation turns individual labours into a social, more productive form. As the directing authority, capitalists are able to extend the working day, accelerate the tempo of work, and make it more continuous and orderly. While this arrangement does not affect the mode of working or the task content, it does increase the rate of surplus-value production: productivity – ultimately, the ratio of surplus to necessary labour value in the commodity – is raised, hence the rate of profit after exchange. In other words, in the simple cooperation model, appropriation of strategic control in the interests of accumulation limits workers to operational control, but the labour process is still only formally subsumed under the capital relation[2].

As competition intensifies and capitalists are driven to further increase the rate of exploitation, they introduce changes into the labour process which shift its mode of organisation from simple cooperation to the manufacture model. This proceeds by wresting control of the labour process from craft workers and sub-dividing the craft division of labour to forge a detail division of labour. Marx offers two illustrations of this development (1954: 318-347) both entailing a shift from a workshop to a factory (although not yet a mechanised factory) setting. The production of complex objects such as carriages (heterogeneous production), requires the coordinated combination of several types of workers such as tailors, locksmiths, painters, wheelwrights, upholsterers and carpenters. From working on one carriage at a time, production is expanded and permanent employees work on several simultaneously under the authority of the capitalist. Craft skills are reshaped and narrowed, turned into a form

---

2    Some have expressed doubts concerning the value of Marx' notion of the 'for-
     mal' and 'real' subsumption of labour under capital (e.g. Littler and Salaman
     1982: 253-255). Whilst I partly accept this assessment, if only because of Marx'
     sketchy and ambiguous account, I would argue that real subsumption is best
     understood not as referring to fixed, irreversible outcomes, but as an abstract
     polarity on a continuum. It is therefore an historical position which capitalists
     have to achieve – and maintain against reversals. In other words, the ongoing
     struggle between capital and labour may shift the degree of subsumption back-
     wards and forwards between the two polarities, depending on the balance of
     class forces at any conjuncture. Equally, the passage proceeds in stages. Differ-
     ent elements – labour, raw materials, task structure and content, objects pro-
     duced – and relations between them, can be worked upon separately. At any
     time, some of these may be formally subsumed, others thoroughly capitalised.
     Historically-grounded studies are needed to restore any value Marx' di-
     chotomy might have.

applicable only to carriage-making, and made the exclusive function of workers functioning as detail labour. In the second case, Marx examines the employment of identical craft workers employed to do the same kind of work (homogeneous production) such as the making of paper, type or needles. From workshop organisation where each works in a handicraft way and makes a complete object in a succession of stages, the capitalist disconnects each stage of the object's manufacture, takes over the planning function and redistributes each partial, manual operation to detail workers. Each needle or piece of paper or type is now the product of detail workers working in combination.

By reconstructing the division of labour and in effect, reducing the value of the labour-power employed ('deskilling', in recent terminology), the capitalist increases the rate of surplus value production applying in the workplace. Moreover, manufacturing capitalists exercise firmer control over production than under the simple cooperation model; they have reconstructed the setting and tempo of work and are beginning to determine its type. Manufacturing, detail work in a factory setting and directed by a capitalist manager, represents a decisive shift from formal subsumption towards (although not yet attaining) a stage of real subsumption of the labour process under capital.

Before turning to Marx' arguments concerning the development of the mechanised factory, the modern industry model of capitalist production, a brief but important comment is necessary on the two already discussed. He seems to treat the simple cooperation model as a transitional phase which quickly gives way to manufacturing. Historically, that may or may not be the case, depending on conditions applying in a particular type of production. For reasons which will become evident when examining the particular characteristics of the culture industry, I want to suggest that Marx glosses over this model too quickly, because it is possible to speak of an 'early' and 'mature' form of simple cooperation where the latter takes the form of a capitalist workshop (cf. craft workshop). In this situation, the owner has legal possession of the technical means of production (hence cutting off the possibility of independent artisan production), functions as directing authority within production, and employs the labour force under wage-labour relations. Because technological innovation of the means of production has progressed only a short distance, the division of labour is still identifiably craft-*based*, though subject to relatively minor technical reconstruction depending on the type of commodity being produced. In short, compared to medieval and early capitalist forms, the mature capitalist workshop reflects a *transformation* of the relations of and in production, but evidences *identifiable connections to craft forms of work and their division of labour*, although still falling short of the technically reconstructed detail form associated with the mature manufacturing model or the industry division of labour of the mechanised factory. My use of the term 'capitalist workshop' in later discussion should be understood to refer to the mature form of simple cooperation.

Consolidation and development of manufacturing increases the flow of products onto the market and creates diversity in the types of commodities available. This goes hand in hand with the generalisation of commodity exchange throughout society and increasing numbers of capitalists each attempting to expand their capital. Heightened competition is again the agent of change, feeding pressures back into production. In order to gain advantage over their competitors, some capitalists initiate a new cycle of development by building large-scale factories and equipping them with newly-invented machinery. These machines have been designed to absorb workers' tools and skills, bringing a dramatic increase in labour productivity. Mechanisation of the labour process in the factory setting marks the transition from manufacturing to modern industry. It obliterates the final remnants of the craft division of labour, thereby undermining existing structures of worker resistance and ushering in the real subsumption of the labour process. Production is organised now not with reference to traditional skills and crafts but around relations between machine and labourer, based on an industrial division of labour defined in terms of the machines it is built around. Differences between types of work are minimised. Most are operative in character, transforming the labour force into a mass of deskilled labourers. Mechanisation also heralds new and more comprehensive structures of labour control. Capitalist organisation is objectified in continuous-flow production and automatic machinery which confronts workers as an impersonal imperative to labour, severely diminishing their power to influence what is produced and how (Marx 1954: Part IV, 1976: 1021-1023).

## 4.2.2 Braverman and the 'Monopoly Capital' Model of Capitalist Production

Using this general framework, Braverman (1974) examines the organisation of the labour process under conditions of 'monopoly capitalism' and details aspects of what he refers to as 'the degradation of work in the twentieth century'.

In contrast to Marx, Braverman suggests that only with monopoly capitalism does the logic of capitalist development come to fruition (Stark 1980: 26), and proposes that this most recent stage of capitalist development has a characteristic form of labour process (Littler 1982: 26). This I will refer to as the 'corporate' model (which I am taking to be a mature form of Marx' modern industry model). At the end of the 19th century, he argues, there were still significant areas of production in which craft work was pivotal to its organisation. Since workers conserved skills through unions and trade associations, they retained effective if residual control within the workplace despite the industrialisation around them, and only scientific management, the principles of management as espoused by Taylor and its implementation by capitalists in the early decades of the 20th century, completed the transition to real subordination. Taylorism was founded upon several principles. They included, first, the dissociation of the labour process from the skills of the worker via the collection of workplace knowledges and their classification and standardisation into rules of practice; second, the separation of conception and execution; and third, the use of this monopoly over knowledge to control the labour process and its mode of execution (Braverman 1974: 85-123). Throughout production generally, technology is highly sophisticated and largely automated, and the previous industrial division of labour has been thoroughly fragmented into partial, machine-minding tasks requiring only unskilled or at best semi-skilled labour – what I will refer to as the 'corporate' division of labour – and organised under these modern forms of control.

There have been important critiques of Braverman's analysis (e.g. Elger 1982: 32-33, Littler 1982: 25-35)[3], most of which challenge his use of the craft worker as the measure of skilled labour, the unilinear deskilling effect of capitalist development, the timing and acceptance of scientific management, and the absence of a working class politics in his account of the making of 20th century conditions of work. Whatever is specifically problematic in *Labor and Monopoly Capital*, this work does, in my view, capture something of the immanent tendencies of corporate capital in relation to the labour process; that is, the point towards which corporate capital is propelled in attempting to realise the law of value; or obversely, the objective pressures against which labour employed in corporate sectors of the economy has to struggle. In this sense, Braverman's is a useful model, since it enables analysis of recent developments in the workplace from a Marxist perspective (cf. also Littler 1982: 27-30).

In the light of these criticisms, Littler (1982: 30-35) indicates a number of directions for further theoretical and empirical analysis of the labour

---

3    The post-Braverman literature is too extensive to indicate in full. Important examples which have contributed to this work include Boreham, Clegg and Dow (1986), Burawoy (1978, 1979), Clegg and Dunkerley (1980), Edwards (1979), Elger (1982), Littler (1982), Littler and Salaman (1982) and Stark (1980).

process in general and in particular instances, all of which are important to this study. The labour process, he argues, has a relative autonomy in relation to the mode of production; that is, "though the labour process takes place within an economic and historical context, the context nevertheless rarely provides a precise determination of work organisation" (1982: 30). I take Littler to mean here that since Marx built his model of the capitalist mode of production by elaborating its internal laws of motion, it is important to insist on a *tendentially* determinant relation between context and labour process. Detailed research is needed, however, to examine the historical forms of capital and labour which enabled the establishment of particular industries, the history of their relations and the forms through which they presently exist, and perhaps just as important, the conditions external to production which impinge upon and mediate the structure and content of work organisation. Research which identifies variant labour processes emerging under specific social conditions can begin to offer explanations for these deviations from the Marx-Braverman models.

Furthermore, there is a "central indeterminacy of labour potential which must be resolved in other ways" (Littler 1982: 31). The capacity to work can be purchased on the market but must still be realised in the labour process itself, and to remain profitable and competitive, capitalists have to face the ongoing problem of extracting the preferred type and productivity of labour. Labour, in other words, remains an active agent in the capital relation and an unwilling presence within mechanisms of accumulation (see also Elger 1982: 24). Braverman's one-sided structure of control is simultaneously a system which stimulates, motivates and harnesses labour's creative and productive powers; and under changing conditions on the factory floor and in the wider society (especially in relation to the state), its foundations are constantly shifting (Boreham, Clegg and Dow 1986, Burawoy 1979, Edwards 1979). In an era of widespread unionism and state-sanctioned industrial rights, corporations cannot simply exercise despotic control over labour but must bargain and compromise with workers and adapt to changing competitive and labour market conditions; in short, they are forced to grapple with the tensions and conflicts which beset their arena of operation.

The third issue Littler raises relates to the "structural dynamics of capitalism" (1982: 33-34). Beyond their production concerns, corporations have various financial strategies for increasing income and expanding their capital base, including currency speculation, cumulative acquisition, asset stripping, taxation minimisation, and credit manipulations. More fundamentally, accumulation requires that surplus value has not only to be *produced* but also *realised*; Littler reiterates Marx' argument that production and circulation are the two necessary cycles of capitalist accumulation. A branch of industry producing similar product lines produces a mass of surplus-value which circulates in the market under given conditions of effective demand, and surplus-value is returned only if and when goods are exchanged. Accordingly, companies compete via marketing and merchandising strategies to realise the largest possible share of the total mass of surplus in circulation; not only the full value of the surplus-value created in their own production but some of that produced by their competitors – that is, surplus-profits (as in the case of publicity profits discussed in chapter 3). Consequently, it is entirely feasible that given the state of competition and the marketing and merchandising resources at its command, an industry or sector can produce commodities at an adequate rate of surplus-value in production to ensure a satisfactory rate of profit. There is no immediate pressure in these circumstances to degrade production conditions further – indeed doing so may cause industrial conflict – even though not doing so may mean, for example, conceding significant control to particular sections of the labour force, or paying wages above the social average. In this situation it is more profitable for capital to concentrate on creating efficiencies in circulation through the sales effort. This point becomes important later in examining the relation between production and circulation in cultural commodity production.

In short, while flawed, Braverman's work is a seminal contribution to an understanding of modern work organisation. Future analysis, however, should:

emphasis first, the complex character of the development of the real subsumption of the labour process to capital, as the development of a large-scale collective organisation of production which dominates any specific form of labour; second, the importance of analysing the development of the complex organisation of collective labour in relation to specific strategies of valorisation and accumulation and their characteristic contradictions and forms of class struggle....[In other words] A more adequate account of the transformation of the labour process would involve a more complex and sustained analysis of the historical development of capital accumulation, the contradictions to which accumulation gives rise and the manner in which such contradictions develop and are resolved in class struggle within and beyond production (Elger 1982: 32-33, cf. also Edwards 1976: 124).

While this chapter focuses not on the capitalist labour process generally but the organisation of work in one industry, and draws on the general thrust of Braverman's ideas to do so, it accepts the spirit of this injunction.

## 4.2.3 The Specific Conditions of Capitalist Cultural Commodity Production

To recap the arguments presented in chapter 2, the historical constitution of art and the artist has given rise to a form of practice with constituent objects, relations and rules of combination, the totality of which contradicts the capital relation. Art is work conventionally regarded as requiring the imagination and talent of gifted and named individuals who require space to work, free from expectation especially of commercial kinds. Under these conditions, guided by profound if capricious inspiration, artists can create works of genius. It is, therefore, a fundamentally irrational process which conflicts with the calculating, accumulative logic of modern capitalism. The industrialisation of cultural practices which gathered pace from the early 19th century, expanded and diversified the recognised range of cultural forms and in doing so, reconstituted the artist as an enormous variety of specialised but still craft-based occupations; the writer, for example, was sub-divided into a range of types including biographers and novelists, playwrights and screenplay writers, copywriters, journalists, and so on. Nonetheless, to a greater or lesser extent, cultural workers such as these are treated by their employers, co-workers and publics and most of all by themselves, as artists, as possessors of rare, expressive and individual gifts and unconventional personalities, and are accorded the organisational status and conditions of labour these attributes are said to deserve. This gives rise to immediate tendencies in production. Depending on the extent to which a particular activity has been technically or bureaucratically redefined, employers must preserve artistic conditions of work and the costs and conditions associated with the search for originality. Artistic labour personifies a demand for personal autonomy in the workplace and the high value of creativity and originality, which provides a material basis for resistance by artistic workers to subordination and control, and against which capital has to struggle. The historical problem facing capitalists engaged in the production and circulation of cultural commodities has been how to devise a system of employment which enables artists to create genuine original and marketable works of art which are stamped with the signs of genius (cf. Miège 1979: 305), but which also disciplines the creative process and brings it under the control of the firm, such that management may set the standards, rate and timing of creation and keep labour costs to a minimum.

Rather than the history, what will be examined here is *the form of organisation which characterises the corporate era of cultural production*, explaining its peculiarities in terms of the contradictions of its art-capital relation. This will entail going inside the corporate labour process to look at the structure and content of the practices which comprise it; to note that it reveals some of the general characteristics of all developed capitalist labour processes as well as the specific contradictions and strategies of accumulation and resistance which reflect the particular form of practice. Its corporate form, in other words, represents the historical compromises achieved by artists and capitalists in their ongoing struggle and shows how capital and art have been reshaped in the course of this encounter.

## 4.3 The Organisation of Corporate Cultural Commodity Production

As indicated in chapter 1, and following the work of Garnham and Murdock and others (e.g. Garnham 1979, Murdock 1982)[4], the primary empirical assumption of my argument relates to the market dominance of the corporations of culture across the culture industry especially in the decades since World War II, and the distinctiveness of the form of cultural production which operates inside them. My search for the corporate form, however, is not based on naturalistic, empiricist assumptions: this is a critique of its *institutional* conditions.

Accordingly, investigation demands more than identifying the major corporate groups at the international and national levels and examining their internal organisational characteristics. Quite apart from anything else, production for transnational corporations such as Thorn-EMI, 20th Century Fox, Philips, Sony, News International and RCA, while based mainly in Britain, the United States, Western Europe and increasingly Japan – and curiously, in the case of media corporations, Australia – is carried out at the regional and local subsidiary or divisional level, and it is these firms which must be the primary empirical site for any analysis. Moreover, it is not easy to empirically bound the corporations of culture; they reveal many connections through ownership and exchange into other economic spheres, to each other, into the periphery of the culture industry, and into state forms of cultural production. As indicated in

---

4    For general discussions of concentration and conglomeration within the culture industry see, e.g. Garnham (1979), Mattelart (1979), Murdock (1982), Murdock and Golding (1977), and Schiller (1969). For more specific studies within particular forms, see, e.g. Coser *et al.* (1982) for publishing, and Frith (1978) for the recording industry.

chapter 1, I am treating the figure 'the corporations of culture' as an institutional term realised empirically as a complex of corporate offices, subsidiaries and divisions articulated through various transactions, sub-contracts and engagements to other sectors of the industry[5] and economy; and within that, I am treating 'the corporate form of cultural production' as the characteristic and dominant institutional form through which production is organised in this context. Having said that, it is worth noting that the corporate form may also be found in some of the smaller firms operating in the semi-periphery of the industry. Through its outwards connections, the corporate form of organisation has 'imperialised'[6] other sectors to a greater or lesser extent. The market power of these oligopolies tends to refashion production systems throughout the industry as a whole, generalising the corporate version of capitalist cultural commodity production even throughout the extensive independent sector (cf. Miège 1979: 309).

---

5   A significant volume of production is carried out by independents ranging from owner-operators (e.g. freelance writers and directors) to medium-sized firms (e.g. publishers, creative shops, recording companies, film and recording processing and post-production companies). Most perform specialised capital or labour intensive functions in a manner which spreads financial risk throughout the industry. Much of the creative experimentation takes place in the independent periphery, partly because their production system tends to be closer to a form of artisan or craft-workshop production.

6   This imperialism occurs, as Boyd-Barrett (1977: 119-120) points out, as much by dissemination, where clients either adopt or absorb changes as a result of contact, flowing through the shape of the communication vehicle exported, the set of industrial arrangements which goes with it, and the body of values concerning ideal practice, as well as specific media contents – to which might be added the impact of corporations on the cultural marketplace as in the formation of particular taste communities, modes of consumption, and a range of labour market conditions.

## 4.3.1 The Organisational Division of Labour in Corporate Production

Figure 4.1[7] represents the essence of the organisational division of labour in corporate production systems[8]. The first and most important point to note is that it is divided into two distinct stages; creation and reproduction. Artistic, creative work entails both conception and execution, the end result of which is an 'original'. This must be commoditised, which involves 're-producing' it in quantity. The reproduction stage has two phases; transcription, in which the original is converted into a master, from which in the duplication phase, copies – the commodities proper – are struck. These are then packaged and distributed to retail outlets.

I want to examine the creative stage of production first, overviewing its technology/labour nexus and technical division of labour, and the structures of management. By looking first at creation then reproduction, points of comparison will become evident which in turn become key issues in subsequent, more detailed analysis of the creative stage of production.

The creative stage is the beginning point of the cultural labour process, wherein musicians, writers, dancers and actors of various types, using only their ideas and techniques, voices, props and costumes and instruments (in some cases, small-scale and specialised technologies such as studio consoles, word processors and synthesisers) to create an original. Whereas

---

7    This model has been constructed from field observations as indicated in chapter 1. Published studies which have also contributed include Elliott (1972), Frith (1978), Macdonald (1979), Moran (1984), Powdermaker (1950), Tebbel (1981) and Tunstall (1971). See also insider accounts such as Baker (1980a, 1980b), Dessauer (1974), Fowles and Mills (1981), MacGowen (1965) and Ravage (1978). Staiger (1982) is a useful case study which indicates but does not develop some of the ideas canvassed here.

8    This model is most applicable to the manufacture of private cultural commodities; e.g. published goods and recordings. Note that the precise nature of the labour process varies according to the form of the final commodity. In the case of movies, for example, as quasi-private goods, since only a few copies are taken for distribution to theatres, there is no need for an extensive duplication phase. Public goods (broadcasting media) are presented live. The final stage of creation is an assembly of selected pre-recorded items linked by commentary. Microphones, replay units, studio consoles and so on transcribe the original programme into electromagnetic signals which are then transmitted; if networked, various technologies are used to duplicate the original signal. In this case, the assembly, transcription, duplication and distribution phases all occur more or less simultaneously and automatically. The four phases remain, albeit in a truncated form.

| Stage | Phase | Object | Publishing | Recording | Filming |
|---|---|---|---|---|---|
| Creative | Creation: production of original | preparation of original (plan) | Idea (draft) | Composition (score) | Writing (screen play) |
| | | Performance of original (performance) | Redrafting & editing (type script) | Rehearsal & performance (performance) | Rehearsal & performance (performance) |
| Reproduction | Transcription: production of master | Transcription of original (transcript) | Type setting (proofs) | Recording studio (recording) | Film studio set (filming) |
| | | Editing & mastering of transcript (master) | Plate making (plate) | Post-production editing etc (master) | Post-production editing etc (master) |
| | Duplication: production of copies | Copying from master (copies) | Printing (pages) | Pressing (disc, tape) | Printing (copy) |
| | | Packaging of copies (commodities) | Binding & covering (book) | Packaging labeling (recordings) | Packaging as film print or video cassette |

Figure 4.1  Division Of Labour In Production

capitalist development usually proceeds by introducing more complex, inclusive and productive technologies which dissolve the existing craft division of labour, creation seems to have been impervious to this transformation. Because art is conventionally held to be a product of the imagination and talents of identifiable individuals and an expression of human experience, artistic work cannot be mechanised: that would be a contradiction in terms, since, according to its conventions, art flows only from the inherently human talents. Although there are some technically-specific permutations of cultural practice such as screenplay writing and film acting as opposed to writing plays and theatrical acting, radio announcing as opposed to compering, electric as opposed to acoustic (especially classical) musicianship, they retain close connections to the original crafts – writing, acting, singing, dancing, and so on. They represent, according to earlier discussion of Marx' models, a workshop division of labour within the labour process. In fact, the relative absence of technology and the craft-based division of labour is one of the most obvious and noteworthy features of the organisation of creation in the corporate context (cf. the remarks of Adorno, Garnham and Miège cited earlier)[9], and is a centre-piece of the following analysis.

Nonetheless, it is not a simple division of labour – and here we see the first signs of the complexity and ambiguity which will become part of the picture of corporate creation drawn in this and following chapters. Like all forms of work, creation has two phases, preparation and performance (cf. Staiger 1982: 97-100), and as art developed as an autonomous practice, so

---

9   While it is generally true that creative activity cannot be absorbed into a machine, technologies are having incremental effects on artistic practice which are worth briefly noting. Some detail aspects of performance work such as rewriting, redrafting, drawing and colouring, involve repetition. These can be mechanised and even automated, and computer-based technologies are increasingly substituting for labour either by eliminating tasks or by reducing labour-time and hence raising productivity; as in journalism and other writing (e.g. Marshall 1983, *The National Times* 3-9 May 1985: 40-42), in announcer-operated radio stations, and in the graphic arts ranging from advertising layouts to animation (e.g. *The Australian* 21 May 1985: 30). Even where new technologies enhance rather than replace labour, there are ambiguous long-term effects. Some cultural forms are being reconstituted in terms of the capabilities of equipment manufactured and marketed by the capital and consumer good sector; as in the case of the keyboard synthesiser (e.g. Towers 1976, *The Australian* 15 May 1984: 20-21) and the impact of special effects generators on filmic and televisual techniques (e.g. *The National Times* 28 December-3 January 1985: 36-37). Additionally, accepted average standards of performance are constantly rising, partly because of the type and quality of instruments and capital equipment available; as in the case of audio recording equipment which permits creation of impossibly perfect recordings. Because artists themselves often utilise technical improvements to their artistic and material benefit, does not alter the consequences. Modified cultural forms develop around innovations. On the one hand, this offers opportunities for emergent artists but on the other, further fragments the artistic division of labour; production – and consumption – becomes dependent on increasingly complex technology. Each new round of innovation chips away at existing forms and progressively devalues artistic labour by raising the average ratio of constant to variable capital employed in the creative stage. While to the present, creation remains labour intensive, these developments threaten to turn the artist into the human shadow lurking behind the machine, like 'the robot drummer' (Towers 1976: 84-95).

it underwent functional specialisation. During the 17th and 18th and into the 19th century, playwrights, composers, choreographers, writers and other designers – i.e. those who do the initial work of imagining an idea and materialising it in a plan such as a score or script – progressively divorced themselves from performers such as singers, actors, dancers, musicians (e.g. Hartnoll 1967: 277-278, 336-337, Raynor 1972: 67, 97-98). These stages are easily distinguishable in music, theatre and dance, but barely so in many forms of writing. Thus, for example, when a song is being prepared for live or recorded performance, a melody must be composed, lyrics written and an arrangement scored before singers and instrumentalists can perform it. Under corporate conditions of production, the division of labour is based on this functional rather than technical distinction. Preparation and performance represent two different regions of specialised skill. Usually it is the case that preparers are not the same individuals as performers, and even where some contemporary composers perform their own compositions, the function remains distinguishable.

Specialisation has also developed along another axis, that of 'cultural form' (cf. Williams 1981: 148-180). In acting, for example, some are known for their comedy skills, others in westerns, dramas, adventures or romances, and so on; similarly in music, composers, singers and instrumentalists are normally associated with a particular field such as opera, rock 'n' roll, jazz, chamber music and country and western. This modifies but is still connected to the craft division of labour within which artists train and work, a situation quite unlike the industrial or corporate division of labour anticipated by the corporate model of capitalist production which is found in most present-day workplaces.

Returning to the general features of the creative stage and the issue of its management, according to Braverman's argument, capitalist control of the labour process proceeds partly through alienation of worker skills and knowledges and their formalisation in sets of procedures. Their application on the shopfloor is supervised by layers of managers and supervisors acting as the agents of owners. Although the cultural forms which artists use have conventional elements of structure and content, generally speaking, the arbitrariness of creation defies reduction to precise, universal, operational rules. Originality presumes innovation and experiment, with artists playing around with possible elements and their customary combinations. Reorganising the creative process around the principles represented by scientific management is barely possible. A 'creative management' stratum, however, is present; editors and others in publishing firms, producers and directors in film, radio, television and audio production, and so on. This aspect will be dealt with in detail shortly, but it is worth noting at this point that creative management is remarkably benign; cultural workers such as studio announcers, composers, screenplay writers and journalists, are initially briefed by creative management but then complete their work with minimal supervision. Elsewhere, when actors and musicians rehearse, for example, management intervenes more actively, but in neither case is artistic direction a matter of giving orders and applying inflexible rules. It revolves instead around collaborative relations and is characterised by discussion, negotiation and compromise, with much of the input coming from workers themselves – although management represents the final, responsible authority.

The picture already beginning to emerge is that the creative stage of production in the corporations of culture has a general configuration unlike those forms discussed by Braverman. Given the existence of a craft-based division of labour, relatively low-level technological composition and mildness of management, all of which reflect aspects of handicraft production (Marglin 1974: 63-82), it would seem that the *creative stage of corporate production approximates to the capitalist workshop model of capitalist production*[10] – although it should be signalled immediately, that subsequent and more detailed analysis in this and following chapters will lead me to modify this conclusion. The truth is that the corporate form of cultural production is complex and ambiguous and its shape can only be progressively discerned from different angles, and then only in outline.

Turning to the non-artistic reproduction stage, the conditions here are more typically industrial. This work originated with the industrialisation of cultural production first in publishing and then from the late 19th century in the performing arts, of a labour process which was already organised as capitalist commodity production albeit in a relatively undeveloped form. It was a decisive intervention. It converted quasi-public goods into partly or fully private goods; for example, books and later periodicals and newspapers progressively became objects of private domestic consumption (Williams 1965: 177-236); similarly, filming and recording technologies introduced between the 19th and 20th centuries reproduced and trans-

---

10  Miège (1979) and Garnham (1979) are strictly incorrect to argue that this is artisan production. Thompson (1968: 279), for example, suggests that artisans even as late as the 19th century ranged from master-craftsmen employing many journeymen to sweated labourers: but that all were defined by their possession of the entire skill of their craft. Conversely, at the point where capitalists have acquired ownership and control of the general conditions of production, and especially where they have installed a management stratum, the artisan as defined by Thompson, ceases to exist, *having been replaced by detail and later industrial labourers in various types of employment relations*. As this and the following chapter demonstrate, to a large extent, this is the situation in the present-day culture industry.

formed musical, theatrical and dance performances which had been staged in various types of venues ranging from theatres, ball-rooms and gardens, into new, more mature cultural and commodity forms (cf. Cowie 1971: 184-187, Raynor 1976: 188-192). Commodities produced in developed private form are suitable for large-volume manufacturing methods, in the reproduction stage at least. Industrialisation divided transcription from duplication as the printing press had previously differentiated the skills of compositors from those of press operators. Press work was easily mechanised and by the beginning of the 19th century, mechanical presses had reinforced this division (Marshall 1983: 10-24).

The duplication stage therefore quickly became capital intensive and from its inception has been the one phase of the cultural labour process which has shifted towards the forms of production discussed by Braverman, as found, for example, in press rooms and recording manufacturing plants (e.g. Marshall 1983: 28-40, 72-89, Schicke 1974: 173-189, 222-227). Historically, technical innovation here has been oriented towards labour substitution and deskilling, resulting in complex, large-scale and automated machinery incorporating various tasks. Workers carry out ordained, repetitious, industrial tasks; setting up equipment, preparing materials for the production run, fixing process problems as they occur and shifting output to the next stage of production. Work is manual, semi- or unskilled and closely supervised.

Transcription work is more varied, ranging from traditional composition previously carried out by printers, to the operation of cameras, lights, sound equipment, set management, console and control-room operations, as well as the editing, mixing and effects post-production work which is part of film and television production (Macgowen 1965: 409-422, Marshall 1983: 21-42, Schicke 1974: 219-220). The industrialisation of transcription developed alongside that of duplication, although taking a less capital-intensive path until recently. Where technological innovation in the duplication phase has been directed towards labour reduction or replacement, the tendency in the transcription phase throughout most of the 20th century has been to enhance and multiply forms of labour by improving, extending and decentralising each functional unit; the development of film and video production and post-production systems is a good example (e.g., Cowie 1971: 245-248). Transcription equipment is composed of small-scale specialised and complex units each operated by a detail form of labour but integrated into a larger system.

Much of the work involved in transcription[11] is little more than

---

11  Transcription-support workers such as technicians, engineers and computer
    programmers have high level industrial craft-like skills which require extensive

routinised and supervised equipment operation – although in some instances (e.g. operating 32-track recording studio mixers with a full range of effects equipment) calls for considerable dexterity and a broad knowledge of operational possibilities. Some aspects of this work, however, involve a limited degree of discretion in a manner which partially blurs the distinction between creation and reproduction. Photographers (still and moving), film and television and text editors, effects creators, graphic reproducers, audio production operators, etc., like compositors of the pre-electronic type-setting era, whilst principally operatives, are called upon occasionally to bring a degree of creative flair to their work. They are encouraged by creative management to suggest, for example, camera angles, sound mix, lighting, layout, effects, editing cuts and so on (e.g. Firth 1978: 85, Tulloch and Moran 1986: 119-129, 146-170), contributions which add to the aesthetic value of the transcribed original.

Thus, if duplication work seems like any other form of modern factory production, transcription appears less so. While machine-based, routinised and positioned within an industrial division of labour, there are occasional moments of reprieve. The situation, however, is changing. Since the post-war years and especially since the 1970s, costs within the transcription phase, especially wages, have risen sharply. Companies have begun reconstructing transcription by computerising the operation of cameras, editing machines, vision mixers, switches and so on (e.g. *The Australian* 6 June 1984: 30-34). Time-consuming manual-mechanical operations (especially in post-production activities) are being replaced by computer-assisted and largely automatic processes which bring productivity and sometimes quality gains for the company. In cases where jobs are not eliminated – recording-studio operators are an example – employees are enskilled and acquire wider skill repertoires (cf. Penn and Scattergood 1985). Elsewhere, deskilling and massive job losses are the rule: printers are the paradigm case (Marshall 1983: 65-110). Compositors of previous eras have been replaced (in Australia) by deskilled graphic reproducers who cut and paste electronically type-set transcripts of the stories input by journalists. As pagination technologies are improved, these last vestiges of the printing craft seem likely to be eliminated (Bonney and Wilson 1983: 120-123). While conditions in transcription seem less industrialised than those in duplication, competition and cost pressures are diminishing their differences and driving it further towards the corporate model of capitalist production.

Clearly, from this overview of the creation and reproduction stages, the

---

training. Since their work does not enter directly into the labour process, it is not discussed here.

corporate cultural labour process has a complex form, neither homogeneous nor uniform throughout its various phases. What is more, it *combines* two different models of capitalist production. Reproduction workers as a whole are positioned within a corporate division of labour, their work organised as a series of routinised, industrial and fragmented tasks built around transcription and duplication technologies, and subject to close management. In contrast, the creative stage has withstood technological reconstruction; a craft-based division of labour remains, and relations between workers and creative management resemble those of the capitalist workshop more than the industrial or corporate factory.

This difference reveals the principal valorisation strategy adopted by capitalists in the culture industry. Their preoccupation has been reconstitution of the labour process in an attempt to raise the rate of surplus-value production, but standing as a barrier to this goal has been the special status and character of art and the artist. Like other workers in the capitalist labour process, artists are employed to create surplus-value, but given the intensity, duration and quality of labour the creation of art is supposed to require, the ratio of surplus to socially necessary labour value embedded in the original is comparatively low. Any attempt by employers to reduce the necessary component by demanding less time and devotion by the artist, runs the risk of a shoddy or mediocre and hence unsaleable artwork. Valorisation, however, is still feasible. Obversely, reproduction work is not surrounded by the mystique of art. With the exception of some aspects of transcription, it is repetitive work which can be routinised, mechanised and automated (cf. also Williams 1980: 58-59). This, in fact, has been its history. Capitalists have succeeded in increasing surplus-value production throughout cultural commodity production system as a whole, with the brunt of increased exploitation borne by reproduction workers. It is they who have carried the cost of preserving artistic conditions in the creative stage of production.


## 4.3.2 Creative Management: Producers and Directors and the Negotiation of Creation

If the creative stage of production seems to take the form of the capitalist workshop, more specific questions about its internal aspects arise. If capitalists have had only limited success in subsuming artists under capital as suggested by the perseverance of this relatively simple form, does the continued existence of a craft-based division of labour imply related problems in managing this work? If a management stratum has been

| Function | | Position In Project | Occupations |
|---|---|---|---|
| Conception | design (outline) | producer | managers, producers editors etc. |
| | realisation (plan) | realiser | writers, composers, arrangers designers etc |
| Execution | interpretation (directions) | director | directors, chiefs-of-staff, sub-editors, studio directors, floor managers etc |
| | execution (performance) | performer | actors, musicians, presenters, dancers, journalists; illustrators photographers etc |

Figure 4.2  Creative Division Of Labour

successfully installed, how and to what extent does it achieve control? And what are the form's dynamics and its present directions of change?

To begin, a brief note is necessary on functional differentiation within the creative process itself. The workshop division of labour separates those who design an original and those who perform it, but further sub-division is possible, as indicated in Figure 4.2. Outlining an idea is divisible from the task of realising it in a plan, and while *design* and *realisation* are both technically part of conception, each can be allocated to different types of workers and one made subject to the other. Equally, *performance* based on a plan must be preceded by its *interpretation*. Designers, realisers, interpreters and performers appear as divergent forms of labour; in theatre, film and television production, for example, as producers/designers, writers, directors and actors.

In the corporations of culture, this workshop division of labour is bisected by the authority relations associated with juridical aspects of the firm. Since profitable commoditisation requires product policies consistent with market trends, and since design and interpretation are crucial in determining the output of creation, capitalists appropriated these functions and backed them with the legal authority attached to proprietorship, transforming them into positions of hierarchical control over the creative stage of the labour process. *This consolidated a creative management stratum as the agents of capital in creation, fulfilling the functions of design and interpretation, and appearing as producers and directors respectively*[12] (cf. Clegg and Dunkerley 1980: 470-475, cf. Miège 1979). Obversely, the effect of this development has been to relegate realisers and performers to the position of directed executant. This is well illustrated by the transformation of radio programming and presentation (the following applies mainly to the U.S. and Australia; cf. also MacDonald 1979, Walker 1973). From its inception till the 1950s, recorded music programmes were generally prepared and presented by announcers; they selected and ordered recordings according to the principles of variety and compered their presentation (cf. vaudeville, music hall). Under the impact of competition from television, the development of format radio was initiated with 'Top 40' programming where a programme head took responsibility for overall programme planning. Increasingly since then, and especially from the 1960s, all-music stations have a music policy set by a (Australian terminology) programme manager who also prepares playlists with a music director. Announcers are employed merely as format presenters with their work overseen by a studio director – this is the situation in Station FM-RADIO, a model of radio station operation presented in the following chapter.

For the capitalist, there are a number of pretexts for installing a creative management stratum. Profitability in a competitive context demands reduction in the value of unit and aggregate labour, regularising the duration and rate of work, and ensuring the production of marketable commodities (price, type, quality). Artists, as we have seen, represent high-value personalised labour, but wresting away design and interpretation reduces some of that value. Equally, artistic work is essentially erratic

---

12  These terms are used as to denote *functional positions in a structure of relations* and as such do not necessarily correspond with industry usage. In fact, as abstractions they incorporate and aggregate a variety of occupations ranging from executive film and television producers to floor managers, talent scouts, editors, studio arrangers, artist and repertoire managers, programme and studio managers, etc. Creative management supervises the creative stage of production and is to be distinguished from general management of financial and administrative kinds, and production management which oversees the reproduction stage. Of particular recent importance has been the extra-organisational extension of this function into external firms such as talent, booking and personal management agencies who take partial responsibility for preparing and rehearsing artists. Note also Garnham's comments on his translation of Miège's term *'editeur'* as 'producer' (Miège 1979: 303), which corresponds to my 'creative management'.

and the output arbitrary. By conceptualising and directing the process of creation, producers and directors can bind working artists to the organisation's mode of rationality; originals of a preferred type and quality are more likely, with less labour-power consumed in their production than might otherwise have been the case. The historical significance of this development is considerable. Unable to exercise technical control over artists through reconstruction of the division of labour, the installation of creative management indexes the specific approach to bureaucratic control taken by capitalists in degrading the creative stage of production as they embedded the social and organisational structure of the firm (cf. Edwards 1979: 111-162). The full extent of its bureaucratic character is seen when the conjunction of creative management and formatting are discussed in the following chapter.

The daily production of editions carried out in metropolitan newspaper newsrooms as examined in the course of fieldwork and represented by a model which I will call *The Daily Courier*[13], illustrates the structure and operation of creative management. The stratum involves a layer of managers and supervisors of various forms. An editor (Australian terminology) and an (executive) editorial manager fulfil the producer functions of overall planning and coordination. The director function, those tasks associated with operationalising the plan (editorial policy) and supervising

---

13   This model is based on amalgamated observations and interviews conducted of several newspaper companies, but primarily on a large multi-media corporation which was at the time also the publisher of two daily and one Sunday newspapers, and the parent of several suburban newspaper companies. It also had substantial cross-media holdings in metropolitan and regional radio and television. Additionally, it was itself a subsidiary of one of Australia's (then) four major media groups, but also a major interlocked shareholder in its parent. Data was collected in a series of interviews and observations in the workplace and with the general manager, deputy general manager (also the financial director), editor-in-chief, and editors and staff of each paper. The model assumes the production of a single masthead. *The Daily Courier* is essentially characteristic of all major Australian newspapers (cf. also Mayer 1964) and broadcast newsrooms (e.g. Baker 1980b). In fact, newsroom organisation is similar throughout most of the Western world; compare this account with, for example, Tunstall (1971) and Gans (1979). Observations in radio and television stations, advertising agencies and recording companies indicate definite parallels in the structure and operation of the creative stage. For the record industry also see Frith (1978), television production Moran (1984), and film companies Macgowen (1965). In book publishing, creative management may not be so intrusive – but frequently are: editors and authors discuss their workplace relations in *The National Times* (8-14 March 1985: 36-38) and *The Weekend Australian* (12-13 March 1988: Magazine 6-7). See also Dessauer (1974).

workers in their tasks, extends across several organisational positions; namely, the chief-of-staff, section editors (business and finance, politics, real estate, foreign, women, arts and entertainment and sport) and the chief sub-editor. Executants comprise general and specialist reporters, sub-editors and staff photographers. According to the editor, he and the editorial manager in consultation with general management, set editorial policy for the paper. Content (story selection and placement) for each edition is determined at daily editorial conferences involving the entire creative management stratum; these conferences are marked by considerable discussion with input from all, but final decisions lie with the editor. In the period leading up to copy deadline, directors supervise the collection and processing of stories; the chief-of-staff and section editors select from the large number of leads available from various sources, allocate them to journalists and coordinate their completion. The chief sub-editor supervises the backbench (sub-editors) in checking journalists' copy and compiles an edition according to the sketch roughed out at editorial conference.

A formal hierarchy coincides with the division of labour: producer, director and worker fulfil the tasks of design, interpretation and execution. While there is some task overlap within creative management (policy formulation and editorial conference), there is little between creative management and workers. What is more interesting is what we might refer to as the 'softness' of these authority relations especially at the interface of management and workers. To illustrate: when asking a journalist to follow up a lead, the chief-of-staff supplies available information (e.g. background, event, contacts) and suggests an angle from which the story might be approached. The presumption seems to be, by both director and executant, that these propositions are not definitive and are offered more as guidelines. In the course of the (sometimes very brief) discussion, reporters sometimes accept the suggestions without comment, sometimes offer their own ideas, and even argue outright. On other occasions, journalists may initiate the lead and angle, a suggestion taken up and developed by the chief-of-staff. The eventual brief represents an amalgam of input from both parties – although the ultimate right of managers to advocate and decide is generally acknowledged. Journalists are then left to get on with the job, relatively free to work up whatever possibilities emerge. They may later seek further advice or discuss progress with the editor or chief-of-staff, but generally, on-the-job supervision is relatively sporadic and unstructured; in the case of feature writers, columnists and commentators and sometimes senior rounds reporters, direction seems even less explicit. Observations suggest, in fact, that this kind of informal, collaborative management style is replicated to varying degrees in all forms of corporate cultural production; with actors in films, writers of books, musicians in the recording studio, copywriters in advertising agencies, announcers on radio stations, etc. Despite operating in an organisational context which seeks to discipline the labour process in the interests of accumulation and appearing in it partly as agents of capital, creative management seem unwilling or unable at the decisive moment to exercise their legitimate organisational powers against the labour-power they are supposed to be managing[14]. While directors direct at the operational level, much tactical autonomy is ceded to workers themselves. Creative management seems unlike the inflexible, top-down supervision found next door in the graphic reproduction and printing sections; instead, its tenor resembles negotiation, built around apparently reciprocal exchanges which belie the subordinate position of the worker. In that sense, while the presence and structure of the management stratum gives creation a corporate flavour, the style of management seems more appropriate to a simpler model of capitalist production, even in substantially bureaucratised practices such as journalism (cf. also Dreier 1976, Tunstall 1971) and in other media (cf. also Elliott 1977). The question is, why?

While I do not want to trace a history of creative management[15], it can be said that part of the explanation lies in the form in which it evolved. Capitalisation of cultural practices developed slowly. After an initial period of merchant production, from the late-18th century onwards, as socially dispersed and differentiated audiences began acquiring a taste for regular public performance and the habit of reading, the role of impresario was taken up increasingly by leading artists of the period. Here, artistic leadership operated through example, not guidance. Only with the

---

14  The general argument stands even though some creative managers are authoritarian in their manner. Considered from an ethnomethodological perspective, executants' complaints concerning overbearing intrusion indicate the strength of the conventions discussed here (e.g. *The Weekend Australian* 2-3 April 1988: Magazine 11-12, 25-26 July 1987: Magazine 4). During entrepreneurial periods where economic and artistic management are combined – as in the case of the early stages of the cinema and rock 'n' roll, a more forceful form of face-to-face 'simple control' (Edwards 1979: 25-27) is common.

15  A history of creative management as such has not been written, but its outline is discernible. For the emergence of the newspaper editor see Smith (1978: 165-166) and management of book publishing, Steinberg (1955). For actor-managers and later the producer and director, see Hartnoll (1967: 766, 1968: 244). A comprehensive account of the court-based composer-musical director and then, from the turn into the 19th century, the orchestral conductor, is provided by Raynor (1976: 25-28, 35-45, 100-124).

expansion of production during the late-19th and early-20th centuries did explicitly capitalist financiers and entrepreneurs assume dominant positions in publishing, theatrical and musical companies, and later in film and recording companies. From this point, the contracted or partnership relations which owners and speculators had previously established with performer-managers[16] were transformed into employee relations, therein subordinating creative management to general and financial management. Creative managers were now expected to explicitly guide and develop the work of others. Nonetheless, they were still regarded as artistic in orientation, something like a master-craftsmen concerned primarily with excellence and originality and the state of their art; hence, they were absolved from responsibility for business management and granted a relative independence in the production process[17]. As competition intensified and the business became more complex, this now-consolidated stratum was sub-divided into the specialised functions of producing and directing (as previously defined) and the former obligated to organisational goals. Their history, however, located them irrevocably as comrades-in-arms with the artists under their control and the tradition of guidance, collaboration and artistic leadership remains the essence of creative direction, even to the present.

---

16  Without developing the point, it is interesting to note that these 'performer-managers' (e.g. actor-managers, conductor-managers) beginning around the eras of Garrick, Goethe, Racine, Händel and Haydn, were crucial to the development of new cultural institutions. They frequently took up partnerships or associations (e.g. Händel with Heidegger and others in England – see Raynor 1972: 265-289) in which they were the direct employer of artists. This seems to have been an internal sub-contracting system not unlike that of the gang boss applying in other industries, and which remained important until the turn into the 20th century.

17  This point is of particular interest in news production, where media proprietors such as Rupert Murdoch still occasionally intervene in editorial policy making in order to promote their own views (Bowman 1988, McQueen 1977). I would generally suggest that accounts of present-day media barons overemphasise their argument to the point where it becomes almost conspiratorial. In fact, usually, with the decline of entrepreneurially-led companies, direct face-to-face and self-interested control is replaced by bureaucratic management control realised through creative management (Edwards 1979, cf. also Murdock and Golding 1978). To that end, Frank Devine (presently editor of *The Australian*, previously the *Sun-Times* and *The New York Post*) provides a provoking although ingenuous account of his dealings with Murdoch, suggesting that as editor, he is much more independent of his employer than accounts such as Bowman's suggest (*The Independent Monthly* August 1989: 3). Bowman replies sceptically in *Australian Society* (September 1989: 10-11).

The muted and accommodating style of creative management also flows in part from the inherent character of the creative process itself, as given by its Romantic constitution. Creation requires the labour of artists, the work of individuals with unalienable and irreplaceable talents and skills, who conjure up exciting and novel works. By definition, it cannot easily be reduced to systems of rules, or the personalised labour of particular artists substituted by abstract labour-power. This necessarily endows artists with powers to demand a voice in production and, if they need, to resist direction. Further, with their appropriation of the conception function, creative management is confronted by an additional problem; not only must executant labour-power be engaged, it must also be motivated. No matter how brilliant an idea, how original a score or script, its promise remains dependent on the capacities, willingness and aspirations of those employed to perform it. In achieving that goal, producers and directors, especially those dealing with actors, musicians, dancers and writers, are forced to contend with the identity and psychology ascribed to artists. Their personalities and expectations are said to require supportive and careful handling; that they perform to their best when workplace structures are relatively loose and their individuality given free rein; when worker-management relations are based on mutual respect and cooperation; and that artists at work seek inspiration not administration – i.e. criticism, advice and assistance from a constructive and trusted leader who will help them evaluate and perfect their efforts (e.g. Ravage 1978). Management only consents to this, however, in so far as artists work in commercial or professional ways; that is, they reproduce the rationality of the corporate culture industry. By providing such conditions, producers and directors hope to unlock the potential productivity of talent, to create those moments of chemistry when the give-and-take of artist and director, of talent and leadership, produce an outstanding original with which they can all be pleased[18].

In other words, creative management at the operational or tactical level can only procure what they seek through what is literally a process of negotiation (Gallagher 1982). Depending on the cultural form, negotiation occurs in a variety of formal and informal settings; the rehearsals through which creative management take theatrical, film and television casts, and

---

18  Many artists are also considered by creative management to be psychologically difficult to handle, ego-driven and self-interested (e.g. Ravage 1978: 19-20). This may or may not be true, but it also reflects the increasing outmodedness of romantic conceptions of the artist in the corporate entertainment industry. It is also typical of the derogation of workers by managers generally, as an expression of their opposing class interests.

musical groups and soloists, are the most obvious examples (e.g. Tulloch and Moran 1986: 46-63, 104-117). Equally, from observations, the briefings given to journalists, radio and television presenters, advertising copywriters and graphic artists, the editorial conferences publishers arrange with writers and so on, are all sites of rehearsal where both parties negotiate the direction of the outcome. Whatever the setting, the remarkable fact is that artistic direction runs the full gamut from tension, conflict and compromise, to rapport, concordance and agreement – but in all cases, manager and worker confront each other less as commander and commanded than as collaborating peers, and the outcome of their relation is preceded by a significant element of uncertainty. While the creative stage of production has the general form of capitalist workshop production, and the presence of an authoritative management stratum differentiated from owners reflects an industrial or corporate context, the ubiquity and necessity of negotiation represents a paradox. Installation of creative management represents an attempt by capitalists to impose hierarchic control based on formal (legal) authority, on an otherwise irrational labour process – to increase the degree of subsumption via the medium of management. The organisational purpose of artistic and creative direction is to ensure achievement of prescribed outcomes and goals, but that process necessarily demands negotiation and compromise with the very workers management are supposed to govern. This is what gives the creative stage of production its indeterminacy.

Despite these potential difficulties, from the capitalist's point of view, it is evident from the growth of the industry that the 20th century consolidation of a creative management stratum, combined with appropriate employment policies and control of the circulation system, has disciplined labour in creation to a level sufficient for organisational purposes. In taking over planning activities and allocating them to their agents, the corporations of culture have acquired effective control of the key moment in creation, which enables regulation of the type and quality of work reproduced in response to shifts in market demand. In a competitive market, this is crucial. In terms of valorisation, their function as coordinators governing the direction and integration of work within the labour process reduces the total time during which otherwise high-value and unreliable artistic labour is employed at creating an original. Thus, all other things being equal, corporations can minimise the proportion of investment in labour in the production cycle thereby raising their rate of surplus-value production to a level which permits satisfactory rates of accumulation.

In that context, it is important to note the tightening of control which is presently in progress throughout the corporations of culture, as indexed by the repositioning and redefinition of creative management. The fact that producers and directors traditionally addressed artistic concerns in their work even at the cost of financial over-runs, brought them into conflict with general management. As economic and competitive conditions have threatened profitability, especially over the second half of the 20th century – for example, in film and radio in the 1950s (e.g. Cowie 1971: 241-244, Walker 1973: 91- 97, 159-184) and even earlier in publishing (e.g. Gedin 1977: 53) – creative managers have been forced to professionalise (cf. also Ravage 1978: 1-11). Now they are expected to temper artistic sensibilities with business acumen and organising skills. One effect of this movement has been to further separate producers and directors (the mechanisms will be discussed shortly). The former is increasingly located within the executive hierarchy and primarily involved with administrative work. Directors have less organisational power and are still regarded as part of the artistic team. This is associated with a more general movement towards controlling creation through rationalisation; bureaucratising the process by crystalising canons of practice and their supervised application as formats. This development has dramatically reduced the level of negotiation possible within creation, turned it into rule-bounded work, and moved it decisively towards a situation which resembles the corporate model of capitalist production. This development is of considerable significance in so far as it modifies our picture of the corporate form of cultural production, and will be dealt with in detail in the following chapter.

## 4.4 Labour Organisation in the Creative Stage of Production

I want to now leave behind the crude models of capitalist production used so far and begin fashioning a more precise historical model of the corporate model of capitalist cultural production. The remainder of this chapter is concerned with its basic structure, allowing subsequent chapters to progressively fill out its various dimensions. Elliott's (1972) study of the making of a television documentary series captures the essence of what will be called here the 'project team' form of labour organisation, which is the corporate form's single most important characteristic.

He speaks of how after initial planning by executive producers, a production team comprising producer, director and researcher was set up.

Once the producer had designed the general programme framework and finalised budgetary and scheduling matters, the team selected a presenter then set about substantive pre-production concerns; preparing subject areas and interviews (researcher), writing scripts (producer), collecting and preparing film inserts (director). They were later joined by the presenter, a well-known and highly-regarded performer, who reworked the scripts and some of the content to suit his style and interests. The producer and director coordinated the final assembly and editing of components (1972: 22-107). Elliott outlines some organisational features of the production team[19], noting how they were brought together to work specifically on the particular project and which became their exclusive occupation. Centred around the producer, the team comprised a number of different formal roles and an accepted division of labour and responsibility, but considerable overlap in task allocation at certain times during production. He also notes what he calls 'status' factors, the origins of which lay partly outside the organisation – presumably, what I will later call 'artistic authority' – which entered into relationships between members and modified the formal hierarchy (1972: 128-129).

## 4.4.1 The Project Team

While Elliott is dealing with a single cultural form, his empirical account reveals something of the essential configuration of labour organisation within creative stage of production, as found in corporate newsrooms (press, broadcasting and news agencies, also magazine and journal production), film studios, advertising agencies, music recording, the production of daily radio and television programmes, the writing and publication of books especially those designed for the popular market[20]. It centres upon

---

19  Note that he uses Burns and Stalker's (1961) distinction between organic and mechanistic organisation to compare the production team and the studio crew respectively. While I am using a different conceptual approach, their description of organic forms of organisation parallels the features I am attributing to the capitalist workshop form of capitalist organisation.

20  This claim is primarily based on field-work observations but other published work seems to support it. For other television production see Tulloch and Moran (1986); newsrooms Tunstall (1971), Glasgow University Media Group (1976) and Baker (1980b); film production Macgowen (1965), publishing Tebbel (1981) and music recording Frith (1978). The successful, serious novelist, poet or classical musician who seems to work almost autonomously, represents a limit case, but it is important to remember that even for freelancers (see later discussion), pre-transcription work also involves creative management

the project team[21], the corporate form of collective cultural labour[22] which represents the artist in historically specific form in the corporations of culture (cf. Clegg and Dunkerley 1980: 470-475, cf. Miège 1979: 304); i.e. the specific form of cooperation which characterises cultural production in this setting, as constituted around various task and authority relations, and similar to the gang-labour necessary for unstandardised production (Edwards 1976: 113)[23].

Where production under the classical corporate model is based on an assembly line (as found in the reproduction stage of production), the creative stage of production has the organisational logic of a project. This is unit or small-batch production, necessarily so, because by definition, originals have neither consistent nor standard form, and it is difficult to

---

(e.g. editors, arrangers, producers) who offer advice on content, sometimes suggesting final revisions, arrangements, interpretations, and so on, even if only retrospectively (e.g. the comments of Australian author Thomas Keneally reported in *The Sunday Mail* 7 November 1987: 15).

21   The project team is a *structure of positions in the creative stage of production.* As such it is not necessarily coterminous with the creative department of an organisation, nor is it restricted to its staff. Being corporate production, creation may spread across several firms. The task of creation sometimes involves general management in so far as they contribute to conception as artistic leaders. It always includes creative management for the same reason. At the other end, in ambiguous fashion, it includes the work of creative-operatives in transcription who work under the director in transcribing the originals and which contributes to its cultural value. In that sense, the project team represents the collective (artistic) labourer in production, a complex structure of roles defined in functional terms (cf. Clegg and Dunkerley 1980: 479).

22   I am iterating here a particular version of Wolff's argument that despite ideologies of individual creation, art is a social product and fundamentally collective in origin (1981: 27, also Williams 1981: 112).

23   It is worth noting that the model of corporate cultural production built up in this and following chapters has similarities to the post-Fordist flexible manufacturing systems associated with niche-based marketing of specialised products and small-batch production (e.g. Bramble 1988, for an overview, see Murray 1988). Much corporate cultural production is divisional production of specialised products governed by a specific format. Rather than being *post*-Fordist production, however, for the reasons outlined here, the creative stage has *never* taken the form of fully industrialised production. It is also worth noting that in the same issue of *Labour and Industry*, Lever-Tracy (1988) examines the importance of part-time workers in installing flexible systems. Again, the culture industry seems to have anticipated this: from its institutionalisation around the beginning of the 19th century, part-time and casual creative workers have frequently been employed to fill minor parts in the project team.

splinter the labour process into discrete, repeatable tasks which can be routinised and rationalised. The production cycle in the creative stage of production begins with the planning of a specific object and has an explicit moment of completion, the result appearing as an exceptional, unique and original object – a work of art. This applies to the creation of a single work such as a novel, a song, film or television play as much as it does a series of related works such as a television series composed of episodes, or editions, as in the case of the editions of a daily newspaper or the daily programmes of radio and television stations.

It is not only the inherent features of the original as an artistic object which underlies the logic of the project. The corporation has organisational concerns which also contribute. The original must appear in a technical form which can be efficiently transcribed, and be produced at a rate which has it reaching the transcription phase as scheduled in order that unproductive down-time in the reproduction stage is minimised. It must be potentially marketable; as an instance of a cultural form, it must have features and qualities which meet the demands of potential audience and industry consumers, and to whom it can be effectively marketed as an object of cultural value. As a project then, creation is conducted through a matrix of organisational and artistic imperatives which impinge upon and constitute the work which must be done, and the corporation sets up a team to achieve those objectives.

The first point to note is that the team is partly constituted around a division of labour. As previously noted, the primary distinction is between conception and execution; in Elliott's study, preparation was handled by the producer, director and researcher, and performance by the director and interviewer-presenter (depending on the cultural form, each of these two positions may be sub-divided into any number of specialist detail occupations). The producer and director have an additional task. All developed forms of cooperation require a coordinator who dovetails the efforts of all employees into a production unit by having them work concurrently, in the same direction, and to common standards. Equally, the unit must be integrated with other components of the production system; originals must be supplied in appropriate form and according to schedule.

As the culture industry matured as a mass of capital, coordination was combined with conception, then appropriated and allocated to a management stratum. Accordingly, these types of work are no longer carried out for purely artistic purposes but are overlaid by the logic of capital. Management actively intervenes in the labour process so that minimum time is spent creating the original, that it is of a marketable type and quality, and that its completion interlocks with the transcription schedule.

These aspects of creative management reflect the demands of commoditi-sation and accumulation. What is compelling about this relates to task allocation *within* the project team. As a form of labour organisation, the project team is partly constituted by the presence of creative management employed simultaneously as workers and agents of capital[24]. This is the point of Miège's argument that:

The producer [read: creative management] *in fact is not only an intermediary* between cultural labour...and industrial capital...In fact his (sic) intervention is decisive in that operation which consists in making out of unique and contingent cultural use-values, products which can be exchanged on the market. To do that he not only concerns himself with marketing problems...but *he also intervenes in the very conception of the product* (1979: 304 – emphasis in original).

The interests of capital are not something external to an otherwise independent labour process. The rules of valorisation and realisation enter into its very constitution, as personified by creative management and realised through their decisions and directions. The creative stage of production in the corporate workplace, therefore, whilst ostensibly a purely artistic process, is significantly mediated by its articulation to organisational – i.e. corporate capitalist – goals. The imperatives of accumulation are *built into* functional relations between the different types of workers which comprise the team itself. This diminishes any separation of art and the market, and incorporates creation within the capitalist goal of expansion of value[25].

---

24  They therefore occupy a contradictory position in the labour process (Wright 1979), appearing in part as creative management, that is, as the agents of capi-tal fulfilling the functions of global capital; and in part as workers, that is, as functionaries within the collective worker stratum. The structure and dynamics of the project team within the corporate form of cultural production, particu-larly in so far as they are intersected by organisational, workplace and market imperatives, make an interesting case study of classing effects within produc-tion – although I do not intend pursuing this here. For a useful discussion of the character of the new middle class and working class under corporate condi-tions, see Clegg *et al.* (1986: chapter 6 and 7).

25  Because of persistence of idealist notions concerning the autonomy of signify-ing practices (cf. Hall 1977, Murdock and Golding 1977), it is necessary to labour this point. Not only do some academics seem unwilling to accept deter-minate connections, the same applies to many practitioners; the Glasgow Uni-versity Media Group (1976: 60) noted, for example, "Participants themselves were unaware of the many factors...that govern and shape their output". The above account, however, only indicates one of the mechanisms – perhaps the most decisive – whereby organisational imperatives enter into cultural produc-

## 4.4.2 Authority Relations in the Project Team

Given this, and returning to the issue of artistic autonomy, the character of the project team emphasises the importance of recognising how the corporate era has articulated the structures of art and business within the labour process. Not only are the rules of accumulation embedded deep in the routines of production but they are daily realised through the capitalist authority relations which stratify the team. This indicates a more extensive incorporation of the process under capital than its external resemblance to the capitalist workshop might suggest. Nonetheless, it must still be recognised that for reasons previously discussed, despite the penetration of capitalist control via the person of creative managers, as artists, cultural workers have a relative independence within the creative labour process. Creative management cannot simply rule on the basis of ownership rights alone. This is not appropriate in the milieu of art. There must be material bases for winning worker consent (and maintaining the relative independence of creative from general management). Producers and directors have to negotiate and compromise with workers in order to achieve their goals. They do so by demonstrating possession of artistic leadership and administration skills[26] – in other words, control within the project team is achieved via a combination of charismatic and bureaucratic, organisational authority (cf. Weber 1970: 196-244, 245-252, cf. also Edwards 1979: 130-162).

The legitimacy of creative management depends partly on their ability to exercise artistic leadership, a form of talent possessed by some as an element of their charismatic personality. It entails a substantive contribution to the search for originality through any of a number of means; it may involve creating designs and interpretations which are themselves original and exciting, perhaps being able to recognise talent in others, or being able to inspire performers to great heights of achievement. It may be the ability to direct transcription in novel and imaginative ways. For some it may mean sensing changing taste communities and producing originals which consistently bring popular and/or critical acclaim with various audiences.

---

tion. It says nothing about specifically cultural determinants of content, although some aspects will be indicated in the following chapter.

26  See also, for example, reported comments by performers on various types of
creative managers in *The National Times* 8-14 March 1985: 34-35 (screenplay
editors and film producers), *The Weekend Australian* 12-13 March 1988: Magazine 8 (book editors), 19-21 March 1988: Magazine 13 and 2-3 April 1988: Magazine 1 (conductors), 25-26 July 1988: Magazine 4 (film directors), and Frith
1978: 79-80 (A & R managers and record producers).

Whatever the path, providing recognised artistic leadership accords creative management the legitimacy to assert their organisational authority. On the other hand, administration skills are also important – perhaps more so in the eyes of general management than performers. Experienced creative managers can efficiently and effectively coordinate operational aspects of creation; the movements and application of equipment, labour and raw materials across the project so that it proceeds without delays, achieving completion on schedule and within budget and interlocks with other phases of production, marketing and merchandising. Because they have a stable, rational setting in which they can work, artists consent to their bureaucratic control over the creative stage of production: it gives them a tension-free environment to exercise their talents.

While these skills must be distributed throughout the management stratum as a whole, the recent tendency has been for companies, through their employment policies, to allocate those with administration skills to producer positions leaving directors to specialise in artistic leadership (herein lie the origins of the recent *auteur* movement in film and music; e.g. Frith 1978: 201), which partly explains the tendency towards freelance rather than permanent employment amongst directors especially in film and record production. Moreover, producers are being increasingly located within the executive stratum as executive producers, which tends to concentrate and strengthen organisational control over the operations of the project team.

So it would seem that despite connotations of equality between members, the project team is stratified in complex and interacting ways, but that not all authority is centred upon creative management. There is a further division which accords influence to workers based on *artistic authority*[27], the specific form of power wielded by cultural workers which flows from recognition of their capacities as various forms of artist. This is a central axis of management-worker relations in creation operating alongside and articulated to the organisation's bureaucratic power structures.

Executants in the project team are sub-divided into leading roles (lead actors, senior journalists or announcers, top places in a list of authors,

---

27  There seem to be parallels in this discussion with Bourdieu's (1977) notion of 'cultural capital'. He argues, for example, for the convertibility between economic and cultural capital in both directions (Garnham and Williams 1980: 216). This is similar to my argument concerning reputation as a means for improving workers positions in relations of distribution or even buying workplace independence. It is beyond my concerns, however, to pursue possible connections between Bourdieu's arguments and my own.

soloists, principal players, and so on), supporting roles and extras. Leading positions (this also applies in some instances to freelance directors) are normally allocated only to those with established and distinguished reputations, as indexed by the familiarity of their names. Film companies look for stars for leading roles, music publishers for a name singer for a new song, radio stations offer prime-time shifts to recognised personalities, record and book publishing companies give top production and marketing priority to manuscripts or recordings from the top names in their catalogues, and newspapers put highly-reputed journalists onto headline or front-page stories. The reasons for this are two-fold. Reputation in the culture industry indicates socially recognised possession (mediated through the market) of the talents and skills of the artist, which promises corporations an exciting and profitable original. By attracting audiences, the name of the star adds to the potential commerciality of the commodity (cf. Staiger 1982: 101). To workers, having a name in an industry founded upon reputation is an index of the value of their labour, and the greater its value, the more artistic authority they can claim in the labour process. In that sense, personal reputation as signified by a name represents artistic authority and is the basis of an alternative power structure within the project team. It endows a capacity to counter the organisational power of creative management. It legitimates and enhances the artist's right to be heard – in other words, it is the ground on which management consent to treat the artist as a collaborator in production (cf. also Elliott 1977, Gallagher 1982).

In fact, there seem to be two intersecting foundations for reputation, *commercialism* and *professionalism*[28], which, while reflecting corporate rationalities imposed historically on workers through the market – in that sense, they function as vehicles of control – workers can also use them to make their names known and improve their position in the project team. These normative orientations correspond approximately to the production relations differentiating stars and professionals (cf. Frith 1978: 162-3). A commercial reputation indicates that a cultural worker has a history of or

---

28   Elliott (1977), Tulloch and Moran (1986: 46-64) and Gallagher (1982) all provide useful discussions of professionalism. Elliott (1977: 144, 147, 149-51) provides a useful account of how the logic of professionalism in journalism leads to certain values and attitudes, and bargaining power inside and outside the organisation, and how high-level professionalism affords opportunities to develop a public persona, to become a personality or star. Despite this last point, he does not seem to fully understand that even in journalism, professionalism and commercialism are intertwined: workers are able to turn both logics to their advantage. Thus, to sustain long-term careers, stars must also be professional, and top-flight professionals need something of the star in them.

potential for success in the marketplace, that they have a talent which appeals to audiences, and deserve the appellation 'star'. Stardom is predicated on market ascription of claim and title to the talent and persona of the artist[29]. Professionalism has a different logic. These names are known throughout the industry but not necessarily by audiences; professional reputations flow from recognition by peers and employers of all-purpose, high-level craft skills of more general applicability than the idiosyncrasy of talent, that they are reliable and experienced and able to apply those skills quickly, effectively and consistently in performance (cf. also Elliott 1977: 148-150).

To the corporations of culture operating in a competitive marketplace, a commercial reputation has more value that a reputation for competent but not inspired work. While the latter is a cheaper, more predictable and adaptable form of labour-power, the mere presence of a star gives the original a potential for marketability. Creative management choose from the available pool of labour, those who they think are right for their project as envisaged, and offer them the high-visibility leading roles, encouraging them to work in their style, to provide their particular brand of originality as a marketable sign of their participation. Accordingly, they must be given considerable freedom to exercise their talents, to reproduce the act which is the basis of their reputation. Hence during rehearsals, creative managers collaborate with starring performers to work up the

---

29  The claim is often made that 'genuine' talent and market success are mutually exclusive, or more specifically, that a commercial logic in cultural production subordinates, diminishes or excludes 'real' artists. Frith (1978: 162), for example, argues that in rock music, "anonymous players are bought, their personalities and all, to meet a perceived demand" and that there are musicians who "sell [themselves] to a manager or producer who uses [their] talents to realise a predetermined image or sound or music". While there are valid elements to his critique, the situation is actually more complex than he makes out. The prevalence of 'hyping' (extensive publicity and promotion) obscures the fact that on the whole, creative management recognise that long-term market success demands 'genuine' talent. In the corporate era, originality and talent are judged relatively by various types of *consumer* groups via sales, not by those of an accredited artistic sensibility and according to the internal rules of art: i.e. the community of artists. Market ascription offends idealist and absolutist notions of art. In fact, *commerciality demands a combination-in-balance of artistry and market appeal,* but since artistry may be dressed up as appeal, or appeal dressed up as artistry, *my discussion of stars necessarily includes both the major recognised talents of an era and its great pretenders.* Further to these points, the relation between formatting, cultural forms and cultural use-value, and the operations of the publicity machine are fully discussed in the following chapters.

original. For example, the interviewer-presenter in Elliott's study (1977: 86-107), chosen for his popularity and experience, was allowed – in consultation with the producer – to adapt scripts and interview schedules, to reflect his perceptions of his image, capabilities, and that of the programmes – and in one programme, even succeeded in convincing a dubious producer to change the topic, approach, and guests to be interviewed.

If stars are usually allocated leading roles, professionals are valuable to companies in supporting roles. Their work is not as important in marketing the original, but is in maintaining a high level of background performance. Production budgets demand lowest possible labour costs by minimising production time. Professionals capable of efficient, high-standard work are required to provide an underlay of competence over which the star adds the touches of originality which attract market attention. Thus, for example, radio stations hire back-up announcers for secondary shifts, recording companies employ session musicians to accompany a star's recordings, and so on. Their task is to perform as directed; to choose appropriate skills and techniques from the diverse range they have acquired in the course of their experience, so that their part adds to the type and quality of the original.

The result within the executant component of the project team is a structure of artistic authority built around a combination of reputation and position and which can be mobilised by workers to counter organisational authority (see Figure 4.3). Stars in leading positions appear as personalised labour accruing considerable power to shape their own performance and to some degree the work as a whole. Professional labour-power is highly-skilled but more widely-available, more abstract in kind, and without the market-based reputation possessed by stars. While allowed a performer's discretion in their own less visible tasks, they are necessarily more subject to creative management and have less artistic autonomy. Below them are extras; minor positions filled by those attempting to develop their talents and skills and hoping to acquire a name. They are expected to learn from the talents and professionals surrounding them and perform exactly as required. In other words, both organisational and artistic authority are concentrated at one end of the project team in creative management and starring positions, although a weaker power to mobilise and/or resist is diffused throughout the whole structure.

The starting point of this discussion has been the resemblance of the modern creative stage of production to the workshop model of capitalist production, but as details have been developed, it has become increasingly obvious that the similarity is only superficial. It is certainly true that a craft-based division of labour survives – and is likely to, since technologi-

| Position | Production Relation | Basis Of Authority | | Form Of Control |
|---|---|---|---|---|
| producer | manager | bureaucratic (executive) charismatic (artistic leadership) | | managerialism commercialism |
| director | contracted artist | bureaucratic (organisational) charismatic (artistic leadership) | *FORMATTING | managerialism commercialism |
| leading executant | contracted artist | artistic (commercial reputation) | | collaboration commercialism |
| supporting executant | professional creative | artistic (professional reputation) | | direction professionalism |

*Formatting as a system of control to be dealt with in chapter Five.

Figure 4.3  Project Team Positions & Conditions

cal substitution of the artist is very difficult, but its stratification has different foundations to the skill hierarchies of craft workshops. Leading positions in the project team are usually filled by those with talents of more ephemeral kinds, which are linked to the sphere of appearance, of publicity and promotion. Further, there is a powerful management stratum who, as artistic leaders – like masters and journeymen of the earlier era – are still part of the collective labourer, but with the additional function of directing creation towards commoditisation and accumulation. Unlike the relatively straightforward structure of the craft workshop, the structure and dynamics of the project team is aligned around a complex grid of authority relations and patterns of consent which are derived from the nexus of economic, political and artistic imperatives underlying this stage of the cultural labour process.

It would seem then that the project team is a form of labour organisation which reflects the imperatives driving both capitalists and workers in the corporate era of the culture industry; an historic compromise between artist and capitalist in the heart of production. In some respects the directed project team has evolved out of the corporate need to discipline the creative process politically and economically and to take advantage of the productivity gains flowing from a workshop division of labour, with work coordinated by their agents. The specificities of its structure and operation, however, are also a consequence of worker resistance. By working either through the market or the rehearsal room to build personal reputations which signify their artistry, executants have consolidated an alternative power structure based on the traditional values of their work. Under it, they have managed to preserve something of the freedoms and autonomies normally accorded to those who possess the extraordinary and specialised abilities which ascribe them the status of artists, and a countervailing power to the managerial and bureaucratic intrusions of capital into the process of creation.

Of course it is the stars, those with commercial reputations, who have benefited the most. They are the more powerful form of labour, which shows up in their collaborative relations with management – unlike professionals who are restricted and subject to direction. The question is why? To examine this further, we need to look in detail at the types of production relations under which stars and professionals work.

# 4.5 Production Relations in the Creative Stage

The two main forms of capital-labour relation underlining the creative stage of production in the corporations of culture are *contracted artists* and *professional creatives*, built upon sub-contracting, and waged and salaried employment respectively. Both need to be examined separately in terms of their differences across three criteria; ownership of particular means of production, control over phases of the creative process, and ownership of the original, as summarised in Figure 4.4:

## 4.5.1 Contracted Artists

To fill the leading positions in the project team, companies sign contracts with *stars* and *freelancers*. In fact, this relationship is more accurately described as *sub-contracting*, since the general conditions in which the artists work are owned and/or controlled by the company (and the term differentiates this production relation from contracted production carried out by an independent firm as a commercial transaction).

Freelancers are 'independent' artists, usually conception workers such as composers, screenwriters, researchers, directors and designers. (because

| Dimension | Contracted Artist | Professional Creative |
|---|---|---|
| Form of relation | intermediate producer | wage - labour |
| Conditions<br>Payment | sub-contract<br>fees, royalties | employment<br>wages, rates |
| Duration | seasonal, single<br>project | continous, permanent<br>casual |
| Means | talent, originality | versatility, skills |
| Negotiation | collaboration | direction |
| Artistic<br>Authority | commercial<br>reputation | professional<br>reputation |

Figure 4.4  Production Relations In The Project Team

of the solitary character of writing, a large proportion of authors work as freelancers), usually hired for one project at a time by consecutive employers. They are frequently well-known inside the industry although not necessarily outside. Stars are the high-profile, public names of the culture industry, the subjects of media publicity, the well-known and highly-reputed performers of the time. They too are usually contracted for the duration of a single project, but where an individual has a proven sales record, she or he may be signed to a long-term contract. Their terms of engagement enable some to achieve considerable wealth and prestige.

The contract is a legal agreement between artist and company which effectively acknowledges the artist's ownership of the original but assigns reproduction rights to the company. It may refer to a single work or cover a period of time; in the latter case it will usually specify the type and volume of work to be produced by the artist over a period of time. Clauses also cover the type and level of fees, rights and royalties to be paid by the company as applicable (Frith 1978: 77-78, Hill 1983: 137-147).

Contracts express juridical recognition of the personalised labour which has gone into the original's creation and its inseparability from the artist's *persona* and *oeuvre*; it gives them strong residual ownership rights and beneficial interests in its ongoing success as a reproduction (Hartnoll 1967: 814-815, Scholes 1955: 249-250). The differences between sub-contracting and employment relations are the key to understanding the kind and extent of the power and freedoms accorded contracted artists[30] – whether in leading executant or management positions – and just as important, their economic interests. To elaborate: under the terms of the contract, the company leases the artist's individual talents and the right to reproduce their work. The price set in the contract is not a rate for the purchase of labour-power but a measure of relative market value of their talents and reputations, and is a rent paid for their relative creative and market appeal[31]. They are contracted to provide their personal labour and/or performance and/or an all-but-finished original, as an object to be worked up by creative management and whose potential value cannot be realised until reproduced as a commodity. Contracted artists are therefore positioned in the labour process not as labour personified or even personified labour, but as *personalised labour* engaged as suppliers of intermediate artistic goods, of originals which wholly or partly contain their singular labour. In other words, these are not wage-labour relations but relations between an *intermediate goods supplier* and commodity manufacturer. Contracted artists, therefore, appear in the labour process not as labour-power but as petty capitalists, as an independent unit of capital, hence able to stand against the pressures of corporate production.

There are, however, a number of qualifications to their powers. Perhaps the most important flows from the fact that the company owns both the master transcribed from their original and the means of its reproduction. Work which does not meet corporate creative policy will neither be reproduced nor released. This places stars and freelancers is a dependent position in relation to the corporation sub-contracting them. Further, contracted artists have no rights beyond transcription, no capacity to stop the company modifying the master in post-production, or over the marketing and merchandising of the resulting commodities[32]. As suppliers

---

30  This discussion of the contracted artist, although similar in certain respects, is preferable to Williams' discussion of post-artisanal and market professional relations (1981: 45-48). Its *conjunction* with the following discussion of waged and salaried professional creatives (cf. also Williams (1981: 51-2) on corporate professionals) enables examination of the relations between these two forms of employment under corporate conditions of production.

31  For example, record royalties vary widely according to individual performers. In Australian rock music, an unknown band gets about 8% of the retail price and a top name about 15% (*The National Times* 21-27 June 1985: 9-10, 25).

32  This is partly why contracted artists in some cases establish themselves as independent companies: to gain control not only in production but also a measure of control over circulation and the higher share of profits which ensue. For

of intermediate products, stars and freelancers have no alternative base for economic or artistic accumulation; their powers are constrained and circumscribed by the ownership relations governing other phases of the commodity producing process.

Other conditions reinforce their independence. The corporations of culture rely on their stars, especially those with commercial reputations, to create the major works which go on to become best sellers and set new stylistic trends. If talent is to provide what corporations seek, as decreed by the ideologies of art, they need freedom of expression and the right to negotiate creation in the search for originality. If restricted, they are unlikely to perform to their utmost: worse than that, they might take their talent elsewhere and sign with a competitor who does not. This confirms their practical independence in the workplace, allowing them a degree of creative autonomy, time to work on their art, and perform in other contexts. For that reason, winning contracts has been and continues to be the most consequential arena of struggle against capitalists for reputed artists of every type[33]. Its terms underwrite the collaborative negotiation which name artists can sustain with creative management and provide a counter to the bureaucratic structures within which they are increasingly forced to work.

That same contract aligns their economic interests with those of the contracting company. Since it positions them in direct market relations with their audiences and makes their income dependent on sales, contracted artists must take some responsibility for the artistic quality and/or marketability of the original. This creates pressures to compromise with producers, directors and personal management to create an original which their audience is likely to find appealing (e.g. Macgowen 1965: 321-323). The logic of commercialism, therefore, limits their desire to experiment and control and is the common ground on which contracted artists and creative management meet. Further, the powers of contracted artists in the workplace are contingent on artists replenishing their reputations. Their economic prospects and artistic authority are reciprocally determined by the market power of their names; the logic of commercialism

---

examples in the recording industry see *Time* (12 February 1973: 40-43) also Frith (1978).

33   For historical details of the struggle over rights see Laurenson (1971: 131-132) and Rickword (1979: 21-29) for authors; Raynor (1972: 237, 345-349, 1976: 31-33, 186-190) for composers and musicians; Hartnoll (1967: 201, 814-815) for playwrights and actors. Hollywood screenwriters and directors were recently engaged in strike action over residuals (*The Weekend Australian* 4-5 July 1987: 24).

demands that they keep its value spiralling upwards. Accordingly, they must publicise their name. In entrepreneurial fashion, aspirant and established names alike engage in a constant round of promotion and publicity activities contrived by creative management and personal agents – although conversely, for some, the enigma of invisibility or distanced, artistic integrity produces the same effect.

What does a knowledge of contracted artist conditions add to our knowledge of the corporate form of cultural production? From the point of view of the corporations of culture, these production relations return a significant degree of control to the artist within the creative process, reintroducing the indeterminacies of the art/capital relation the project team is supposed to reduce. Nonetheless, because of the terms of the contract, corporate management can be confident that pursuit of individual interest will coincide with theirs and will temper their artistic ambition with the hard edge of business calculation. Most importantly, it transforms stars and freelancers into small units of capital who must live by the laws of the marketplace or fail – a marketplace dominated by the companies which engage them. In that sense, while the creative stage of production appears generally to be only formally subsumed under capital, this particular element of the collective artist has been transformed into capital: not variable capital, but capital itself – a living personification of value in motion – and made subject to the demands of the corporate form of production.

## 4.5.2 Professional Creatives

The supporting artists in the project team are employed on wages or salaries in permanent or casual positions. These are the un-named professional creatives who carry out most of the behind-the-scenes work – the studio musicians and arrangers, staff writers and designers, advertising copywriters and graphic artists, dancers, journalists, actors and screenplay writers, radio announcers, photographers, graphic artists, and so on – and who make up the bulk of cultural workers in the corporations of culture.

In contrast to contracted artists, professional creative work is substantially rationalised, and subject to creative management. Those who take up professional creative employment exchange artistic freedom and an ethos of experimentation for financial security and bureaucratic working conditions. By embedding the employment relation in the organisation of the labour process, the corporations of culture have transformed the nature of artistic labour; it turns artists into a generalised capacity to perform creative work – it positions them in the labour process as *creative labour-power*.

Professional creatives are possessors less of the innate and extraordinary talents of the artist than acquired, generalised craft-like skills of a cultural worker. By virtue of their experience or the formal training (increasingly the latter)[34], professionals are expert and versatile practitioners of a range of artistic skills and techniques. What makes them valuable to their employers is their ability to perform across a range of cultural forms, on cue, and to a high standard. Since creatives are defined in terms of ownership only of their labour-power, they are paid not market-based rights or royalties, but hourly rates, wages and salaries based on average not individual labour value, which are set as minimum standards in union awards and industry agreements[35]. Compared to stars and freelancers, they appear in the labour process not as an inspirational, recognisable

---

34  The reconstitution of cultural practices as generalised skills – and hence the possibility of transforming artistic labour into creative labour-power – has been made possible partly through developments taking place outside of production itself. Particularly important has been the role of the modern democratic state in providing educational institutions which introduce students to aspects and institutions of cultural practice, hence directly or indirectly training them as a potential labour force (cf. also Miège 1979: 305). Equally, the state itself in its function as patron, has led the way in providing secure employment for many forms of artist in national opera, dance and theatre companies, national and regional orchestras and national broadcasting systems. Note the contradiction confronting the state in its dual function as patron of the arts and supplier and regulator of the creative labour market; its educational and performance bodies are infused with the traditional ideologies of art, yet these bodies are expected to operate in a context which is dominated by commercial forms and production systems.

35  Despite the formation of various unions, guilds and associations since the late 19th century, membership amongst artists is generally low, although highest in those sectors (e.g., media) where employment predominates (e.g. Australia Council 1983: 62-65). This indifference reflects prevailing ideologies of creative individualism which flow from the constitution of art, where worker strategies have been geared towards individual negotiation with employers on the basis of personalised labour-power, or by setting up as a freelancer or independent company. However, as the proportion of artists employed as professional creatives increases and there is wider recognition of changes in the cultural workplace as discussed here, there may be wider reliance on the value of collectivism. To that extent, the recent experiences of journalists (media concentration, impact of technology) and their changes of attitude (e.g. Bonney and Wilson 1983: 110-123, Windschuttle and Windschuttle 1981: 236-241, 301-309), may be a sign of things to come.

talent but as an un-named but trained capacity to consistently labour in a supporting role. In so far as professional creatives reveal the extent of degradation of artistic labour, they approximate the detail worker of Marx' manufacturing model of production – *labour personified* rather than personal labour, variable capital to be put to work across continuous cycles of production[36].

Creatives are expected to work under direction. Creative managers personify organisational demands for a type and quality of original created at a price, and the task of cultural workers is to dedicate their skills efficiently and competently in the manner required. Casuals employed in part-time work or as extras, such as weekend announcers, stringers, chorus singers and dancers, are the most explicit case – their obedience motivated by long lines of unemployed hopefuls looking for 'their big break'. Permanent professionals such as staff writers, designers, and musicians, ensemble actors and musicians, general reporters and continuity announcers and so on, possess the craft-based skills and competences needed by companies to support the stars, which accords them a restricted operational right to negotiate creation within their own contribution. The terms of their negotiation, however, are of a different order. This is less collaboration than *direction*; guidance and teaching as opposed to cooperation between equals. To creative managers, professional creatives represent a different subject to contracted artists, a versatile and capable instrument at their disposal.

Ideologies of professionalism provide grounds for their consent to subjection. Employment is more secure than the market-mediated situation of contracted artists, less subject to the whims of fashion. Professional job performance can bring long-term employment in an industry which is notoriously fickle, and there is pride to be gained from a difficult job competently done. Moreover, they can win returns beyond their station; top-rank professionals with significant reputations – names within the industry – can appropriate a measure of the rights due to stars, at the very least, the right to contribute to the strategic planning process. Under some circumstances, they can demand and get naming rights to their contribution, as in the case of reporters writing by-lined features, television presenters identified in the programme title, or the key workers listed in

---

36 As befits their historical constitution, some express a worker consciousness which is antagonistic to their subsumption, but since commercialism is the specific focus of attack, an artistic idealism is projected as a counterfactual. Hence, for example, session musicians search out opportunities to play 'real' music (e.g. Frith 1978: 162-163) and journalists harbour aspirations to write plays, novels, poetry and so on (e.g. Glasgow University Media Group 1976: 71-72).

film or recording credits. These high-status creatives work not as anonymous creatives like most of those employed in the project team, but as personified labour – although naming makes them appear like personalised labour. While bringing no entitlements to royalties, this indexes the significance of their reputations and entitles them to air their views at the planning level. Furthermore, if their names appear regularly on successful products or they win industry awards, individual creatives can build the sorts of reputations which attract promotion or job offers from competing firms, enabling them to convert their artistic into organisational authority and/or higher salaries – perhaps even to break free of salaried employment and establish themselves as freelancers or stars (cf. also Elliott 1978). Accordingly, professional creatives have material foundations for cooperating with creative management in creating originals of a high standard while simultaneously asserting the value of their own contribution. Since it indexes accretion of reputation, the struggle to be identified, to be publicly recognised as a name of note in an industry which thrives on reputation, is an important goal for professional creatives. It modifies the dynamics of authority within the project team, by providing a foundation for the authority to claim a more gainful position within the relations of distribution, a path towards relative freedom from workplace control and in some cases, escape from the wage-labour relation itself.

## 4.6 Conclusion

Using the essential relations posited by labour process theory, this chapter has examined the organisational conditions under which cultural commodities are produced in the corporations of culture. Because of the artist/capitalist contradiction, the creative stage of production is organised along apparently simpler lines than the corporate form of the reproduction stage. The degradation of creative work has proceeded only a short distance because of the historical constitution of the artist; artistic workers have a structured capacity to resist the inroads of capital, especially the typical path of technological reconstitution of the division of labour. As a result, it takes a form somewhat like the workshop model of capitalist production.

The essential feature of the corporate form of capitalist cultural commodity production is that the position of the artist in the production process appears historically as the project team, constituted by its structure of relations based on a producer and director as creative managers, and leading and supporting executants who are engaged or employed to perform the originals they design. Again, because of the form of labour, relations between creative management and workers is characterised by a style of management based on negotiation rather than direct command. Intersecting the organisational structure of authority relations are the orientations of commercialism and professionalism, representing alternative power bases which impact variously upon each of the positions in the team and which, while representing a form of external control over the collective artist, are also a resource which members can mobilise against the powers of capital. They are also aligned with the two fundamental production relations cutting across the project team, whose members are either engaged as contracted artists, generally directors and leading executants (a sub-contracting relation with the artist as an intermediate goods producer), or employed as professional creatives, usually supporting executants (wage labour relations). Producers are generally employed but are increasingly appearing as executive managers.

Despite having the general form of a workshop form of organisation, as we begin to look closer, the project team in some of its dimensions seems to represent significant degradation of artistic conditions of work. On the one hand, the consolidation of creative management within the project team represents appropriation by the corporations of culture of the conception function within creation, thereby relegating the rest of the team to the position of executant and making them subject to its authority structures – even though stars and freelancers, by virtue of their reputations, are allowed to participate in planning of the original. But the clearest indication of inroads by the capital relation is seen in the conditions of professional creative work. Once having transformed the traditional artistic leader into creative management and reserved for them the right to imagine, and preserved the traditional freedoms of the artist for the contracted artist – in return for a market-oriented approach to creativity – the way was clear for capitalists to reorganise the conditions of artists – whose indifference to unionisation meant few barriers were erected. These workers, especially since the 1950s, have had many of the traditional artistic autonomies and controls stripped from them. They have been asked to exchange the status of labour-power, direction by creative management, and work in the shadow of stars, for secure employment and regular paypackets – although top-flight professionals with significant reputations seem able to win conditions close to those of the stars. Nonetheless, it should be remembered that artists' conditions have been substantially preserved because capitalists have increased the rate of surplus-value production primarily in the reproduction stage of production, transforming duplication and transcription into unskilled and semi-skilled forms of work.

The project team, therefore, still represents considerable indeterminacy in the labour process for the corporations of culture. However, its controls have been tightened considerably since the 1950s – the period marking the maturation of the corporate form of production – through the bureaucratisation of creative management and its planning techniques, the effect of which has been to significantly rationalise the process of creativity. 'Formatting', as I call this development, is the focus of the following chapter.

# Chapter 5
# Rationalising the Creative Stage of Production: The Formatting of Creativity

## 5.1 Introduction

Even within the project team around which the corporate form of cultural production revolves, an indeterminacy persists in the relations between artist and management. Although its organisation restricts and reshapes the rights bestowed upon artists by their history, strong residues of their constitution remain embedded in its structures, allowing artists a relative autonomy in their work.

In principle, this openness should enable the creation of a wide and variant range of originals. We find, however, a multitude of artists, critics and audiences complaining of the tendency within corporate cultural production towards formulaic production. Observing the increasing concentration of ownership in publishing, one writer has commented:

Concentration will mean...a more homogeneous product, which will mean more gardening books, more Fonda workout books, more diet books and more Wilbur Smith books (*Times on Sunday* 31 January 1988: 13).

Similarly, Simon Frith has argued that domination by a few major corporations has turned present-day popular music towards "production to formulas which limit individual creativity...market choice rather than artistic judgement...an obsession with fashion...and flattery of mediocrity" (1978: 192), creating "a culture of predictable market tastes and indulgent superstars, of slick radio shows and standardised sounds...in short, music business as usual" (1978: 209). Early and sustained arguments of this kind permeate the work of the Frankfurt School writers, of which Adorno and Horkheimer's *Dialectic of Enlightenment* - especially the essay 'The Culture Industry: Enlightenment as Mass Deception' (chapter 4 in 1979) – is a classic example (see also Adorno 1978a, 1978b, Marcuse 1972). Their bitter and pessimistic attack on the "mass culture of advanced, monopoly capitalism" is sprinkled with their concerns: "Films, radio and magazines make up a system which is uniform as a whole and in every part"; "Under monopoly all mass culture is identical..."; "...the achievement of standardisation and mass production..."; "The ruthless unity in the culture industry..." (1979: 120-122), and so on. At one point they assert that:

Not only are the hit songs, stars and soap operas cyclically recurrent and rigidly invariable types, but the specific content of the entertainment itself is derived from them and only appears to change (1979: 125).

Adorno's celebrated attack on "the fundamental characteristic of popular music: standardisation" (1978a: 199) makes similar points.

While many of these accounts evidence an unacceptable elitism, there is a certain empirical truth to their observations. The need, therefore, is to explain the contradiction between the structural indeterminacy inherent to the creative stage of production and the systematic predictability of its products. Without developing their argument, Adorno and Horkheimer suggest that the sameness which characterises modern cultural production stems from:

The assembly-line character of the culture industry, the synthetic, planned method of turning out its products (factory-like not only in the studio but, more or less, in the compilation of cheap biographies, pseudodocumentary novels and hit songs) (1979: 163).

The arguments presented in the previous chapter concerning the work-shop-like conditions of creative production, however, suggest that this formulation is incorrect – although Adorno (1978a: 205) himself seems closer to the mark when he observes elsewhere that "The production of popular music is highly centralised in its economic organisation, but still 'individualistic' in its social mode of production".

This chapter will show that the explanation for this contradiction does indeed lie in the organisation of creation in the corporations of culture: that despite the relative autonomy of the collective artist in the project team, there *is* a tendency towards formula and cliché in creation and that it flows from *the formatting of the creative stage of production*. Corporate creation is underlaid by a structuring principle[1] which articulates economic

---

1    The term is used in the sense of ruled constraint and enablement and is derived
     from the work of Giddens (e.g. 1984: 16-28). The rules of a practice I under-
     stand in his dual sense of rules and resources, recursively implicated in the
     reproduction of social systems. The structuring principles – the formats – I
     discuss are, like Giddens' structures, rule-resource sets, implicated in the insti-
     tutional articulation of social systems (1984: 377). They are systematic clusters
     of rules which both express and constitute the articulation of economic, organi-
     sational and cultural practices in a social field and which in combination, gener-

and organisational imperatives to specifically cultural imperatives in a context of expanded production, realising their combination through company-advocated rules of creative work. As these conditions developed, thereby constituting the corporate form of cultural production, their effect was to substantially rationalise the creativity engaged in production.

## 5.2 Bureaucratisation of the Workplace in the Corporate Era of Capital

An important dimension of recent literature dealing with the reorganisation of work in capitalist firms since the late-19th century has been investigation of the specific forms of labour control they developed; Braverman (1974), Edwards (1979) and Littler (1982) are only some of the more important contributors. Putting aside their differences, the empirical thread linking these works is that during the early and middle decades of the 20th century, a variety of direct and indirect methods were installed to manage the workplace in the interests of profitability. In this sense, the period appears as a distinct phase of capitalist development in which labour rationalisation (Littler 1982: 188) was an important organisational concern.

### 5.2.1 Edwards: The Embedding of Bureaucratic Control

In distinguishing bureaucratic from technical control, Edwards argues that above all else it made workers' behaviour more predictable, and predictability brought with it greater control for the corporation. It:

institutionalised the exercise of capitalist power, making power appear to emanate from the formal organisation itself. Hierarchical relations were transformed from relations between (unequally powerful) people to relations between jobholders or relations between jobs themselves, abstracted from the specific people or the concrete work tasks involved. 'Rule of Law' – the firm's law – replaced rule by supervisor command (1979: 145).

---

ate a specific logic of action. For a specific application of a similar approach in the sociology of organisations, see Clegg (1975: 119-124) and Clegg and Dunkerley (1980: 501-502), especially their notion of the modes of rationality underlying organisations and through which they are constituted.

According to Edwards, bureaucratic control was a corporate response to the fact that technical control had become the seedbed for new forms of shopfloor conflict and spreading unionisation. In essence, it involved the explicit analysis, systematisation, and standardisation of the conditions of labour, resulting in sets of approved descriptions, rules and directions. Specifications were drawn up identifying job entry requirements, starting pay, location, the tasks to be performed, the objects to be used and the pace and quality of work required, promotion procedures and definitions of responsibilities and so on. These were tied to systems for supervising and evaluating workers' performance, distributing rewards and imposing punishments (1979: 136-142).

This approach habituates and sediments day-to-day operations. Once in place, the work of management can proceed without the need of the conscious intervention or the personal power of foremen, supervisors, or capitalists and in ways which reinforce elements of hierarchical and technical control (1979: 131). Its advent marked a shift from the personal and arbitrary preferences of the owner or manager to methodical formulation and application of impersonal rules of practice. Through it, employers extended their control over the work performed throughout the organisation, making worker behaviour more predictable. Despite its coercive power, bureaucratic control did not eliminate struggle between employers and employees but established the terrain of contest as the rules themselves, rather than the form of domination represented by the structure of the labour process itself (1979: 130-132, cf. also Clegg and Dunkerley 1980: 433-482).

This argument demonstrates the bureaucratisation taking place in major companies in the middle decades of the 20th century; how a system of constraint founded upon a combination of hierarchical power and sedimented rules was erected alongside technical forms of control within which work was organised. It completed construction of what was defined in the previous chapter as the corporate model of capitalist production.

Edwards also notes in passing that bureaucratic control establishes the impersonal force of company rules or company policy as the basis of control (1979: 131), a point which becomes important later in this analysis. The rules inserted into production have a content and an object, created out of principles underlying the operation of the corporation, the most fundamental of which is profitability, yet flowing from the type of commodity being manufactured. Each activity within the labour process, each phase and stage of production, is activated through a matrix of rules which appear in the form of a 'policy' comprising strategic dimensions (planning) and operational dimensions (activities) (cf. also Clegg and Dunkerley 1980: 444-450, 501-503). Some aspects of policy are written down – albeit in fragments – in job and task specifications, memos, reports and manuals, while others exist discursively in the culture of the organisation – the everyday understandings and values of workers and management. These refer to the particular types of raw materials, technologies and forms of labour invested in by the organisation, the purpose of the organisation and the character of its output. In the daily organisation of work, as Clegg (1975: 77) points out, these policies are invoked 'iconically', as an idea(l), a standard measure of activity. Their constituent rules become not only a vehicle of control but also a resource within the work process itself (cf. Giddens 1979: 16-28), coordinating the activities of those who people positions in the structure of relations which underlie the production process.

## 5.3 Corporate Control in the Creative Stage of Production

As seen in chapter 4, technical control has had a major impact in the reproduction stage of production but not in the creative stage. Since the 1950s, however, creation in the corporate context has been overtaken by a kind of bureaucratic control as a consequence of moves to make creativity more predictable in the face of changing market conditions and tightening conditions of profitability. A classic example of the outcome is provided by Coser *et al.* in their study of the culture and commerce of publishing. They illustrate their discussion of 'fiction factories' with a case study of Book Creations, Inc. headed by Lyle Kenyon Engel. Over fifteen years, this company had turned out five thousand paperback titles 'authored' by some eighty professional writers by filling out story outlines provided by their employer:

Engel usually dreams up ideas for an overall series and for individual books in the series...When an idea has jelled, he contacts a paperback publisher and hawks the idea. No writer's name is mentioned. Only after the book has been sold will Engel approach a suitable writer from his large stable. Once the book is written, Engel's seven editors see that the formula has been successfully followed. Engel spends a considerable part of his advances on publicity...Engel, like a steamroller, homogenises the products of diverse writers so that they turn out identical products to be packaged and sold in huge numbers (1982: 263-265).

This single instance captures much of what will be discussed in this chapter. Under the corporate form of cultural production, administration has been inserted into the sphere of art. Creative work is performed to a management plan. Specific, fixed cultural rules are formulated as company policy by its creative managers and applied to members of the project team. These are key conditions in the process I refer to as *formatting*[2].

Why has formatting emerged? Why is it coming to dominate mainstream cultural production? To understand these changes, we need to examine the organisational consequences of the contradictions of the cultural commodity as discussed in chapter 2, using publishing firms to illustrate the argument.

## 5.3.1 The Consequences of Expanded Production on Creative Work

One of the chief characteristics of cultural commodities as *commodities* is their sales pattern (see Figure 2.2). Even highly successful works demonstrate, to use a marketing term, a truncated 'product life cycle' (also Escarpit 1966: 119; Dessauer 1974: 30). Because the originality and distinctiveness which attracts people to newly-released works in the first place are undermined by their increasing popularity, as more and more copies are sold and people become familiar with a work, its capacity to excite, inform and amuse diminishes and the urgency of audience interest dies (cf. Escarpit 1966: 128). The initial rush of sales peaks, then declines.

As previously noted, this has a range of organisational consequences for manufacturers. They are locked into recurrent cycles of production (also Curwen 1981: 17) and must organise a procession of new artistic projects through their creative departments[3] (cf. Coser *et al.* 1982: 128), but

---

2    The term is borrowed from the broadcasting media where it is used to refer only to the manifestation of this mode of rationality. My use refers to *the combination of structuring principles underlying the creative stage of production and its manifestations*. The term 'format' is also occasionally used to refer to technical aspects of the commodity; in publishing, for example, in relation to page size and paper type, fonts and font size, binding, and so on. These are essentially aspects of the transcription phase; as such, I am presuming these to be part of formatting, but am ignoring them here to focus on the creative stage of production.

3    To simplify matters, the following discussion presumes that new originals are created in each production cycle. It largely ignores fact that the next original may be a new edition of previously released work (e.g. paperback version of hardback), reissue, translation, novelisation, reprint, collection, even repackaging of work from the backlist. This is work almost entirely carried out by creative management with the help perhaps of some realisation (design) workers

because of the arbitrary character of the creative process, companies need to increase the productivity of their artistic labour force and coordinate its work around a production schedule.

To do so, the early speculative entrepreneurs of the culture industry relied on numbers, by establishing commercial relations with many independent artists. Creation was organised along the lines described in chapter 4 as the 'simple cooperation' model of capitalist production. Based on merchant-artisan relations, it appeared variously as simple exchanges between artist and intermediary, a putting out system, or in some cases, a craft workshop. Economic authority flowed from ownership and/or control of the means of *reproduction*, although artistic control was limited to the cash nexus (labour, finished original). Relations of artistic (cf. economic) production governed the process of creation. Ownership of the talents, knowledges and skills necessary to create, lay with artists, both individually and collectively. There was no social foundation or organisational mechanism for the entrepreneur as owner or controller of the reproduction system, to appropriate the right to imagine or direct the making of the original – to take, in other words, the role of the master.

This arrangement seems to have prevailed throughout the expanding culture industry from its beginnings till around the 19th century (and continues in some areas of present-day non-corporate production such as art galleries and craft markets). It supported the large publishing enterprises of the 15-17th centuries owned by the Kobergers, Plantin, Elzivier and others (cf. Febvre and Martin 1976: 109-166) and the 'slop shops of literature' of 18-19th century English and Western European publishers (Laurenson 1971: 130-136, Steinberg 1955: 142-171). Even early examples of mass employment under artist-entrepreneurs such as Lully at the *Academie Royal de Musique* (Raynor 1976: 156-157) and Scribe's 19th century 'play factories' (Freedley and Reeves 1968: 341) seem to have been built upon this configuration.

Once the size of the company and the scale of production reaches a certain point, as was increasingly the case from about the 19th century to the first half of 20th century, and depending on the costs and/or time involved in producing the original (cf. film, opera), it becomes necessary for owners to engage artists as permanent or seasonal artistic teams

---

(e.g. Escarpit 1966: 132-133, Gedin 1977: 23-24). This is actually an important aspect of creative management work especially in the private goods sector, entailing working through the back-catalogue and stocks of older masters, assessing their potential for re-release in the light of changing market trends. Companies find re-release particularly attractive because of the rate of profit attainable from its low marginal production costs.

working under the independent control of a master; this is the craft workshop model noted in chapter 3. In the performing arts, for example, the 'long run' and touring companies inaugurated by 19th century theatrical entrepreneurs such as Daly, Boucicault and Pastor (Freedley and Reeves 1968: 311-321, Hartnoll 1968: 194-202), and the concert orchestras of Strauss in Vienna and Offenbach in Paris (Weber 1975: 50-53, 110-112), seem to be examples. It even survived, but not for long, into the earliest days of film-making, recording and radio (although it continues to play an prominent role in modern-day small and medium-scale independent production). In the craft workshop approach, the entrepreneur establishes a partnership with an independent artist to head the team, the core of which comprises experienced artists employed seasonally or casually by the artist-manager – though leading positions are sub-contracted to popular artists[4]. Apart from the introduction of wage-labour into the creative phase, its other distinctive feature is the centrality and power of the artistic leader (in some cases also the owner), engaged because of their history of commercial success. While the work of the team is made to revolve around their talents and guidance, their artistic control is separate from and provides a barrier against, economic control.

This craft workshop system with its commercially oriented master-manager, introduces indirect artistic control for the entrepreneur. In organisational terms, it is more rational than the cooperation model;

---

4    This indicates the economic importance of the sphere of 'independent' cultural production (for a discussion in publishing, see Coser *et al.* 1982: 36-69). At little risk to the corporations, these writers, musicians, actors, dancers and so on get on with the business of innovation in small-time venues. Much of the initial work of creative management is carried out by independent personal managers and agents (e.g. Coser *et al.* 1982: 285-307) and the corporations are becoming increasingly reliant on them for these services (e.g. literary agents, authors and publishers discuss their roles in *The Weekend Australian* 21-22 December 1985: Literary Magazine 6). When practiced, and having already primed the market, they are contracted by the majors for volume release. The corporations can pick and choose from those clamouring at their doors as market conditions shift, without having to bear the financial and industrial costs of a permanent workforce.

Equally, of course, where intermediate goods and services are routinely required by corporations at the core, favourable business opportunities exist for independents within the semi-periphery. Thus, progressively, throughout the 20th century, agencies of various kinds, including casting and talent agencies (see Macgowen 1965), news agencies (Boyd-Barrett 1980) and advertising agencies (Fox 1984) have flourished, becoming a significant component of the culture industry.

artistic authority is invested in an individual manager who works over a division of labour. It is still arbitrary in its specifically artistic aspects, operating through charisma; the right of artist-masters to direct other artists flows from their personal talents and reputation and not their organisational position. The originals produced display their personal touch, reflecting their style of work, and are likely to demonstrate the same commercial potential. This makes their artistic *persona* crucial to the commercial goals of the owner, but still there is no foundation for direct company control, much less via impersonal rule.

Within publishing, the growth and consolidation of newspaper companies illustrates the transition from craft workshop to the capitalist workshop. As emerging reading publics in the 18th and 19th centuries provided opportunities for expansion, weekly, bi- or tri-weekly and later daily publication permitted permanent employment of writers with new types of skills (journalists), coordinated by a leading artist, the editor (e.g. Harris 1978, Asquith 1978, Lee 1978; for examples, see Souther 1981). This form did not evolve further until companies reorganised from the late 19th century under the dual impact of new competitive conditions and a push from journalists towards professionalisation. From then, newspaper production was increasingly organised around a more specialised division of labour; journalistic work was sub-divided into sub-editors, specialist and general reporters, rules and conventions were developed governing employer-employee relations, job specifications, gradings, salary levels, and codes of practice, and the position of editor was ascribed a legal-rational form of authority. In combination, these conditions gave companies their present-day, corporate, bureaucratic form with creation organised around a project team (cf. also Lee 1978, Murdock and Golding 1978, Tunstall 1971. For parallels in book publishing, see Coser *et al.* 1982: 97-199, Tebbel 1981, and for the recording industry see Perrow 1979, and film, see Kindem 1982a).

Bureaucratisation within the creative stage of production is therefore partly explained as an organisational response to the economics and dynamics of competitive expansion. The irrationality of creativity was mediated by a division of labour on the one hand, and direction by creative managers employed as agents of capital on the other. This is like Edwards' (1979) model of technical control. However, there is no necessary imperative within the capitalist workshop model to further tighten control over creativity. This is partly precluded by the conventions of art. More specifically, since it is difficult to raise the rate of surplus value production in the creative stage (which had been profitably raised in reproduction), there is more to be gained, as Littler has argued (see chapter 2), by improving the efficiency of circulation. The fact is that formatting represents a tendency towards rationalisation of cultural work as *cultural* work, as a development of the workshop model. The question is why?

## 5.3.2 Consequences of Corporate Commercialism on Creative Work

By focusing attention of the corporate desire to produce immediately saleable commodities in an unpredictable market, we see one of the most influential imperatives underlying the development of formatting. Its purpose is hinted at by Coser *et al.* in their remark that:

> Not only is it hard to predict in advance which will be successful books...it is difficult to plan exactly when a successful author will deliver his or her next manuscript. The vagaries of public taste are not always ascertainable in advance, and the productivity of creative individuals can be equally unpredictable (1982: 182).

Two of the basic problems confronting companies needing regular supply of saleable commodities, are first, that art presumes the free flight of imagination unbounded by non-artistic considerations; and second, that while tastes are reasonably stable, audience response to particular works is quite unpredictable, especially those which are highly original. Historically, the first problem has been confronted by dealing with the second. In essence, corporations orient their production towards *commercialism*[5],

---

5    In those forms of divisional, subsidiary or independent production where the conventions of art or any of its sub-divisions – e.g. scholarship – remain important and the bottom line does not reign supreme (Coser *et al.* 1982: 15), some releases do not appear particular commercial; i.e. no matter how economical their production, because of their strictly limited appeal, the company is likely to make an overall loss (but which can be offset against more successful titles). The publication of poetry and some forms of classical music are frequently cited examples. Thus companies can claim to have met their social responsibilities as 'cultural gatekeepers' (Coser 1976) and provide some artistic satisfactions for the staff concerned – that their "asceticism in this world is the precondition for salvation in the next" (Bourdieu 1981: 284). Coser *et al.* (1982), Dessauer (1974) and Escarpit (1966) all provide examples of innovative publishing which effectively ignores short-term profitability, and emphasise that even within large corporations, an artistic ethos occasionally dominates commerciality.

     Bourdieu offers a more telling observation. In many cases, given the dynamics of the art market, apparently art-based decisions are made, in fact, in the hope of future profitability. It might seem to a company that while an innova-

where audience taste preferences as indexed by existing patterns of commodity sales, dictate the direction of creation. This creates a logic of *repetition* which surfaces as formatting, as a management control applied to the project team and which has the effect of rationalising the creative stage of production.

When sales of their current frontlist titles begin to decline, like other cultural commodity manufacturers, publishers have to replace them. As there are no certain means for predicting audience responses, many of their choices – in fact, the large majority – are abject failures, failing to recover the costs of their production (Dessauer 1974: 36). A work created by a star, however, is a reasonably safe bet for the next release. A small number of artists are defined as the major artists of the times and audiences purchase their works in enormous quantities, turning them into the best sellers which return to companies the massive profits that enable expansion[6] (cf. Escarpit 1966: 117-118, Steinberg 1955: 223-247)[7].

As discussed in chapter 2, and taking books as an example, best sellers typically exhibit a sales pattern which rises sharply to a peak within a matter of months after publication and then go into steady decline (Curwen 1981: 18). Their relative rarity, the speed at which they peak, the magnitude of profits they generate and the rate at which these are returned to the company (cf. Escarpit 1966: 119), are their most important

tive work might not sell immediately, the long-term prospects of this and other works in the artist's repertoire, when finally recognised by the artistic community, are much rosier. Bourdieu cites the case of Editions de Minuit who took the gamble on Becket's *Waiting For Godot*, initially at some loss (1981: 282-283).

6     While obviously applicable to private and quasi-private cultural goods, despite initial appearances, this argument also applies to public cultural goods; i.e. the media and their contents – including broadcasting, although the connection here is analogical rather than literal. Newspapers have best selling days when important, topical news stories break (or they run a popular promotion); so do magazines and periodicals when they lead with articles on topical or relevant public issues. Radio and television stations have days of particularly popular programming, where other days draw only average audiences. Of course, in the broadcasting case, we are not dealing with sales, but popularity does reflect consumption, and their product cycle is measured in hours not weeks or months.

7     Escarpit (1966: 115-134) distinguishes usefully between what he calls 'fast-sellers', 'steady-sellers' and 'best-sellers', in a manner which resembles Bourdieu's (1981) brief but excellent analysis. Since my purposes are slightly different (and there may be more connection between fast and best sellers than he credits), I have collapsed the first and last of these into a single category of 'best seller'.

features, and explain the quest for the golden seller which preoccupies many corporations of culture, publishers included (Coser *et al.* 1982: 18). Compared to many other mass-produced commodity lines such as clothes, packaged foods or cars, their product life cycle is relatively short; a limit case offered by Escarpit (1966: 117) covers less than 18 months – although most actual instances are much shorter. At the point of decline, rather than withdrawing the title, the publisher has several options. Remaining stocks can be kept on the backlist till all copies are finally sold, or if rated amongst the 2 or 3% of books which become the sales successes of the year, it can be reprinted in paperback form and later repackaged as a 'standard' or 'classic', perhaps even transformed into a television series or film – the sale of tie-ins and subsidiary rights are a significant source of additional profits especially for trade houses (Coser *et al.* 1982: 212, Dessauer 1974: 31). Re-release usually brings another spurt in sales although not of the same intensity, but significantly extends the effective market life of the original work. Since the marginal costs of re-release are relatively low, this maintains a healthy flow of profits back to the corporation (Dessauer 1974: 30; Escarpit 1966: 119, see especially the 'anatomy of a best seller', Curwen 1981: 36-37).

Accordingly, the extraordinary, even excessive emphasis placed on best sellers (Dessauer 1974: 46) leads companies inevitably to compete furiously for the work of established and emerging stars as part of the cult of the celebrity (Coser *et al.* 1982: 221). This formula has a long history in the culture industry: for example, like present-day corporations, music publishers from the 18th century sought out the new works of popular composers, late-19th century vaudeville and variety impresarios signed up the major singers, actors and performers of the period (e.g. Raynor 1978: 147-154), and early film moguls offered rich contracts to the major stars their earlier movies had created (Kindem 1982b. See also the case of the author James Clavell, *The Weekend Australian* 5-6 March 1988: Magazine 3, or radio industry battles over 'its million dollar megastars', *The Bulletin* 5 February 1985: 76-78).

Having signed a star, the company sets out to exploit their name by releasing as much of their work as possible, but like the life cycle of the commodity, a star too, is subject to the ebb and flow of popularity. Too many releases, too quickly, leads to overexposure. Audience familiarity breeds a commercial contempt and their reputation begins to wane. Signing stars in order to secure continuous sales of their total output, therefore, is a strategy with limitations: if long-term success is the goal, exploitation must be tempered and release patterns carefully managed.

If unsuccessful in signing established stars, companies have other options. For example, publishers can search out developing but unknown artists by reading 'over the transom' (unsolicited) manuscripts, those referred by agents or patrons, and 'talent scouting', i.e. doing the rounds of minor publishers, clubs, conferences and workshops to identify those with artistic and commercial potential[8] (cf. Coser *et al.* 1982: 129). A one-off alternative is encouraging luminaries from other spheres such as journalists, ex-presidents, stockbrokers or movie stars to put pen to paper (cf. Coser *et al.* 1982: 60). With appropriate marketing and publicity, a best seller can be created from these beginnings (cf. Coser *et al.* 1982: 200-223).

Best seller strategies are predicated on company expectations for continuity; that stars will produce works similar in type and style to those which made them famous (Escarpit 1966: 151-152). Commercial thinking presumes that the strongest predictor of success is to repeat the formula. When, for example, editorial managers assess drafts as manuscripts near completion, they pressure authors to be consistent and adhere to the rules of form – as Dessauer ingenuously comments: "to achieve the best organisation, the most appropriate emphasis, the right tone, the optimal length, the proper slant for his (sic) work" (1974: 38). The logic of commercialism also appeals to the star. Since their contract ties their income to sales, they too adopt a market orientation to their art, motivating them to create more of the same. Name-based approaches to creation, therefore, represent a commercial strategy to rationalise the indeterminacies of the cultural marketplace. Offering audiences more of what they have previously purchased reveals the logic of repetition and continuity that underlies commercialism in culture industry. It demonstrates in weak form the principles guiding corporations towards formatting the creative stage of production[9].

---

8    Ultimately, the decision to reproduce a work depends on the company's assessment of its commercial potential; a belief not only in terms of its artistic worth (the bottom line cannot afford to be the sole concern of creative management), but also its market value, its capacity to meet existing demand and hence attract a profitable level of sales. In some cases it might seem to the company like a 'sure-fire hit'; in others, editorial and marketing staff might recognise an income-producing potential for promotional tie-ins and sale of subsidiary rights; or they might accept that an author's cultural/market potential may not be realised until the second or third book, and will carry the loss on initial publication till his or her talent is recognised and reputation established, whence the backlist titles will acquire a new and increased value (Coser *et al.* 1982: 118-174, Dessauer 1974: 29-49).

9    Even so, signing stars does not guarantee success. Not every work of a recognised artist is a masterpiece, and some which are, do not catch the mood of the audience. Working on the premise that given enough choices, audiences will like something, companies have adopted the 'shotgun' or 'buckshot' approach

In fact, name-based creative strategies aimed at producing best sellers provide only a partial foundation for the expansion of business. Because by definition, great artists/works are rare, best sellers are few and far between. Furthermore, they create stop-start production and sales patterns. To utilise full production capacity and maintain a steady flow of profits, companies also developed a complimentary strategy which filled the gaps in their production schedules: they oriented some of their production towards *type*-based creative policies[10].

Publishers, for example, knew from long experience that audiences also had continuing needs for particular types of books. Some of these were functional works to meet continuing needs (Escarpit 1966: 118), including what Coser *et al.* (1982: 201) refer to as 'staples' such as bibles, dictionaries, texts and instruction manuals. Others fulfilled entertainment needs (Steinberg 1955: 223-258). These were relatively undemanding works based on conventional forms (Wellek and Warren 1963: 235), consumed as recreation – the types of books frequently abused by mass society critics and aesthetes (e.g. Swingewood 1977, cf. Williams 1963). Demand for goods of these types had expanded regularly throughout the 19th and 20th centuries with the consolidation and development of bourgeois society. The growth of new class strata and new reading publics went hand-in-hand with the emergence of different schools of writing. As publishing technologies improved, publishers expanded by exploiting these new markets with various types of books, frequently released in cheap editions alongside reprints of standards and classics and which sold in substantial quantities (Laurenson 1971: 117-139, Watt 1972: 38-65, Williams 1965: 177-194).

Books of a type have a tendency to be steady sellers (see Figure 2.2). The shape of the sales curve in these cases is less spectacular than that of best sellers: sales build up at a slower rate, peaking at a lower level but

---

to product release. This, according to Dessauer (1974: 36-37), is "the lighting-will-strike theory…take a flyer on as much material as seems to hold promise and you can afford – lightning may strike some of it". Accordingly, several stars are signed, each contracted to create a flow of new work – hence the tendency towards overproduction of titles which plagues every sector of the culture industry, publishing including (Escarpit 1966: 132).

10  It needs to be stressed that type-based creative strategies are the other side of name-based strategies. My distinction does not represent a *dichotomy* but a *polarity*. Every artwork represents a combination of artist and form, of performance and style. Stars usually rise to fame on a particular style, and popular styles are usually build around or related to the work of stars. Both exist in dialectical relations. Hence, as creative strategies, type and star approaches are two dimensions of commercialism, two polar positions on a spectrum which operates throughout all sectors of the culture industry.

sustaining sales longer. Escarpit (1966: 117) offers a case study where profitable sales of a title continued more than two years after initial release. Steady sellers recoup the costs of investment later in their careers when compared to best sellers but offer the advantage that their sales patterns sustain useful and orderly cash flows. Their impact is to stabilise annual operations, which suits the corporate search for security. They provide conditions whereby the company can calculate and predict financial performance and plan a production schedule. For this reason, type-based creative policies have come to occupy an increasingly important role – perhaps, now, a dominant one – in corporate production strategies.

In type-based production, once companies know what types of cultural commodities audiences seem to want, they supply more of the same. As in the case of Book Creations, Inc. cited earlier, management draws up a plan for a series of similar works and searches out artists experienced in working in that form, or searches the periphery for emerging artists with the right sort of potential[11]. They are then put to work under the guidance of creative management and directed to create an original which meets the dictates of the plan. This, in its simplest and most interventionist form, is how type-based creation is organised. As a method of managing the creative stage of production, it represents an organisational attempt to shape the process of creativity. Instead of starting with an artist and their inspiration, it begins with a market demand to which an artist must tailor their talent. Type-based creative policies have a kernel which, in recent years, has become generalised throughout the corporate core of the culture industry, as formatted production. In that sense, their increasing adoption by the corporations of culture as a compliment to name-based production, has had a decisive influence on the workings of the culture industry.

## 5.3.3 The History and Structure of Formatting

Historically, formatting developed out of the formation of the project team and institutionalisation of its structure of relations. Craft workshop production in the creative stage had survived even into the vertically-

---

11   This explains why hopefuls working in the periphery need to demonstrate not only commercial promise but also either versatility or representativeness. Companies are interested mainly in those who match their present creative policies; in their own words, those who 'suit their list' or meet its established traditions or overall 'house policy' (Coser *et al.* 1982: 132, 144, 192).

integrated combines of early 20th century, but conditions were developing around them which led to the reorganisation of creation around the organisationally more efficient project team. They included contextual factors such as dramatic fluctuations in the economic fortunes of advanced capitalist societies, especially the post-war boom and subsequent changes in the patterns of urban living, the emergence of new lifestyles, and hence patterns of cultural commodity usage. Equally, there were changes internal to the culture industry, including new technologies which raised production efficiencies and provided opportunities for independents, especially the new forms of cultural production (films, records, radio and later television); rising labour costs; the increasing range and volume of cultural commodities which began outstripping potential demand, and so on. Shakeout and rationalisation followed, especially from the 1950s. The upshot, which filtered through different sectors at different rates, was a shift away from centralised production for the mass market to decentralised divisional production based on product differentiation and market segmentation – i.e. an increasing focus on type-based creative strategies.

Within the new semi-autonomous divisions and subsidiaries, creative managers, especially producers, had claimed a professional position, power and responsibilities, and adopted a new manner of working. Professional creative management took its power primarily from its *organisational* position. As a form of creative management – note: no longer 'leadership' but now 'administration' – it reflected the impact of commercialism and the calculated use of method and rule. Like bureaucratic control generally, as Edwards has argued, it flowed out of the existing organisational hierarchy. These developments simultaneously reshaped working conditions for other members of the project team. Under their rule, executants were increasingly employed to follow the plans their managers devised. Rehearsal gave way to learning what management want. In return, they were offered security of employment, with reasonably comfortable material rewards. In short, institutionalisation of the structure of the project team, professionalisation of creative management, and the generalisation of type-based creative policies, were fundamental conditions which completed the construction of the corporate form of cultural production.

Formatting can be characterised as a form of creative control based on corporate attempts to confront the uncertainties of the cultural marketplace in a context of expanded production (cf. also Escarpit 1966: 120-135, on 'programmed publication'). Presuming that audience preferences can be known in advance by measuring what already exists, a manufacturer begins not with an author or idea but by using market research to identify potential areas of demand and the size and propensities of the target audience. Since the index of consumer preference is patterns of commodity purchases, companies scan various types of market information ranging from sales reports, to observations of competitors, to newsletters and trade publications, identifying those types which seem to be popular. Sociological and psychological studies are mounted to investigate purchasing patterns, motivations and attitudes; profiles are drawn up of audience segments, which management relate to tastes or preferences for particular types of works. 'Strategic product planning' – the marketing language captures the shift in cultural practice – is based on specifically targeted 'creative policies' which are imposed upon the project team as the in-house rules of creativity.

Under this system, creative managers have the task of operationalising creative policy by preparing plans for the required types of works and ensuring staff adhere to them. Preparing the plan is a crucial stage in this process. While intended to generate an original, it is based on rules of its type, the conventional frameworks of knowledges and techniques which make up the craft and its object; i.e. what literary theorists refer to as 'genres' – or more generally 'cultural forms' (Wellek and Warren 1963: 226-237, Williams 1977: 180-185, 188-191; 1981: 148-180[12]). These repre-

---

12 Both Williams and Wellek and Warren speak of the formal classification of works according to kind by differentiating between (in Williams' words) 'outer form' (specific metre or plot structure, characters and setting) and 'inner form' (attitude, tone, purpose), to derive historical categories such as tragedy and comedy, within ultimate categories such as poetry, fiction and drama, from whence further sub-divisions or second-order groups can be identified.

The problem with such typifications is that the stockpile of known instances includes a surplus of features not included in the model, and the reality of artistic practice (as opposed to formal, academic classifications) is that forms are constantly undergoing change. Thus a cultural form has to be understood as the totality of first-order conventions (ultimate or core categories, such as poetry, fiction, drama, etc), second-order conventions (enduring historical categories such as romantic comedy and comedy of manners, jazz and rock 'n' roll, the symphony and concerto, spythriller and biography and so on). In an age of marketing there is also a third-order of features which are further sub-divisions of second-order forms; i.e. the variant forms which are presently being constructed in the sphere of art (and which, of course, may not last). Some of the schools of late-1960s-early 1970s literature such as superfiction, the fabulists, moral fiction and minimalism (e.g. *The Weekend Australian* 6-7 February 1988: Magazine 3) probably illustrate this last category. Perhaps most important of all, these three layers are linked in dialectically determinant relations.

In fact, in a context of ubiquitous product differentiation and marketing strategies, third-order forms have multiplied unbelievably. Some of these may be transitory, stylistic variations of a second or third order form, derived from

sent the structured conventions which characterise different types of
artistic work and which link audiences and artists in a common universe of
meaning. Creative managers design an original by working around the
rules and objects presupposed by the form, but adapting them in the light
of commercial trends. The plan they produce is the operational manifestation of the underlying structuring principles, the organisation's format,
containing the rules for creating the types of books wanted by the
company. Backed by the power of creative management, it is presented to
executants as a set of instructions, who are employed as its subjects and
bound to do its bidding. This is formatting in its fullest expression: a
system wherein commercialism determines creative policy which directs
the project team towards predictable, marketable outcomes. Guesswork,
intuition or arbitrary inspiration is minimised. Form has been transformed
into format. Art is made subject to administration. Conventions drawn
from the past are imposed in the present as a rule which dictates endless
repetitions of itself and the conditions of its making. Under formatting,
everything is fixed around experience and commercial calculation, alienat-
ing and reifying relations within the project team, and between the project
team, the collective artist, and audience.

Before looking at the organisational dynamics of formatting, several
points need to be made. To be socially recognised, a cultural object must
be identifiably original, otherwise it will not appeal. Since formatting is
oriented towards echoing the past, companies must ensure that originals
they reproduce display a new and unique array of stylistic markers[13]. This

---

an individual's style but masquerading as significant breakthroughs. Others,
more substantive and relevant to the times, may be in the process of embedding themselves in the fabric of art, recognised first as styles and becoming
themselves enduring historical categories. Much of the discussion here will be
concerned with formatting at the second and third levels (the most empirical)
but what complicates this even further is that stylistic variations are frequently
linked to the major artists of the time which contributes considerable fluidity to
the situation (see the following footnote). Given its importance in the present-
day marketplace, marketing attempts to reify what are after all transient stylistic variations and make them appear as definite styles, as sub-forms in the making, in order to maximise their cultural and economic value; this will be discussed in the next chapter.

13  Style, or rather stylistic devices or markers, like the term cultural form (to
which it is connected in practice), plays in important role in later discussion.
Since a style identifies the work of an individual or group (taken together, their
idiom), the creation of stylistic markers (which are reinforced in marketing) is
important in signifying originality to a competitive market. These may range
from the signs of an individual's expert and distinctive talent (their brilliance

gives them an idiomatic cast as versions of familiar cultural objects; they have, literally, an appearance as *stylistic variations on known themes*.

To the company, one of the benefits of formatting is that it generates successive production of similar items, all with known market appeal. Since tastes for these types are reasonably stable at least over the short term, editorial management can organise a continuous series of books with a common overall theme (Coser *et al.* 1982: 261; in the film world the "Carry On..." films are a classic example, see Jordan 1983) which promise high aggregate sales across several successive releases. If a series enjoys long-term demand, production may be concentrated in a strategic production unit (division, subsidiary, department or team). Doubleday, for instance, is a leading hardcover trade publisher, but through divisions such as Anchor Press, Dell Publishing, Delta Books and Dial Press, is also involved in general publishing, special interest publishing, religious books and paperback publishing (Coser *et al.* 1982: 49). Each organisational unit is characterised by a single format identified under a rubric; for example, the 'New Accents' series from Methuen (see 'The General Editor's Preface', Hebdige 1979: vii), or Jove's (a subsidiary of the Canadian-based publisher Harlequin) 'Second Chance At Love' series of light romances.

A brief comment: Escarpit and Coser *et al.* seem to think that formatting is restricted to 'popular' but not 'serious' publishing – if this distinction makes any sociological sense, other than displaying the aesthetic values of the writer (Hall 1981, Williams 1976a: 198-199). A simple dichotomy of this (elitist?) sort misunderstands the commerce/art *duality* which flows through corporate decision-making, a point which Bourdieu, on the other hand, seems to recognise when he comments: "A firm that is much closer to the 'commercial' pole (and conversely, that much further from the 'cultural' pole), the more directly and completely the products it offers correspond to a pre-existent demand, i.e. to pre-existent interests,

---

as, say, an actor, singer or writer), to contrivances of dress, mannerism, speech, etc., which speak of novelty but not creativity, and difference without substance (as in the case of a singer affecting a style of dress or manner). One of the difficulties here (and this becomes more obvious in the next chapter) is that in an era of market segmentation and product (type) specialisation, and hence the proliferation of second and third order cultural forms referred to in the previous footnote, the external appearances of popular forms are often mixed up with the stylistic characteristics of popular stars and are difficult to distinguish (for both analysts and the corporations), such that individuals can come to personify a form (e.g. the 'magic realism' of authors such as Gabriel Garcia Marquez and Salman Rushdie). In this way, the stylistic attributes enter into conceptions of forms via the artists who popularised them; the relationship, in other words, is dialectical.

and in pre-established forms" (1981: 280). For the reasons indicated here, commercialism and formatting cut across all forms of cultural production, whether 'serious' or 'popular' (cf. also Steinberg 1955: 223-258). Commercialism is only more explicit in the latter.

# 5.4 Formatting the Creative Stage of Production

The operation of formatting is realised in corporate relations in production. The format has both strategic aspects (general premises) and operational aspects (particular rules) as manifested in the cultural work of management. Each of its aspects is associated with a division of labour within management (see chapter 4, especially Figure 4.2). Taking the terms 'owner', 'manager', 'producer', director' and 'marketer' in the following discussion to refer to positions in the form of relations comprising the corporate organisational structure[14], general managers attend to the strategic business of making creative policy (the corporate version of 'designing the concept'), which is operationalised by creative management, with producers 'realising the plan' and directors 'supervising its execution'.

---

14   This point is stressed again here since the power to decide is only rarely tied to individuals or occupations – the latter reflecting no more than the contingencies of a technical or even company division of labour. While hierarchically-ordered, occupations have their independencies, organisational power is exerted collectively within the loosely-defined territory these individuals occupy (cf. Clegg and Dunkerley 1980: 470-475). Consequently, there is overlap. For example, a General Manager or Chief Executive with recognised experience in artistic leadership may also legitimately participate in the work of creative management. Increasingly, individual divisional and departmental managers also hold seats on local or corporate boards whether as individual shareholders, shareholder nominees or executive directors. With the professionalisation of creative management, the producer component increasingly functions as part of general management. This point is relevant to debates in media studies concerning intervention by general management and/or owners in editorial work (e.g. Bowman 1988).

## 5.4.1 Developing Creative Policy: 'General Management'

Strategic policy making can be illustrated by returning to the model of newspaper operation introduced in the previous chapter, called *The Daily Courier*[15]. The general management stratum – in structural terms, a combination of the manager, the marketer and the producer – does the work of designing the concept. Like Doubleday's 'enclave of cardinals' (Coser *et al.* 1982: 139), strategic creative planning in the case of *The Daily Courier* involves the general manager and his deputy, the marketing manager, the editor-in-chief and the editor (although not the chief-of-staff who works exclusively as the creative director). It is their prerogative to decide what type of cultural object will be produced.

There is some debate in the media/cultural studies literature concerning the relative input of the owner and manager into creative policy, especially in the media (cf. Bowman 1988, McQueen 1977), but like most corporations (cf. Dahrendorf 1959, Blackburn 1972), although precise demarcations between board and management are frequently blurred, the owner and manager positions in *The Daily Courier* have formally differentiated although partly overlapping functions. Board members preoccupy themselves primarily with the financial operations of the company and are only marginally concerned with content. As a matter of routine, throughout the corporate sector of the culture industry, general management is the centre of decision-making on creative policy. This is the case at *The Daily Courier*. As the general manager commented:

I don't think our board members are very strong policy makers. Most of the policy initiatives come from below rather than above and they're accepted by the board[16].

---

15   This model reflects the situation generally in the press and television (e.g. Gans 1979, Schlesinger 1978), and is paralleled with minor variations in the production of books (e.g. Coser *et al.* 1982, Dessauer 1974), popular recordings (e.g. Denisoff 1975, Frith 1978), television programmes (e.g. Moran 1984), and films (e.g. Powdermaker 1950) – and, as later models will show, advertising agencies and radio and television stations.

16   The general manager's comments here may be ingenuous. Since company management had considerable board representation there is considerable overlap; the general manager and his deputy sit on both the subsidiary and corporate boards (they are also small shareholders, "5% and "1% respectively) and the editor-in-chief is an executive director of the subsidiary board (although the editor is closeted to avoid charges of influence). Notwithstanding, on the basis of field work evidence and despite some confident arguments to the contrary (e.g. Bowman 1988, McQueen 1977) and allowing for variability between firms, as a matter of routine, relations of possession effectively distinguish –

In explanation, one of the company directors argued:

What would I know about newspapers, apart from what I've picked up over the years doesn't amount to much. You don't look for top editors and managers and tell them what to do. That's what they're good at, putting together good newspapers. You let them get on with it.

Creative policy is not formulated purely or even primarily on artistic criteria. Of the options entertained by the producer stratum, general management make the final decision within the constraints of the operating budget approved and monitored by the board. Although not forcing particular choices, this structures out expensive experiments. Commercialism is a more important influence on decision-making since it effects long-term profitability; in the words of the editor-in-chief, "Whatever else, the bottom line is the paper has to sell". *The Daily Courier* management circle rely on marketers to bring a wide range of up-to-date market information to their collective deliberations: daily, weekly and monthly sales figures form the circulation department, market research conducted by specialist agencies, advertising revenue figures, information and opinions gleaned from trade press, observations of competitors' activities, and feedback from readers. These are examined to discern which types of papers and contents are being bought by whom. In this way, considerations of profitability enter directly and deeply into the formulation of creative policy at the strategic level and are constructed as a framework for the operational directions built over it.

Since *The Daily Courier* is a long-established paper, creative policy is thoroughly etched in newsroom conventions, the library of past editions and memories of its history, and is only amended and reiterated as required. Where modification are proposed, they are channelled around this stratum, discussed, argued over (there is considerable conflict between marketing and editorial managers although the marketing manager ruefully acknowledged, "Editorial is an untouchable god around here, but perhaps that's the way it should be"), until a more-or-less coherent consensus emerges.

Strategic dimensions of the format are characterised by their generality. Expressed as a broad injunction concerning the type of originals to be created, it represents the understandings of company (that is: divisional or subsidiary) production goals sustained within the general management

---

although not divide – the relative contribution of owner and manager in the making of creative policy. Coser *et al.* (1982) reach a similar conclusion for the book publishing sector. For a case of board intervention during financial difficulties in the press sector, see Souther (1981: 553-555).

stratum. While its economic premises are hidden behind the overlay of cultural parameters to which they are articulated, it provides an umbrella under which a series of projects – in the case of *The Daily Courier* a daily flow of editions – are initiated. In the words of the general manager and editor, it proposes:

A serious newspaper, a quality daily...for the average reader who lives in this city and state, but who is also aware of national and international affairs...A paper which serves the interests of these citizens....A family newspaper...which serves the personal and public needs of different members and interests, by providing different segments for them to read; for example, local, national and foreign news, real estate, finance, the women's' section, sport and racing, the arts and entertainment.

Once agreed, the task of creative management is to turn this strategy into operational reality. Since its breadth leaves spaces for journalists to write discordant stories, editorial managers devise a plan to guide reporters in the types of leads to follow and the writing style they should use. In their dual strategic-operational role of creative management, we see one of the principal mechanisms whereby corporations have tightened control over the creative stage. As noted earlier, professionalisation of creative management has separated the producer and director, locating the former (in the case of *The Daily Courier*, the editor-in-chief and the editor) within the executive stratum and incorporating them in the strategic planning process. As *cultural* managers, they have a vested interest in devising a plan which meets the dictates they have helped to draw up and approve as part of *general* management. Their potential power as artistic leaders within the project team to counter the inroads of capital is dulled by their structural incorporation in the strategic aspects of formatting, binding their efforts to the corporate commercial goals of viability and marketability.

The capacity of the format to direct creativity operates partly through its personification in the producers and directors, and also through the (brand) name designed to cover the series of originals produced under its jurisdiction. Earlier, I noted Clegg's arguments that organisational policy operates iconically when projected as an idea(l) to orient the activities of its subjects; policy is formulated by appropriating a cultural form for organisational use and reifying its conventions[17]. Designing a variation on

---

17   We should also note Williams' (1977: 187-188) observation that cultural forms are common property of both artists and audiences – to which we might also add the mediators who control production and circulation. Appropriation, therefore, can never be more than borrowing: it remains joint property with cultural actors beyond the organisation such as audiences, critics and review-

a theme to shape the type of creation carried out under its auspices – for example, a uniquely styled daily broadsheet – and giving it a legally-registered brand name – *The Daily Courier*, for example – which is heavily publicised internally and publicly, iconisises the symbol and the combination of qualities it connotes, and naturalises its hegemony in creation. This enables the company to not only direct its labour force towards the ideal it desires but also to create the impression of monopoly possession over the form. Mastheads, labels, imprints, logos and so on become literally part of the company's assets. As a kind of constant capital, the format appears to the project team as an objective apparatus, its rubric constituting the identity of their purpose, and enables the management stratum to press its will on the process of creativity.

Creative policy, therefore, expresses company strategy, a general, authoritative proposal embedding a cluster of organisational imperatives, the general framework upon which the format's operational dictates are constructed. Forged by general management, confirmed by owners, and designed to guide producers and directors in managing the project team by incorporating the impersonal laws of the marketplace as necessity into its constitution, it limits the play of artistic imagination to predictable arenas. Both the impersonality and force of its rules and the locale of its making, reveal something of the historical specificity of formatting. The right to imagine, once the preserve of the artist, is structurally relocated and authorised as the (cultural) task of general management (including the producer), and transformed into the bureaucratic power to determine what will be reproduced.

## 5.4.2 Operationalising Policy as a Format: 'Producing'

According to the editor of *The Daily Courier*, once having been presented with the general policy, he selects sets of news values which serve as a mould for the paper. This motivates the types of stories to be chosen, their relative concentration, significance and placement within particular editions. As in other newsrooms (cf. Baker 1980a, 1980b, Schlesinger 1978), these news values are clarified, developed and affirmed in daily editorial conferences, in memos and discussions, until sedimented as the house rules which identify the particular paper.

---

ers, and other workers within the sector and who retain some control over its terms. The danger for the company is that audiences may reject their definition of the form or its manifestation, or that company staff may draw upon external influences in the course of their work and challenge the dictates of policy.

This is the artistic work of the collective producer in the corporate context: to operationalise strategic creative policy handed down from general management (but which they also played a part in making) by making a plan based on sets of performance rules intended to guide the work of the project team towards production of predictable originals. How this is done is illustrated by a case of script development within a television production house (The Grundy Organisation) for a drama series (later called *Bellamy*) created for the Australian TEN network (Moran, 1982, see also 1984).

The Grundy Organisation has a reputation for producing "reassuringly recognisable formats, characters and plots that keep coming round like the washing on a rotary line" (*The Weekend Australian* 23-24 January 1987: Magazine 12). After requests from the Ten Network for a drama series to fill a vacant weeknight slot, Grundys proposed another police action series. Despite some concerns about their falling popularity, advice from a market research agency – not an indigenous organisation but the London-based TAPE (Television Audience Potential Evaluation) group – suggested that a series similar to Australian programmes *Homicide* and *Division Four* or the American *Streets of San Fransisco* or the British *Z Cars*, still had the potential to hold up in the ratings. An executive explained to Moran that:

a police action show of the genre and style has been very successful in television... [because] the market seemed very appropriate to have a good, straight-down-the-middle police show. We set out to develop one (1982: 33).

The production executive in charge of the project (here functioning as the producer) contracted an established writer with a reputation for this kind of work to jointly develop a blueprint and pilot scripts, and decide on tone, style, content and approach for the series. The early format[18] visualised the general framework around which each episode was to be constructed and stipulated the performance rules to be used in their making. A short extract serves to illustrate its character:

Series Style: The series is intended to be one-hour, once-a-week episodes in the lives of the personnel of the Special Crimes Squad. Each week shall contain one self-contained story, under which other investigations are simultaneously in progress, one of which might well become the main story three episodes later. Also there will be an on-going development of human relationships within the series...of

---

18  Moran uses this term only in its operational sense, referring to the plan. My use, as indicated earlier, refers to the combination of the structuring principles underlying the creative stage of production as well as its most evident phenomenal form, the plan.

say, the relationship between Stevie (Bellamy's girlfriend) and Bellamy, plus the satisfaction from the viewer standpoint of being able to see a complete story in one episode.

We intend breaking new ground in a number of areas:

1. It will not be necessary to follow the formula of seeing a crime committed then plodding along until it is neatly resolved...                             .
2. Maybe three investigations are in progress at the same time, at various stages of development, and one of them results in the police getting their man, while others are plants for future stories.
3. In keeping with real life, the police may not get their man (1982: 47-48).

This set of instructions are similar in form to those reported by Coser *et al.* (1982: 264, 272) for a series of romances ("...The hero and heroine make love even when unmarried, and with plenty of sensuous detail...the fadeout will occur before actual intercourse...") and a 'managed [geology] text' ("...The reading level appropriate to the student in this market is grade nine or ten. This means short sentences and words...They will not follow long explanations...They just want to know the 'rule' and how to apply it..."). They appear as operational rules to eliminate artistic 'irrationality' and maintain continuity and style.

As development of the *Bellamy* concept proceeded, details were clarified. Pre-production work in all cultural forms can be a labourious, conflict-ridden and frustrating process[19]. A later draft of the 'Format and Writer's Notes' indicated that it was to be very much a 'partners' series, focusing on the action adventures of the two main characters, Bellamy and Mitchell. Because strong characters with whom Australian audiences could identify were crucial to the success of the series, considerable effort was put into characterisation. Of the two, Mitchell was to be slightly more 'up-market', but ten years younger and the supporting partner, whereas Bellamy:

likes a good meat pie, and fish and chips, but wouldn't be out of place in a decent restaurant. He's a beer drinker for preference...If we ever considered his politics, he would be a rightist Labor supporter, or a leftist Liberal. He believes in a fair go, not an open slather...But when it comes to contact with crimes which are committed without regard for human life...Bellamy is implacable. He is very much for the little bloke, and sees himself, not as being able to stamp out crime single-handed, but as making sure that society is menaced (1982: 51).

---

19   The film *Tootsie*, for example, took 7 years and 10 people working on the script to bring it to the screen (*The Weekend Australian* 26-27 March 1988: Magazine 8). For examples of frequent conflict between editors and authors, see *The Weekend Australian* 21-22 December 1985: Literary Magazine 6.

Plot lines too were prescribed. A typical *Bellamy* script was to have the central characters hunting for the villain with Bellamy turning it into a personal quest. As they worked their way through a collection of murders, kidnaps, hostages, bombings, and so on, a pattern was built into the rules where he would seek to help others but in doing so would fall into situations of extreme personal danger (1982: 51-52).

In other words, the collective producer work of realising creative policy and developing a plan – in this case, comprising an executive producer, producer and writer (but which may in other cases include various types of freelance or staff designers, arrangers, directors and independent agents) – culminates in a set of specifications for the project team even before a single original is created. Speaking of television programming more generally, the network programme manager of Channel One (a model of television organisation to be introduced shortly) compared the process to making a patchwork:

You have an encompassing vision of where you want to go...the grand plan of how you could be the marketleader. If you did this and this, you would be unbeatable. And having decided the vision, you then start applying all the bits and pieces to it.

Whether written up in a document as in the case of *Bellamy* and of 'books without authors' (Coser *et al.* 1982: 260-282), or conveyed in a verbal briefing as is more common in say, advertising agencies, newsrooms and recording studios, the operational plan appears as a collage of cultural fragments stitched together into a coherent if not always comprehensive framework. Its single purpose is to ensure continuity across all episodes so that the series as a whole is artistically unified around a pre-determined goal. Its proposals are intended to govern realisation workers in the project team, in the *Bellamy* case, the writers who prepared the scripts for each episode, so that each script materialises the background strategic and operational assumptions of the format.

Artistically, what is going on here? In general, the process can be described as one wherein the producer appropriates the conventions of an existing cultural form but then pastes various stylistic devices over them to mark out its singular identity and confirms their combination as a set of rules.

To elaborate: like any individual artist planning a work, as a matter of practical consciousness (Giddens 1979: 24-25), producers invoke the cultural conventions which underlie the general form of their work. In the case of *Bellamy*, the producer worked up a television adaption (police action series) of an epochal theatrical form (drama) overlaid by at least one variant (second or third-order) of the cultural form (partners adventure). Its inner core of stock characters and their relations, settings, plots and narrative form are preserved; for example, the city cop and his partner as the main protagonists, a selection of dangerous villains, urban crimes and defenceless victims (nieces, prostitutes, Bellamy's girlfriend, house-wifes – note they are mainly female), and routine resolution in favour of the legitimate forces of law and order. Generality and detail are shuffled into a combination which makes the series appear relatively original. For example, in contrast to the impersonality and violence associated with urban crime and metropolitan police forces (and perhaps 1980s filmic and televisual codes based on the tough cop), the main character is drawn as 'a good Australian bloke'; a man who cares about others and has deep emotions which sometimes break through his strong, no-nonsense, action-oriented personality (characterisation here is strongly inflected through idealisations of Australian maleness based on mateship and egalitarian-ism). Moreover, he represents a 'good, trustworthy cop' (wish-fulfilment in an era of widespread police corruption?) with his sense of fair play and personal commitment to justice. Note the particular rule that in contrast to the conventions of television crime dramas, moral goodness and the protective state do not always triumph.

Further, the producer's ambition is to create a fresh approach to an old idea by creating a unique idiom for the series; by attaching to its framework of conventional rules a singular stylistic vocabulary intended to stamp it with the uniqueness it needs to maintain an artistic identity – all of which is reflected in and carried by the name. According to the history of art, of course, these are necessary in order that an object be recognised as such to compete in the cultural marketplace. It must display originality, relative or otherwise. One which is too typical would appear unexciting and unlikely to create audience interest.

Formatting transforms the usual rules of a form into *necessity* in the workplace. While this is work which follows the rules of making art, it is also structured by economic considerations which work behind the scenes. For production and circulation reasons, its purpose is to provide continu-ity across a series of otherwise separate originals produced by the company (in a way which approximates the branding of several product types) so that audiences keep returning and purchasing (or watching, in the case of a television programme). Grundys were creating an intermedi-ate good for sale to a medium which needs to meet advertisers' require-ments for reach and frequency across target segments. To attract and maintain weekly audiences over the duration of the series, *Bellamy* had to be a recognisable and popular programme type yet feature sufficient continuous signs of originality to maintain interest. As it happened, *Bellamy* was only moderately successful on both counts (Moran 1982: 148-154).

This highlights an important dimension of professional creative management. The demands of art are embedded deep in the rules of creative management, but so are those of commercialism. As the naturalised commonsense of professional producing, this combination of antagonistic practices represents a set of unobtrusive controls operating through the embeddedness of the rules of the house, reflecting how the vast proportion of activity in large, established organisations goes on without personal directive and supervision – and even without written rules (Perrow 1979: 146-153). Grundys executive management permitted the collective producer a more or less free hand in creating *Bellamy*, knowing they would keep to the rules. These are conveyed via the plan to the performers hired for the project team.

The *Bellamy* case illustrates how formatting is the corporate lynchpin in bounding creativity within the project team and guiding its energies towards company-advocated goals. Its propositions are authoritatively crystalised in texts of various forms; in memos, notes, proposals, manuals and rule books, presentation logs and mockups, in the habitual procedures and knowledges routinely sustained by management and staff[20]. Each of these objects contains, in more or less complete form, a collection of cultural rules which operate at the level of form and stylistic variation, derived from the past and applied in the present as a template for creativity by a management hierarchy. While the format proposes a desired outcome and prescribes the performance rules to achieve it – in the way that a script, for example, contains dialogue, set directions and so on (e.g. Moran 1982: 46) – it does not – nor *cannot* - tell the performer *how* to perform. The plan, therefore, also represents the *limits* of rationalised control over cultural workers. Corporations remain dependent on performers within the project team to bring the project to life, to possess and select the appropriate level of technique to transform the plan into inspired performance. While the format is borne to the workplace by the director, rehearsing – or rather, learning – the format, still involves spaces within which cultural workers stand beyond direction. This becomes evident when we move to the next stage of creation.

---

20  In the words of a news editor: "In those days we were developing the conventions. Now we merely apply them" (Gallagher 1982: 166, cf. also Tuchman 1978). *The Daily Courier* style book given to each journalist begins with the words "We have arrived at a series of ground rules, mainly through conferences between editors and senior journalists. The result is not a manual of literary style...[but] a few points of guidance, as a general approach to writing for our newspapers".

### 5.4.3 Applying the Format: 'Directing'

Present day all-music radio stations represent one of the most tightly formatted forms of cultural production, and again, I will illustrate my discussion by constructing a model which I will call FM-RADIO[21].

Stations of this type usually set out to crystalise their format within a logo – their call-sign plus descriptive slogan – in this case FM-RADIO *Stereo Rock* - which serves as a management icon within creation, but also functions as a marketing vehicle (I am reserving discussion of circulation aspects for the following chapters). It unifies programming and announcing work on the station in the daily production of originals; i.e. activities carried out by (Australian terminology) the programme manager, music director, programme clerks, studio director, production studio operator and announcers – the members of the project team.

The plan is prepared by the programme manager and music director. Their task is to create a specific station 'sound', known from ratings surveys and attitudinal and call-out research (telephone testing of play-listed selections) conducted by the station to attract specified audience segments (cf. also Hirsch 1970. For rare published accounts of the marketing of a format, see Nicholson Broadcasting Services 1975/76, 3AK Melbourne Broadcasters 1973). Having chosen a target audience, they select a small number of tracks from the existing station library and new releases being promoted by record companies, and classify them according to their perceived stage of popularity into a collection of short, rotating playlists. Some, for example, will be identified as the hits of the moment (Playlist A), recent hits or 'recurrents' (B), new releases (C) and standards or 'golden oldies' (D). Programme logs are prepared for announcers which indicate the sequence in which playlisted recordings are to be played. A half-hour sweep, for example, might require a track from playlist A, then B, A, C, D, A.

Worth noting in passing is how the format is shaped by the mode through which a sector derives its profits, how economic imperatives

---

21  The following is based on observations and interviews at two leading Australian metropolitan radio stations (one an 'adult rock' station, the other 'middle of the road' – referred to as 'beautiful music'). Both were subsidiaries of large, multi-media conglomerates, but while group directors held some positions on subsidiary boards, the local board exercised significant autonomy (partly because of regulatory aspects related to local interests). Interviews were conducted with general and creative management, programme and announcing staff and observations were conducted of the complete chain of program preparation and presentation.

penetrate into the organisation of the workplace and are embedded deep in its daily routines (Granovetter 1985). In the same way that 'books without authors' (Coser *et al.* 1982) and television series (Moran 1982) have formats geared towards generating successive consumption of individual titles within the series, FM-RADIO's format is designed as a system for creating quasi-public goods (as discussed in chapter 3). By repeating popular records at regular intervals throughout daily and weekly programmes, individual listeners can anticipate that if they keep listening on a daily and hourly basis, they will hear something they like. Audiences are thereby pulled across successive quarter hours and days of the work in a manner which makes them continually available to hear advertisers' repeated messages, an effect which improves the station's distributive efficiency which is rented to advertisers.

The programme log listing the items in order of air-play and which is supplied to announcers in the on-air studio, is a primary expression of the format. Other dimensions are materialised in studio manuals or memos on a noticeboard, or more frequently, in the shared culture of the FM-RADIO workplace. The rules of announcing required by this format, including, for example, such minutiae as the presentation of time, front and back announcements, station call-signs and slogans, are proposed in advance by creative management. As the programme manager – speaking here as the director – explained in relation to announcers:

they are regulated tightly because what's said is important and the way its said. For example, locating your call-sign closer to your music than your commercials, little perceptual things like that. For example, coming out of a record, you might say: "Call-sign with Go West We Close Our Eyes, it's 12 minutes past 4, and coming up in a moment, the Beatles", and then commercials. Now if I come out of the record and said "Go West, We Close Our Eyes, it's 12 minutes to 1, coming up next, the Beatles on call-sign", I give our call-sign, the commercials play, and that juxtaposition of our call sign next to commercials instead of music – maybe 99% of our listeners are not going to hear it. But one of them might think "God, this station, commercials, I'm sick of commercials". So just for that person who might perceive it that way, we just structure it out.

This indicates how far organisational design is driven into performance activities through creative direction, how, in the name of commercialism and professionalism, procedural aspects of the format are intended to transform creativity in programme presentation into work routines to be carried out in the on-air studio, positioning announcers more as creative operators than artistic personalities.

Nonetheless, surface appearances can be deceiving. This is an *artistic* workplace, and the contradictions of the art/capital relation lie just under the surface. The format cannot be imposed as a regime but only as a set of propositions. Creative management still depends on the artistic and professional capabilities of the employed talent. "Otherwise", commented the programme manager:

they don't get hired here. I have to know that they have a brain, can speak on the radio, have an interesting sound about them, a certain flair. If they have the personal ability to put together the pieces the way I want them put together, or the way the radio station wants them...[To do so] in a professional manner, as a communicator for a contemporary rock music station speaking to a segmented portion of the demographic groups that exist in our society.

Even under the tightest version of formatting, there is still significant fluidity in the creative process at the moment of performance. How much, is suggested by the manner in which the programme manager – speaking here as director – conducts training and monitoring sessions with individual announcers. In his words: "I'll say, O.K., here's the general picture. I'll listen to you and say, That's great, that's not so great. I don't like that, what do you think of that, here's why I think this." There is a considerable degree of give-and-take in the relation between artists and management, remarkably like the indeterminacy of rehearsals which take place prior to film or music performance or the briefing of journalists and advertising agency copywriters. Formats cannot predetermine every moment of operation. While *strategically* rigid, their *operational* aspects are relatively open; elements of programme presentation, for example, require nuances of inflection, segueing of recordings, timing, and a flow of cheerful personality, all of which demand creative flair from the announcer. Operationally, they exist more like multiple, fragmentary and negotiable parameters which performers can exploit to meet personal strategic goals. This interplay of possibility and practical necessity in the corporate context is captured by the station's top-rating morning announcer who declared that formatted radio turns announcers into "button-pushers. All we do is load, play and unload the cartridges [onto which playlist tracks are dubbed], chat for the required 15 seconds, push another button", but then laughed off its operational constraints with this remark:

Yes, the format does restrict us. Its a struggle for announcers to maintain that spark of creativity. Its a challenge to insert your personality within a tight framework. But the trick is to twist it around so that you can. And if you try, you can get away with a lot.

This is why I have doubts about the claims from Coser *et al.* that the anonymous authors hired to write for fiction factories and the like, are wholly subject to the demands and constraints of others (1982: 261). Even the most regulated of creative professionals cannot be entirely dominated by formula; even writers of the most formulaic books report that there is negotiation between themselves and their editors (e.g. the interviews with Mills and Boon writers in *The Australian* 31 June 1985: 6, *The Sunday Mail* 29 February 1988: 4). Residues of the constitution of art lies hidden in the structures of the corporate cultural workplace and can be mobilised in every moment of creation.

The duality of formatted production is also evident from the point of view of management. Producers and directors are reliant on cultural workers learning the format in the process of rehearsal and using it as a framework within which they think and act. As the FM-RADIO station manager acknowledged: "You can't impose the format too tightly on your personalities. It restricts their creative juices". Because management are anxious to secure originals consistent with creative policy, they create highly detailed formats and use them to regulate the work of the project team to a considerable degree, but because of the constant demand for originality which underlies their industry, they simultaneously hope that the performers they have engaged, especially the stars and top professionals allocated to leading executant positions in the project team, will use the format imaginatively, extending its limits through their own unique contribution. The problem for performers, however, is that the format sanctions the historical limits the corporations of culture place upon their artistic idealism, and the terrain of their contest with managers is confined by its fiat to the operational level of technique and interpretation of its rules.

# 5.5 Formatting as a System of Creative Control

## 5.5.1 The Format

The development and character of formatting as an essay in labour control applied to the project team, is one of the characteristic features of corporate cultural production. Fundamentally tied on the one hand to the emergence of large private companies manufacturing cultural commodities and geared towards regular patterns of release for differentiated markets, formatting is also associated with the professionalisation of creative management. Given recent changes in the conditions of production and circulation, it represents a corporate response to the organisational indeterminacies characterising the form of labour organisation within the creative stage of production, after limited attempts at technical control and reorganisation of their creative departments around the principle of a project team. As a system of control, it exhibits many features and effects of the process of workplace bureaucratisation which major capitalist enterprises in the Western world developed throughout the 20th century, and has impacted specifically on the cultural aspects of artistic creation which had previously been beyond direct company control. By transforming the production of originality into a process governed by company-advocated rules, formatting serves to rationalise the otherwise arbitrary and idiosyncratic play of imaginative creativity and routinely steers artists towards repetition of the particular cultural forms in which companies have invested. To the degree that corporations have been successful in this production strategy, it drives the creative stage of production further towards its structural subordination to the imperatives of accumulation.

As we have seen, the corporate task of creative management entails generating and installing formats designed to guide the work of the project team in pre-conceived directions, and to temper the chaos of the market. In this sense, the fusion of management and rule in the present-day corporate core of the culture industry represents an historically specific circumstance in relations between artists and artistic leaders. In one sense, there are reminders here of much older forms of artistic leadership which prospered after cultural production emerged from court and into the public realm: like performer-masters of the 18th and 19th centuries who were primarily concerned with the aesthetic and artistic excellence of the work being created, today's creative managers still take responsibility for the initial moment of inspiration and oversee its gestation, although in a weaker and more mediated manner. Now, as creative *management*, and having lost much of the latitude and motives they once enjoyed, the professional mode of their administration has realigned their interests with those of their employers, turning their ideas towards the dictates of market demand.

To deal with vagaries of market conditions, the format realised by the producer and installed by the director is founded upon the conventions underlying existing cultural forms, but which are given a unique and identifiable form of appearance. Customary grammars are invoked through unexpected vocabularies to generate singular, stylistically-identifiable works of art, but the products of a format are not the absolute originals the traditions of art anticipate from artists. Instead, they appear as variations on a theme, which the manufacturer can be reasonably assured have market potential with particular audience segments. At best, as works of art, they represent a cultural reorientation – associated with the fundamental and complex differentiations of the public sphere of culture in modern, capitalist societies, and the institution of 'entertainment' as opposed to 'art' – around preferences for familiarity and amusement rather than the challenge of originality[22] (cf. Williams 1963: 13-19, 1965: 70-88, cf. also Corrigan 1983). While this bureaucratic system of production might suit corporate proclivities for predictability, formatting produces – at worst – artworks which lack the effervescence and restlessness which are the very ethos of artistic creativity, precisely because the element of uncertainty and the excitement of discovery have been done away with in the interests of financial security (Coser et al. 1982: 281, Escarpit 1966: 122).

The format appears as little more than a collage of loosely-connected parameters stitched together and unified under a rubric, but is invoked in the workplace as an ideal, an icon, and assumes or at least shares the mantle of authorship with creative management to orchestrate the efforts of members of the project team. Where does its power come from?

The obvious answer is that its rules are backed by the organisational power of creative management, but there is more to it than this. Cultural forms are conventional in character. They stretch across and connect an artistic community; not only the corporations of culture but the culture industry itself and beyond to regions of independent and amateur production, academies and journals of art, and less explicitly into audiences themselves. Their conventions are lodged in the practical and discursive consciousness of community members. Cultural workers engaged in a particular type of work inevitably draw upon the customary structures and contents which characterise it. Even the greatest artists of an age, as Wellek and Warren (1963: 235) note in relation to authors:

are rarely inventors of genres: Shakespeare and Racine, Molière and Jonson, Dickens and Dostoyevsky enter into other men's labours...and modern genres...start with a specific highly influential book or author.

Behind the innovations of present day artists lies the accumulated record of the past, embedded in the commonplace cultural forms out of which their work flows, and the practicalities of communication ascribe them a sense of necessity; in that sense they represent institutional imperatives which are coercive in their effects. The same applies in the corporate workplace. If a format is recognisably underlaid by the conventions and

---

22  There may be connections in audience preferences for familiar entertainment to Giddens' (1984: 50, 375) notion of the personal search for 'ontological security' as a feature of contemporary everyday life, but I do not intend pursuing this here.

standards of its type, its propositions will be accepted as the commonsense of cultural work. The difference here, however, is that where cultural forms are freely malleable to independent artists depending upon their biases and ambitions, company policies are presented to corporate cultural workers as impersonal rules, personified by the managers, producers and directors with organisational authority over the terms of their employment. This gives the format its apparent objectivity. The organisational fetish which attaches to its terms, confronts executants as an apparatus, demanding that rehearsal and performance become a matter of learning and reproducing its approved procedures.

Despite corporate efforts to influence creativity, formats are not and cannot ever be monolithic. They can never be more than loosely-connected parameters pointing to preferred outcomes – if the company is to compete in the cultural marketplace. Because the objects they manufacture are still artistic objects, companies rely on their project team playing around with its rules and their combinations to impart a minimum quantity of originality to each original. The coercive power of formats, therefore, seems to partially dissolve in its application – but more so when confronted by the *persona* of stars than creatives: its organisational determinacy varies across the project team, a fact which warrants further consideration.

## 5.5.2 Formats and the Project Team: Creative Management

Perhaps the most important organisational effects associated with corporate rationalisation of creativity have been felt by creative management. Since producers have historically reserved the conception function, their relocation within the executive hierarchy was a crucial move for corporations needing more control over their project teams. In this way their artistic inclinations were made more subject to the logic of business, resulting in their enforced professionalisation. In the case of editors, for example, we find that:

In place of the personal and idiosyncratic style found in houses run by a single individual, publishing houses, particularly in the textbook market are adopting professional management principles and techniques that allow houses to grow in complexity, while at the same time they are attempting to maintain coordination and control (Coser *et al.* 1982: 199).

An important element in the construction of the corporate form of cultural production has been the shifting 'upstairs' of the centre of creative control. The rise of executive-status producers has been crucial in consolidating and legitimating the format as a vehicle of routinised company control. In this way, company management have ensured that the unstable market conditions they needed to respond to were accounted for in creative project planning – even if it meant diffusing management control. It served to establish effective company control at the strategic level of creative planning by connecting producer work to administration (involving matters such as budgets, revenue, staffing and equipment), and rationalising their creativity.

In one sense, formatting has impacted most on the structural position of the director. Previously involved with the producer in both the planning phase and the rehearsal room, professional directors in the corporations of culture are being reduced to the nominal function of supervisor. This is especially the case in television, press and radio production, where permanent employees direct many types of in-house continuity or series television programmes (directors) (e.g. Ravage 1978), or coordinate the gathering and processing of daily news (chiefs-of-staff, or news directors) as in the case of *The Daily Courier*, or direct announcers and programmes in the on-air studio (studio directors). They are little more than the hired hands of the producer who designed the format. In these cases, the organisation of formatted production has had the effect of limiting directors to operational aspects of the execution phase, binding them like other executant-employees to company concerns by restricting the play of their imaginations to the prescribed terrain of the format.

The situation, however, is complicated. In film and musical recording, professionalisation of the executive producer has encouraged some directors to claim new territories of skill within the creative stage. Some have made themselves invaluable by becoming specialist leader-executants, interpreting formats in exciting ways and eliciting performances from others which transcend its creative restrictions. Others, in their function as coordinators of the performance-transcription and post-production processes, experiment with the expanded technical capacities of equipment such as cameras, recording consoles, effects generators and electronic type-setting equipment, in ways which contribute to the overall aesthetic and commercial qualities of the original (in this sense they are redeveloping in new directions, the artistic contribution once made by now deskilled transcription workers, but from an authoritative position of management). More recently, oligopolistic domination of production within segmented taste markets has created many opportunities for freelance operators, both individuals and teams, allowing them to recapture lost ground. Some producer-directors have reputations which define them as superstars in their own right – but as creative *managers*, not performers (e.g. interviews with Mike Nichols and Stanley Kubrick in Gelmis 1970: 265-327). Their artistic authority enables them either to take full responsibility for their projects seeking only distribution agreements and/or perhaps some invest- ment funding from the majors (the advantage of this for the majors, of course, is that it shifts much of the risk on to the independent), or to be sub-contracted by the majors to create special projects (which by defini- tion are not tightly formatted). In either case, beyond a necessary concern for commercialism, they have complete artistic control in a manner much like the entrepreneur/artist-manager partnership of the 19th century (the craft workshop model). This development has been of immense impor- tance in film (e.g. Gelmis 1970) and popular music (e.g. Frith 1978), as well as in advertising, and in some instances, has countered the corporate tendency towards formulaic creativity.

## 5.5.3 Formats and the Project Team: Executants

In considering the impact of formatting on the executant component of the project team, we need to distinguish between the stars who are sought out for leading and supporting roles and the professional creatives who back them. Formatting has separated superstars from minor stars. Corpo- rations also need originals which break new artistic ground and which become best sellers. While expecting continuity in an artist's work, they still need them occasionally to strike out boldly, whether by developing their talents in new directions or putting their trademark on an otherwise tired and faded work or form. Accordingly, major stars have a powerful structural potential to transcend any format. Theirs' is a space where talent is allowed to fly freely, if they have the conviction, idealism and talent to challenge its limits. They can force their way into strategic project planning, whether invited by creative management to participate, or in spite of creative management, during arguments over interpretation of the form or plan.

If formatting cannot be imposed on stars it may still be present in its effects. Economic relations also mediate the star/format relation. Stars are engaged as a contracted artists: if they wish to maximise their earnings and preserve their commercial reputations, they must take some responsibility for its market appeal. Since the format is also predicated on commercial- ism, economic self-interest encourages them to collaborate with creative management in their plans and keep their inspiration within conventional bounds. Theirs' is a joint venture in formatting, and their cooperation legitimates its reign.

The danger for major artists in adhering too closely to commercial formulae and accepting company attempts to format their creativity is that they are locked into endless cycles of marketplace fashion which, without warning or good reason, can redefine them as worn-out talents and replace them with the latest issue of the publicity machine. This can substantially shorten what might have potentially been a life-long career based on the gradual maturation of their talent. Equally, since formats are derived partly from their previous works, it mimics their talents. With a popular format, corporations can substitute major talents with lesser and cheaper names who can be guided in the right directions and dressed up in the marketing process to appear as the latest fashion. This may bring temporary success for minor stars, but they lack either the artistic or organisational authority to challenge the limits the format places upon their talent and employment. In having their talents defined through its terms, it becomes a set of chains, typecasting them throughout the course of their careers (cf. Escarpit 1966: 151-152).

What of professional creatives? Their structural location presupposes artistic anonymity, subjectivity to creative management, and an exclusively executant role. Plainly, there are historical connections between the development of formatting and the consolidation of creative professional conditions. Associated with the regularisation of production and the attempt to stabilise the cultural marketplace – especially in the media, where by far the majority are employed under these conditions – it can be defined as work based on 'following the format'. If this requires resigning the customary freedoms usually associated with artistic work, the structural consent of creatives is bought by the professional working conditions they enjoy; the security, regular wages and the possibility of promotion – all of which are significant material benefits in an industry notorious for its instability and insecurity – and the craft-like pleasures of performance at high levels of professionalism. Nor do these bureaucratic conditions necessarily bleed their work of all its artistic freedoms. As we saw earlier, even in the most heavily formatted forms such as the media, the system creates its own contradictions. While the format brings common identity to a collection of projects, each is a complex apparatus calling for high-level skills with each project requiring its own touches of originality. Creative management are reliant on professional creatives not only to exercise skills of the highest order (and in many arenas throughout the culture industry, professional skills have reached extraordinarily high standards), but also to exhibit their personal flair. Those who build substantial reputations for professionalism are able to claim a qualified version of the same strategic freedoms and financial returns granted to major talents. If their employer markets their work, they soon acquire a name and attract some of the prestige and recognition usually reserved for stars. For professional creatives, therefore, formatting is a double-edged sword. For most, it brings the security of regular work and a weekly salary, but at the cost of relinquishing the idealism that is constituted as part of the artist's makeup and forces them to accept the frustrations of being an artist in a bureaucratic and capitalist context.

## 5.6 Conclusion

If formatting was introduced as the corporate answer to problems of labour control in the creative stage in an historical context of regularised production and the carving out of market share, then measured by levels of consumption of the goods they produce, it has been substantially successful. While stars can escape their regimes, formats have played a crucial role in consolidating the conditions of creative (as opposed to artistic) work and sedimenting professional cultural practice. Despite the fact that they are unable to exert total control over cultural workers, since formatting operates as a superstructure over existing structures of creative management and a specialised division of labour, corporations can administer the creative stage in a manner which systematically supplies them with the originals they need to expand in an unpredictable and competitive market.

From the perspective of the corporations of culture, however, this limited victory in production has been won at the cost of introducing significant problems of realisation in the sphere of circulation. Cultural goods produced under the formatting system reveal a marked tendency towards typicality and repetition. The problem with this is that, in the publishing sector, for example, it can generate objects which are "bland and uniform, if not outright uninteresting. As a result, some have sold very poorly" (Coser *et al.* 1982: 278). Consequently, corporations are forced to spend considerable sums of money in marketing their otherwise homogeneous releases in order to make them distinguishable and attractive in the marketplace. This is not only expensive, it also reconstitutes the contradictions of the art/capital relation at a higher level of complexity. These are the matters to be covered in the following chapter.

# Chapter 6
# Rationalising the Cultural Marketplace: The Marketing of Cultural Commodities and the Making of Stars and Styles

## 6.1 Introduction

The contradictions of the cultural commodity constantly confront the corporations: they are unable to predict either the market behaviour or financial yield from the goods they invest so much in producing. Their search for security has driven them towards formatting the creative stage of production; this chapter deals with another important strategy, the adoption of marketing techniques to discipline the cultural marketplace.

To organise a regular supply of commercial originals to the reproduction stage of production, manufacturers have adopted name-based and form-based creative policies and have formatted the work of the project team. The commodities they manufacture, however, still have to be sold. Not only is the cultural marketplace overstocked and highly competitive, but because the qualities of cultural commodities as artistic objects deteriorate quickly, companies need to create an immediate, conspicuous and persuasive impact for them immediately upon release. Marketing, therefore, has come to play an important role in the circulation of cultural commodities[1] – but in a specific form, centring upon 'the making of stars and styles'. This is the outcome of 'positioning' cultural commodities, of constructing their 'identity' and 'promoting' them to a position of 'significance'. Under these conditions, stars and styles come to function in the market like 'brands', serving to order demand and stabilise sales patterns, allowing the corporations of culture to engage in a degree of planning. The importance of marketing is such that the position of 'the marketer' has

---

1   Given their existence as the suppliers and distributors of marketing goods and services, sections of the culture industry were crucial to the growth of corporate marketing. It may even be that currents in the culture industry played a constitutive role in the practice of marketing, hence making conglomerations of capital possible, although I shall not specifically investigate this question.

become institutionalised within the structure of relations which constitutes the corporate form of production and is the vehicle whereby the demands of marketing are made to reach back into the creative stage of production and play a determinant role in the shaping of creative policy.

# 6.2 Marketing: Culture at the Service of Capital

The emergence and consolidation of marketing is associated with the rise of the corporate phase of capitalist development. Many industries are dominated by giant conglomerations of capital, usually transnational in scope and which represent enormous productive capacity. These corporations need to stimulate demand so that production can be maintained and output sold. In order to "reduce the *autonomous character* of demand for its products and to increase its *induced* character" (Braverman 1974: 265), corporations expanded their 'sales effort', built around "the advertising, research, development of new product varieties, services, etc., which are the usual means for fighting for market shares" (Baran and Sweezy 1966: 117-144, cf. also Braverman 1974: 257-270, Galbraith 1970: 124-164, also Ewen 1976). Understood historically, therefore, modern corporations developed partly through the construction of specific technical means, the techniques of marketing as an extension of sales activities, to order and expand their markets. In that sense it represents an extension of the rationalism which underlies modern capitalism (Weber 1976) but applied in the sphere of circulation.

A socio-cultural critique of marketing is needed to derive appropriate concepts that will allow us to examine its specific form in the culture industry. As a complex practice, marketing involves several related activities including research, product planning and design, packaging, publicity and promotion, pricing policy, and sales and distribution, and is closely tied to merchandising and retailing (e.g. Baker 1985a, 1985b). Because I am interested in the cultural mechanisms of marketing, I will deal only with the first four of these.

## 6.2.1 Segments, Science, Brands, and the Business of 'Product Positioning'

By the middle decades of this century, modern corporations were characterised by a marketing rather than production orientation (Baker 1985a:

17-19, Galbraith 1970: 143) wherein marketing strategies began to play an important role in shaping design and manufacture (Baran and Sweezy 1966: 134, Braverman 1974: 266). Now, product differentiation and market segmentation have displaced prices as the primary form of competition. In the search for long-term market share and hence long-term profit maximisation, companies manufacture a range of specialised goods and services, each targeted to a specific consumer group (Baker 1985a: 139-141, Baran and Sweezy 1966: 73). This provided conditions for the expansion of advertising and marketing agencies and the commercial media, especially radio and television, which also established transnational linkages to service their clients' needs (e.g Fox 1984, Smythe 1977).

In its research aspect, marketing represents in part the application of science to the service of capital. Basic, internal analysis of sales trends is now combined with systematic research into consumers and consumption. Some is sociological, wherein socio-economic and demographic factors are clustered to identify various consumer segments which are correlated with purchasing patterns, and more recently, lifestyles. Some research is psychological, examining consumer motivations, attitudes, and desires (Baker 1985a: 141-165, Packard 1957). These data are fed back into product planning and design, whence a range of differentiated products are created for different market niches, then packaged and advertised to attract consumers according to their needs or wants (Galbraith 1970: 148-149).

Brands are particularly important in the competition to establish market share, and because they become important in later discussion, warrant brief examination. Each incorporates a range or family of goods and is extensively marketed so that something of its reputation rubs off onto every commodity which bears its mark. To the potential consumer, brands are made to appear as if a guarantee of worth (Baran and Sweezy 1966: 123), signifying that the commodity bearing its name possesses known attributes and properties, and is superior to or at least the equal of its competitors, and represents value for money (Baker 1979: 59). If successful, it generates brand loyalty, where branded product lines attract repeat sales which, if sustained, build market share and sustain annual turnover and profits. Companies also seek to maintain year-to-year sales within each brand line. This partly involves creation of new models supposed to meet changing, emerging or potential wants amongst different consumer segments. Equally, fashion has been made a crucial part of marketing (Braverman 1974: 266); this is the business of 'aesthetic innovation' (Haug 1986: 42) wherein the design, style and/or packaging of the commodity are regularly updated, and the 'new' model is advertised around fantasies of upward mobility which their purchase is supposed to bring (Galbraith 1970: 140-152, Haug 1986: 39-44).

In many ways, the key to the marketing process lies in packaging and advertising. Here we see how marketing brings science and culture together in the service of capital to regulate the process of circulation. Their purpose is to stimulate demand, "to wage a relentless war against savings and in favour of consumption" (Baran and Sweezy 1966: 132). Specialised cultural workers are engaged to produce signifying objects designed "to *position* products in order to create a new market or segment an existing competitive market" (Bonney and Wilson 1983: 159) and engage in the "competitive manipulation of consumer desire" to attract sales, to "create desires, to bring into being wants that previously did not exist" (Galbraith 1970: 150). If successful, a company's products become the leaders in their respective market niches.

With this general framework in mind, I want to examine the workings of marketing as a form of socio-cultural activity. The following draws on recent cultural studies analysis (e.g. Barthes 1967, 1977, Eco 1976, Williamson 1978)[2], but it differs in an important respect. Unlike most cultural analysts, I am not concerned with the ideological functioning of signifying objects, of the semiological relations between their contents and the subjectivities they propose[3]. Instead, my concern is to examine the sociological determinants of marketing practice; i.e. how the specific corporate political-economic objectives underpining marketing are realised in packaging and advertising.

## 6.2.2 Product Packaging: The Textualising of 'Identity'

If we take the term 'positioning' to refer to the goal of design, packaging and advertising, it has two constituent phases; 'packaging: the construction of identity', and 'promotion: the allocation of significance' – which

---

2  It draws especially on works which link the semiotics of particular types of texts to their social, institutional and organisational contexts; e.g. Bonney and Wilson (1983), Dyer (1982), Glasgow University Media Group (1976, 1980) and Hartley (1982). For a prescriptive and programmatic 'application' of semiotics in marketing, see Umiker-Sebeok (1987). Myers (1983) is a useful contribution of similar intent to mine.

3  I would argue that the conclusions of semiotic analysts in this regard are important, but that they represent hypotheses awaiting empirical examination. Further, I would suggest that my analysis identifies important determinants in cultural production which may be relevant to examining outcomes in consumption, although I do not attempt to draw these out here.

correspond approximately to signifying the commodity's use and exchange value respectively. In socio-cultural terms, the first seems straightforward, the second more complex. By examining both in detail, I will demonstrate later how marketing techniques affect the production and circulation of cultural commodities and the reverberations these have in the creative stage of production.

If potential consumers are to be attracted to a commodity, then its purpose and properties must be specified. Some rationale must be provided as to why it should be purchased. This will refer primarily to its potential 'uses' – understanding this term broadly, whether in a technical and/or social and/or psychological sense (it will likely be a combination of all three)[4]. The commodity must promise to satisfy potential purchasers by fulfilling their specific wants and needs; what marketers speak of as its 'consumer benefits'. Accordingly, an 'identity' – or in the anthropomorphic talk of marketers, a 'personality' – is constituted for the product through various languages, in exchanges between seller and buyer. In itself, this is not new. Previously, shopkeepers explained the possibilities of their unpackaged, unbranded stock to customers and persuaded them in their choices. In that situation, the medium was the personal interaction between individuals. The difference in the modern era of depersonalised merchandising and self-service retailing, is that the commodity is designed to sell itself, to make a spectacle of itself in order to attract the attention and interest of shoppers (e.g. Davis 1966). Hence the necessity for 'commodity aesthetics' (Haug 1986: 8); the construction of a desirable appearance around the commodity, intended to stimulate the desire to possess and the impulse to buy.

Under oligopolistic conditions, this is an increasingly problematic task, as reflected in industry complaints, voiced regularly, for example, in the leading Australian periodical, *b&t advertising, marketing and media weekly*. For example:

Products and brands are becoming more increasingly (sic) homogeneous and it is

---

4    Bourdieu (1984: Part III) shows clearly how positioned commodities are purchased and consumed to mark out distinction as part of a individual's life(style) project (cf. also Featherstone 1987). I disagree with Baudrillard (e.g. 1975) who argues that packaging and advertising obliterate use-value. First, a functional notion of utility is still important to most purchasers; clothes, cars, durables, etc. must still work properly. Second, the utility that lies behind consumption is broader than mere technical purpose. Purchase to maintain class or stratum differentiation, positioned consumption, is use, a constituent, transformative moment of agency (i.e. purchase/consumption as a mode of appropriation; cf. Featherstone 1987, Hebdige 1979) – however socially undesireable it might be.

becoming more difficult to find a product or service benefit which enables marketers to create a meaningful identity for their brand in consumers' minds (3 February 1983: 22).

Making the product stand out in a niche full of otherwise indistinguishable products is dependent, according to Baker (1979: 221), on its packaging. "Many competing products are incapable of differentiation on the basis of objective criteria", he argues, "and in these instances packaging and promotion often constitute the sole distinguishing features upon which the product's success or failure depends". Product design and packaging (which I will refer to generally as 'packaging') serve to identify the particular purposes which the commodity is uniquely designed to serve, to posit its marginal differentiation in a manner meaningful to a particular consumer segment. In the language of cultural studies, packaging is part of the process of signifying the commodity's difference (Bonney and Wilson 1983: 125-196).

The marketer dresses up the commodity so that carries signs upon itself which proclaim its form of existence. Symbols are made to surround its physical form, playing upon and becoming, in effect, its external surfaces. Product and packaging are absorbed into each other and operate as a 'text', inviting potential purchasers to 'read' the commodity's value. A good Australian example is the sleek, wind-wedge shape and darkly iridescent colours of General Motors-Holden's new range of *Commodore* motor cars which attest to its combined claims of modernistic, high-techno-logy manufacture, the efficiency of its operation, and its suitability as either business or middle class family transport. Another is the recently repackaged *Penguin Classics* paperback range (for Penguin's marketing approach see *The National Times* 4-10 October 1985: 30-31, *The Weekend Australian* 25-26 May 1985: Magazine 17). The status and seriousness of these books are signified by reproducing paintings on their covers which symbolise the period and setting of the plot and/or characters and/or writer; *Anna Kerenin*, for example features Yaroshenko's 'Portrait of an unknown woman'. Backcover notes elaborate the novel's literary claims: "With *Anna Kerenin*, Tolstoy's most perfect work, the psychological novel of the nineteenth century reached its peak", and so on. These signs speak eloquently and confidently of the commodity of which they are part; in textualising it, they enable the potential consumer to understand its value as a commodity.

Creating the packaging is the task of various cultural workers employed in the creative stage of the marketing process, ranging from designers to artists in marketing and advertising departments to the agencies sub-con-tracted by the manufacturer. They select signs from various discourses and collect them and their conventional meanings around the object[5]. As a text, the packaging becomes a polysemic but powerful voice apparently emanating from the commodity itself. It signifies the specific terms of its identity, offering propositions as to its use-value, and asserting its uniqueness within an otherwise homogeneous range of commodities, serving to constitute "its real countenance, which the potential buyer is shown first instead of the body of the commodity" (Haug 1986: 50). In this sense, packaging is a necessary sales gambit in complex, oligopolistic markets, intended to position the product horizontally along a plane of use-value, as an identifiable and singular promissory within a range of otherwise similar products.

---

5    'Post-modern' cultural practice is often said to be characterised by borrowings, echoings, and repetitions, and the stitching together of otherwise disconnected signs – as *pastiche* (e.g. Jameson 1984). Given the manner in which cultural workers 'do' packaging and publicity, it is tempting to speculate that this 'cultural dominant' is associated with this form of cultural work (I make further comments in the next chapter about the historical and structural ontology of 'communication', connecting it to 'marketing' as a form of cultural practice). Its spread into other forms would reflect the generalisation of marketing techniques into other spheres of social-cultural life. In so far as marketing is a form of cultural practice associated with corporate capitalism, Jameson might be right to connect post-modernism with the logic of late capitalism.

## 6.2.3 Product Promotion:
### The Creation and Allocation of 'Significance'

Product positioning continues in the process of advertising[6]. An advertise-ment signifies a consumption setting for the commodity and creates a fantasy around its use. It offers an idealised display of its promises in action by showing representations of its intended consumer using the product in possible sites of consumption and being wonderfully satisfied; its referent, in other words, is the *significance-of-the-commodity-in-its-context-of-use*. This serves to confirm the product identity proclaimed in its packaging by positioning the product, consumer and context of consumption within specific and recognisable social practices[7]. But in an important sense, this is still horizontal positioning. Identity is insufficient to ensure sales in a competitive market. Because the product is a commodity and sale is subject to the price mechanism, it must also be positioned along a 'vertical' axis of market value; i.e. ranked within a

---

6   It needs to be remembered that "the positioning of products is inseparable from the positioning of audiences addressed" (Bonney and Wilson 1983: 163) – to which one might also add, according to the same logic, the constitu-tion of audience segments. The complex web of social and psychological fan-tasies operating within the advertisement not only project the product's iden-tity and value, but simultaneously seek to locate potential consumers individu-ally and collectively within a grid of individual desires and social desirability. The value of the commodity is represented as its capacity to realise those dreams; the advertisement's pledge is that consumption materialises them. Ac-cording to recent analyses which connect semiotics and psychoanalysis, an ef-fect of this is the structuring of consciousness (e.g. Bonney and Wilson 1983, Williamson 1978). I am ignoring the subjectivity-consumption phase of the ad-vertising process to focus on the economic conditions which necessitate it (cf. also Myers 1983). I have no real argument with the types of claims made by the best of this work (e.g. Williamson), other than to insist that their propositions require some form of empirical investigation based on a notion of consump-tion-as-agency (for extended discussion of the notion of 'agency' see Giddens 1979, 1984). It may be, however, that political-economic determinants which are articulated to the cultural work of making advertisements as indicated in this discussion, have significant effects in both production and consumption of texts and the possibility of analytical readings, which need to be investigated further.

7   In doing so, it also constitutes and naturalises the social significance of the consumer group for whom product is intended. This suggests that advertising and marketing might generate a specific and powerful form of classing effect operating through the sphere of culture.

hierarchy of exchangability. Since money represents exchange ratios, relative cultural values ('significances') between commodities are necessarily stratified. To the potential purchaser, a product must appear not only unique but also value for the price[8]. It must exhibit its superiority compared to its competitors; it must proclaim its significance, its position of value in 'the economy of significance'.

This needs explanation. The battle for market leadership in the market takes place partly in the cultural realm, in the cultural dimension of the economy; i.e. an economy of significance, which operates in parallel with the money economy (cf. Bourdieu 1984, Featherstone 1987: 57, cf. especially Baudrillard 1975[9]). Product positioning entails not only postulating identity but ascribing the product a 'reputation'; in effect, signifying not only its utility but also its market value. Exchange value was defined by Marx as the monetary expression of the abstract labour value consumed in its making – understood in the sense of its manufacture. The advent of marketing has added to this. Reputation is a measure of the commodity's recognisable significance, its cultural value – the importance it is deemed to possess in relations between buyers and sellers. In this sense, analogous to the relationship between value and money in Marx' framework, reputation is the currency of significance, its abstract expres-

---

8    Although advertisers employ master symbols in an attempt to claim universality for their product, in an era of market segmentation, the complex of functionality, desirability and worth that constitutes 'value' varies across different consumer groups (cf. Bourdieu 1984, Morley 1980, Myers 1983). In the following discussion of cultural value ('significance') and its currency, its form of appearance ('reputation'), I presume but do not always spell out these relativities.

9    Baudrillard goes too far in asserting the social disconnection of sign and referent, and that "the code no longer refers back to any subjective or objective 'reality' but to its own logic" (1975: 127). Although there are certain connections in my analysis to his 'political economy of the sign', I obviously have different views (cf. also Featherstone 1987; Lash and Urry 1985: chapter 9), nor can I accept his provocative anti-sociologism. Rather than critique his work, I would simply rather assert that while advertisers might attempt to achieve the effects he deals with – reification of the image, privileging ostensible realities around commodities, etc. – these strategies should not be treated as achieved effects. Marketing, like language generally, involves an unequal struggle over meaning; it is a contested terrain of signification (cf. Hall 1977, Volosinov 1973), and one of the most disabling shortcomings of media/cultural studies remains inadequate theorisation of consumption as agency and modes of consumption (cf. Bourdieu 1984, Hebdige 1979, Morley 1980, cf. also Willis 1983 – see also footnote 24 below). Instead, an unacceptable derogation of the lay actor and the possibility of privileged academic readings, remain primary assumptions of so much of this type of work.

sion (underpined by the cultural work which went into its marketing), and contributes to the exchange value of the commodity[10]. To compete, the commodity is advertised so that it attracts more reputation to itself than that of its competitors. The larger the sum of significance a given commodity accumulates, the greater its reputation, the higher its market value – as measured by its reputation plus price of production. Its total market value is an economic and cultural aggregate. The price asked or which is possible to ask for the commodity is a monetary expression in part, of its market value *in toto* as a manufactured, packaged and advertised item of exchange.

Returning to the process of product positioning, the higher the relative reputation of a product, the more likely it is to seem competitive in the marketplace. The purpose of advertising is to maximise the product's reputation, to *promote it to a position of recognised superiority relative to its competitors,* so that it appears as the most significant commodity within that product range and the only one worth the price being asked. This is the vertical dimension of positioning, and reveals the logic underlying promotion.

To represent the significance-of-the-commodity-in-its-context-of-use, advertisements are built around a rhetoric of comparison utilising visual and linguistic devices such as hyperbole and superlatives (cf. Barthes 1977). Slogans illustrate this: for example, "That's why Hoover is ahead of the rest", Simply the best – from Sharp", and "Toshiba – Guaranteed to be better". As cultural analysts have shown, a deeper and more powerful rhetoric is spoken through the advertisement's semiotic structures. A representation of the product is located alongside signs drawn from discourses whose significance is already recognisable. The product-signifier is ascribed its relative cultural value via its juxtapositioning against them. Part of their value flows over to the product located in their midst[11]; they allocate it part of their accumulated significance. Bonney and

---

10  Significance is also an expression of labour value, that of the cultural workers engaged in the marketing process who signify the commodity's value, and which is added to the cost of the commodity's production. If the cultural dimension of the economy is a parallel system of production and circulation of significance, its infrastructure is the publicity apparatus of the culture industry – especially marketing, public relations and advertising agencies and the media.

11  The significance accumulated by the product being advertised, flows from a number of sources and parallels the flows of economic value. The most important is the value of the cultural labour consumed in the making of packaging and the advertisement, and in the media contents which distribute the message to the target audience. As will be seen in the following chapter, some also flows from the labour which went into making the goods used by the medium in

Wilson's (1983: 172-174) analysis of an advertisement for Benson and Hedges silver-packeted *Sterling Mild* cigarettes, is a good example (although their notion of 'significance' is the simpler and narrower notion of 'meaning' common to cultural analysis than the one I am using here). In it, a photograph of the packet is centrally positioned alongside other signs of a leisured and wealthy lifestyle such as an expensive yacht, champagne, elegant male/female hands; and a socially-valued consumption setting, a tropical island holiday, languid enjoyment of the pleasures of love, and so on. These objects of social distinction become the product's point of reference, the grid of social value within which it is positioned. *Sterling Mild* acquires its putative reputation from the structure of signs within which its sign is located.

In summary, the purpose of design, packaging and advertising as part of the marketing process, is to position the commodity in a specialised and segmented market niche, to confer upon it a singular identity and promote it to the highest rank of market value – to constitute its social status as a useful and significant object[12]. As an effect of the cultural work put into its circulation, its market profile is completed and the commodity readied for merchandising. Thus culture is combined with science in the marketing process and put to the service of capital, aiding the process of accumulation by rationalising the circulation of commodities.

---

making its own commodity. In other words, the form of appearance of promotion, the pre-emptive allocation of reputation flowing to the product being packaged and advertised, derives from the reputation of the signs used in its packaging, of the signs it is located with in the advertisement, the reputation of the medium, and the items of media content alongside which the advertisement is placed. Hence, for example, marketers use signs of high-status objects in packaging and advertisements, from materials to exotica to star-presenters (see the following discussion of *Sterling Mild*), the most popular media, and look for placement against the items likely to be most popular with their target audience.

12   A question raised with me by colleagues concerns the truncated product cycle of cultural commodities and whether or not the product cycles of niche products are also relatively short; in other words, whether cultural commodities are as different as this analysis makes out. Given the cultural character of marketing and the impact of marketing on all types of commodities in recent years, it is tempting to suggest that if they are correct, all marketed commodities begin to behave more like cultural commodities – that they take on some of their market characteristics. While an interesting hypothesis, I do not intend pursuing this here.

## 6.3 Marketing Cultural Commodities: The Making of Stars and Styles

Discussing the popular music business in the early 1970s, American critic Jon Landau complained that:

> As spontaneity and creativity have become more stylised and analysed and structured, it has become easier for businessmen and behind-the-scenes manipulators to structure their approach to merchandising music. The process of creating stars has become a routine and a formula as dry as an equation (in Frith 1978: 191).

Marketing in the culture industry is the focus of the remainder of this chapter. By investigating the *form* it takes, I will suggest that the character of marketing in this industry is systematically connected to the contradictions of the art/capital relation. As might be expected, marketing is most developed in the sector where cultural commodities are manufactured in the form of private goods[13] (see chapter 3); accordingly I will illustrate my analysis with examples from the recording business.

Marketing has been a lynchpin in the development and operation of corporate capital within the culture industry. Predictability and control – in so far as these are possible – are effects of various techniques employed by the corporations of culture to establish and maintain market share. Processes similar to product differentiation and market segmentation, coupled with promotion and publicity, are crucial to these goals. By talking about the process of creating stars, Landau puts his finger on one of the pivotal techniques. Others to be discussed shortly, and their linkages back to production, are hinted at by Tucker in his historical overview of the music business from the mid-1970s:

> It's significant that at the start of the decade, the cant term for music within the industry is *product*: The music had become merchandise to be packaged and sold. Following good capitalist theory, the music industry began to approach its product

---

13  While this analysis is illustrated primarily with reference to the recording industry, occasional references are made to other sectors which produce private goods, to indicate parallel developments there. Contrary to first appearances, the marketing of media products takes similar although less developed form. The following discussion of name-based marketing, is equally applicable in cases where, for example, radio stations promote their product by concentrating on the talents and appeal of individual announcers. Form-based marketing, however, is much more common, parallelling their more marked shift towards formatting; as seen, for example, where a station promotes itself as a rock or beautiful music station.

as a series of alternatives, of choices for the consumer. This was the neatest way to package the growing sprawl of 1970s popular music, and thus the profusion of products lining the record store shelves arranged by neat labels; *singer-songwriters, heavy metal, soft rock, art rock, country rock, disco, reggae,* and *punk.*

Radio, too, was discovering what television had already learned: demographics...The notion of *formatting,* of programming a certain kind of music for a certain segment of the audience to sell a certain kind of product, became the prevailing practice...Radio stations offered listeners a strict diet of [a type of music]. The idea was to attract the ideal demographic group for advertisers (1986: 468-469).

The embeddedness of marketing in corporate cultural production and its consequences, is illustrated effectively by the case of Britain's Stock, Aitken, Waterman, the firm behind the PWL label which was responsible throughout the 1980s for an extraordinary string of 60-70 Top 30 singles with aggregate sales in excess of 37 millions copies. Based on extensive ongoing market research, production is geared towards "High Street pop – bright, bland and easy to dance to", fronted by "Kylie Minogue and other squeaky-clean boy/girl-next-door pinups such as Jason Donovan, Rick Astley and Bananarama". Theirs' is music *designed* for marketing. PWL runs its Hit Factory according to a formula. "This is production-line pop in overdrive, devoted to cranking out the hits", taking full control of the creative stage and "treating its artists like puppets" (*The Sydney Morning Herald* 19 August 1989: 73). As a market-oriented company, PWL is organised around the principles of what the previous chapter characterised as formatted production. Marketing imperatives reach back into creation and link the production and circulation of their commodities. How this occurs and its consequences will be examined in detail later.

Marketing in the culture industry involves a stratum of employees, agents and sub-contractors[14]. In the recording sector, this ranges from company marketing and sales, publicity and promotion and art departments, to the individuals and agents they sub-contract, and the agents who

---

14   For the sake of simplicity, I deal with marketing here as something occurring within and controlled by the corporations of culture. In fact, some of this work is done outside by agents within the publicity sector (e.g. cultural mediators within the media and other cultural institutions, independent publicists and promoters) in elaborating, publicising and promoting the identities of artists and works. Important contributions are also made by personal managers, who in this regard function as an extra-organisational extension of creative management. They assist their clients in developing their act and repertoire, usually in line with commercial dictates, and promoting them to companies and audiences (e.g. Chapple and Garofalo 1977: 123-179).

help artists develop their act. They create objects such as covers, publicity handouts, posters, advertisements and campaigns, and video clips (Denisoff 1975: 144-146) and work on the technique, appearance, act, and repertoire of the artist to develop the image that will best sell them (Frith 1978: 81). In that sense, like the positions which constitute the project team, we can refer to 'the (collective) marketer' as a separate functional position within the corporate structure of cultural relations, and one of recently institutionalised power and consequence (cf. Frith 1978: 86-89). Moreover, the marketing process itself is organised along the lines of the project team[15].

In marketing a release, the corporations of culture can follow either of two strategies; as 'the work of a star' or as 'representing a style[16'] – although many releases seems to combine both. These are the respective counterparts in circulation of the name-based and form-based production policies as discussed in the previous chapter.

## 6.3.1 Marketing Name-Based Cultural Commodities: The Making of Stars

A time-honoured company strategy for beating the unpredictability of the cultural marketplace is to focus on the 'name' behind the release, and market it as the work of a 'star'. Manufacturers of cultural commodities look for outstanding, original artworks – a particular song, book, television programme, or film and so on – to reproduce in commodity form. Under conditions of expanded production, however, a single work has only limited economic value, even if a best seller. From a peak of popularity, sales decline to nothing. The corporation, however, requires continuous patterns of sales: hence, in part, the early development of the star system. The institution of the 'star' is not new. From the beginnings of

---

15  Reflecting the fact that marketing is substantially *cultural* work, labour organisation within the marketing stratum has the form of the creative project team, with the power to plan concentrated around marketing management (a marketing manager and sales manager), and execution carried out by employed professionals (e.g. photographers, graphic artists, copywriters and animators). Furthermore, creation is formatted.

16  I am treating stars and styles here as *two polarities on a continuum of forms of appearance,* as the essential duality of cultural commodities in circulation. Every artwork is related to a style and flows from the energies of an artist. They are never entirely separate and in the middle of the continuum, they dissolve into each other – partly because, as will be argued later, styles generally develop out of the work of stars.

the culture industry, entrepreneurs exploited the popularity of audience favourites to make profits, as, for example, in opera and oratorio, and later in orchestral and instrumental concerts (for examples see Raynor 1978; for equivalents in theatre see Freedley and Reeves 1968). But the making of stars in the modern era represents a fundamentally new intervention in the cultural relations between artists and audiences. It is the corporations of culture rather than audiences who take the initiative in defining and confirming artistic greatness: furthermore, these stars and, as will be seen later, styles, are transformed into brands. This constitutes an historically specific type of relationship between artists of significant reputation and the process of capital accumulation, and one which is characteristic of the corporate era of the culture industry.

In the case of name-based cultural commodities, marketing focuses on the artist[17]. By making them into stars then using them in numerous productions, a repertoire of releases is produced, many of which are likely to become best sellers. To the potential consumer, a commodity bearing the name of a star has immediate appeal. To the corporations of culture, stars and their works are desirable commercial properties which promise to attract long-term sales and bring some financial stability to their operations. Accordingly, companies sign up audience favourites or those with mainstream commercial potential presently working in the periphery or the amateur sphere (Chapple and Garofalo 1977: 130).

Once the original is created, the corporation has to position the release within a highly competitive marketplace. If the artist is relatively new to the mainstream market[18], audiences do not yet know of their talents and/or appeal, hence their work must be packaged by dressing them up in *signs of artistry*. This necessitates working out the basis of their uniqueness and appeal, consolidating them into an image and attaching it to their name. It is work carried out on many sites and through many objects, the

---

17  As in previous discussions, use of the term 'the artist' refers to a position in a structure of relations. Empirically, the artist might appear as an individual or combination ranging from a group to an orchestra to theatrical company. Equally, it might be a project team, where named individuals (the producer, director, leading performers) stand for the collective effort.

18  Note I am making the conventional assumption here that experimentation occurs in the independent sector, where artist 'pay their dues' and prove their commercial potential, before the majors move in and sign them (e.g. Denisoff 1975: 45-49). Whilst this often occurs, as later arguments will suggest, the corporations of culture are not as averse to experimentation as is sometimes suggested. They have a structural reliance on their stars occasionally creating new styles, and conditions in production for first-level stars are such that this can and does occur.

most important of which is wrought on the body and persona of the artist in developing their on and off-stage appearance and personality, their dress, speech, movement, manner, repertoire, style and stage act. Artists themselves do some of this, sometimes under the guidance of personal managers or company management including the marketer. Additionally, in the case of recording artists, for example, covers, sleeve and liner notes, posters and display materials, video clips and publicity materials for media and retailers are prepared by the marketer (cf. Frith 1978: 87-88; the publicity sector also contributes to this work but I will save discussion of the manufacturer/publicist relation till the following chapter).

What are signs of artistry? In essence, the unique array of signs which constitute the image as that of an artist. These are individuals defined as possessors of extraordinary, expressive talents, as human sources of significant creativity, their abilities evidenced by individual indicators which flow through their works and persona. These are taken to be the signs of their artistry, the foundations of their distinctive personal style, their unique vocabulary of stylistic markers – their *idiolect* - which becomes the primary focus of star-based marketing strategies.

The potential audience has to be told and sold on the value of this putative star. Their idiolect is identified; that is, the obvious artistic and extra-artistic signs of their talent are differentiated and defined and their claims to uniqueness highlighted. In a process similar to *bricollage*, the marketing stratum stitches together a rhetorical discourse out of fragments of their work and persona, a discourse which is given coherence by the naturalness of the signs employed. In the case of recording artists, for example, this might include highlights of their act, their songwriting and singing abilities, their instrumental technique, training and experience, musical influences, their biography and how it influences their talent, 'real life' personality and physical appearance, living circumstances and personal life, and so on.

The packaging of Australian television-soap-actress-turned-pop-singer Kylie Minogue is a good example[19] (the following points from *Marxism*

---

19  There is a complex relationship between stars and styles (see later discussion) which creates problems for researchers. All artists draw to some extent on existing styles. This is reflected in marketing, even star-based. Only rarely are artists signed and marketed outside of familiar styles: some, because they *represent* them – yet their work is marketed *as if* they are stars. In these cases, if successful, they thereby *become* a star. Minogue seems to be a good example, but the following discussion of Springsteen seems clearer. Most of the examples in the following discussion seem to be polar examples of star and style-based marketing. Empirically, however, many examples are ambiguous and difficult to disentangle, appearing to feature aspects of both approaches. In the

*Today* October 1988: 64, *The Australian Magazine* 8-9 July 1989: 20-30, *The Sunday Mail* 13 March 1988: 7, *The Sydney Morning Herald* 19 August 1989: 73[20]). The creative manager for Mushroom Records (Minogue's original Australian label) claims that the essence of her image is as a "teen idol symbol. She's a perfect image – clean, healthy, young, and Australian". It has been constructed partly from her acting, partly from her singing but mostly from her personality. Her work as the coquettish Charlene in the television programme *Neighbours* and in her first film *The Delinquents*, caused her manager to comment that "She's a considerable actress, capable of a much greater emotional range than anyone you normally see in the soapies". A product of a hi-energy-pop-disco formula, first at the hands of Mushroom Records and since 1987, with London's Stock, Aitken, Waterman and their PWL label, she is little more than a 'voice', a production factor slotted into her producer's plan – but its cheerful, accessible, child-woman, fun-love-and-money effervescence and immense commercial success, is taken to stand for itself. Far more important in her packaging has been the 'real-life' person, from her "fluffy, suicide blond curls" to her "overwhelmingly pleasant niceness". According to Lucy O'Brien writing in *Marxism Today*:

Kylie Minogue's *persona* is utterly marketable; frothy emotions and down-to-earth pap. She succeeds where a U.S. soap star would have failed. A *Dynasty* kitten would be too knowing, too sophisticated, too sexy. Only Kylie's cardboard 'Aussie' unpretentiousness could seem so accessible...

---

20  It is significant that data sources here include media items. The following chapter deals at length with the symbiosis between manufacturer and publicist in the culture industry. For the sake of simplicity I am dealing with packaging as something done inside the corporations of culture by the marketer: in fact, there is frequent overlap between the work of the marketer and the publicist, with the latter operating outside the corporation. This example is a case and point. Media coverage here, unwittingly or otherwise, is contributing to packaging and publicising this star, to constituting the Minogue image as well as promoting it to a position of superiority in an order of cultural things. As Frank Robson, in his 'Kylie: A Serious Story' (*The Australian Magazine* 8-9 July 1989: 22) observes wryly: "Occasionally there are attacks on the 'Kylie publicity machine' for making something so small seem so big. Only a few media people seem to realise they *are* the publicity machine".

The Kylie story is homespun and sweet. A shy mousse girl brought up in a Melbourne suburb, she was a loner at school. Her mother...encouraged her to take up a life of entertainment...a dad who's a chartered accountant. She feels guilty if she spends too much money on clothes, is never seem apart from her mother...She looks average, sings in tune, and feels happiest in jeans...

[She is] the girl who would have a 'Love Is...' poster on her wall. Kylie is the girl with the frilly curtains and a giggle...She's everything every young girl wants to be.

These are the signs, the fragments of meaning, the signs of uniqueness which have been stitched together in the packaging: they constitute the appearance known as 'Kylie Minogue', as created in her recordings, her films, the publicity handouts, the album covers, the press interviews and photosessions, and so on, in an endless repetition of the same theme.

The packaging of Bruce Springsteen is another and perhaps clearer example – its elements identified by Frith (1988: 94-101) in a perceptively observed piece, as 'The Real Thing'. His image is founded on 'authenticity', how he has been made to stand for 'the core values of rock and roll' in a manner which "most convincingly creates (and depends on) a sense of community". Frith links the singer and his songs with the notion of 'the street', a populist ethos which permeates rock and which Springsteen is seen to personify. It is the centre of every representation of the artist, every appearance, live, recorded or photographed. What 'Springsteen' *means*, his identity and value, is constantly reaffirmed in the same terms. A central signifier, according to Frith, is that he is "a millionaire who dresses like a worker", always seen in worn jeans, singlets, and a head band:

these are working clothes and it is an important part of Springsteen's appeal that we do see him, as an entertainer, working for his living. His popularity is based on his live shows and more particularly, on their spectacular energy...He makes music physically, as a *manual* worker.

But there is even more to these clothes than this. *Springsteen wears work clothes even when he is not working.* His off-stage image, his LP sleeves and interview poses, even the candid 'off-duty' paparazzi shots, involve the same down-to-earth practicality...Springsteen doesn't wear clothes appropriate to his [wealthy] economic status...he's never seen flashily attired...For him there is no division between work and play, between the ordinary and the extraordinary. Because the constructed 'Springsteen', the star, is presented plain, there can never be a suggestion that this is just an act (as Elvis was an act, as Madonna is). There are no other Springsteens, whether more real or more artificial, to be seen (1988: 96).

Other dimensions of the image include his 'brotherly' on and off-stage relations with the members of the E-Street Band – a contradictory signifier, as Frith points out, since the singer is actually their employer (and reportedly, not a generous one, according to his road crew – *The Sunday Mail* 1 November 1985: 7). He is always represented as friendly, a 'superstar-as-friend', evidenced by his manner as 'a 37-year old teenager'. Signifiers of the 'shy exhibitionist' are particularly important: he is considered, as Frith acknowledges, "one of the sexiest performers rock and roll has ever had – that there's a good part of the audience...can't take their eyes off his body". Each of these signs functions to constitute the 'Springsteen' image, an absorbing and totalising text stretching over time and across many sites, giving coherence and significance to its referent through its naturalness.

Image-making is crystalised in several different objects made to accompany product release. In the recording industry, with the proliferation of product, eye-catching covers have become a salient site for elaborating the position being constituted for the artist within various social and cultural institutions (Denisoff 1975: 179; for similar comments on the function of covers in book publishing, see Coser *et al.* 1982: 219-220). Springsteen's album *Born In the USA*, for example, features photographs of the singer clothed in jeans, t-shirts and denim or leather jackets ('the street', 'working clothes'), in poses which openly but not crudely emphasise his sexual attractiveness ('the shy exhibitionist'). Other photographs feature members of his backing band, some as individuals ('the isolated artist'), and some together ('fun', 'brotherliness', 'collective project'). In cases of other artists, if a company sees them as an important 'serious musician', packaging and presentation will reflect this. Lyrics may be printed on the recording cover, accompanied by comments from the artist on their subject matter, personal motivations, their musical project and influences; an example is Paul Simon's *Graceland* album where a dark-toned, serious-face shot of the singer-songwriter on the front cover is supported with extensive backcover notes explaining the genesis of the album, especially its African influences. If the artist is a leader in 'progressive' rock or jazz, the cover design might be built around a futuristic or metaphysical fantasy, as in those for recordings by Yes, Weather Report and Miles Davis. A recording by a major middle-of-the-road star, on the other hand, will likely have them represented in glittering stage performance, or posing with a member of the opposite sex in a mood setting such as a rainforest, candle-lit dinner or rocky coastline; many covers for recordings by singers such as Julio Iglesias, Shirley Bassey and Johnny Mathis are good illustrations[21].

---

21  We see in these examples how the image constructed of an artist refers to the intended site of consumption and the lifestyle the target consumer segment is

The name used by the artist can itself be a telling element in signifying an image; evidence Boom Crash Opera, The Dubliners, New Riders of the Purple Sage, Sting, and The Beach Boys; if the artist's real life name is inadequate for this purpose, it can be changed to a stage name, as Reginald Dwight changed his to Elton John when he went solo (e.g. Tucker 1986: 505-508). To assist the association between name and image, it should have a potentially iconic relationship with the image being constructed; as punk groups, for example signified their confrontational image with names such as The Sex Pistols (with Sid Vicious), Sioxsie and the Banshees, and The Clash. Middle-of-the-road singers are more likely to have exotic-sounding names (bearing in mind the language community they are being marketed to) which conjure up romantic or 'show-biz' images; for example, Engelbert Humperdinck, Whitney Houston, Sammy Davis Jnr., Cher, etc. Pop/rock artists go for the cheerfully outlandish, signifying the loudness, exhibitionism and frivolity associated with the form, with names such as The Beatles, Twisted Sister, Prince, Abba, AC/DC (whose first album was titled 'High Voltage'), Bananarama and Canned Heat – precisely the connotations that serious or conventional artists avoid by using their quieter, more commonplace, real names – Paul Simon, Roberta Flack, Phil Collins Linda Ronstadt, James Taylor, Paul McCartney, Billy Joel, and so on.

Their name is centrally located in every expression of the image, structured into the field of meanings constructed around it and functioning as its focus – in other words, *as its signifier*. Now artist and image are forged into an objective, polysemic and unique identity. The conventionalised relation between name and image, signifier and signified, turns them into a Saussurian sign[22] and the whole package of object and image into a text, operating in and through the grammars and vocabularies of marketing. Thus, the name and image of the artist is ready for promotion

---

presumed to desire. Artist and commodity are inserted into this as a possible object of agency-in-consumption. The referent of these marketing languages, therefore, is the-significance-of-the-commodity-in-its-context-of-consumption and not purely aesthetic dimensions of the recording. This is its material referent, however idealised. It might seem that I am labouring the obvious, but this seems to entirely escape Baudrillard (e.g. 1975) and undermines his claim that the political economy of the sign abolishes the connection of sign and referent.

22  In his influential *Course in General Linguistics* (1974), Saussure distinguished between the referent and its sign. The sign is made up of two elements, the signifier and signified. The first is, in speech, the sound-image, the second, the concept or meaning. Their relationship is arbitrary and their association must be conventionalised.

within the existing hierarchy of talent, to be presented to the audience as a star.

It is worth noting in passing that the signs of artistry attached to an artist must appeal to the target audience (Denisoff 1975: 169). Like Spring-steen's 'common man' signifiers, they must be significant, meaningful, or capable of being made so in their imagined context-of-use, in the context of a consumer's life project[23]. The packaging offers a complex of cultural, social and psychological resources to members of the target audience by drawing from or anticipating aspects of the emerging, dominant or desired art and/or life forms they are taking up[24]. The punk rock groups, for example, which emerged out of alternative musical and class cultures in the late-1970s, adopted clothing, behaviours and language which con-fronted and opposed middle-class culture and the big business methods of major recording companies. In much the same way as the flower children of an earlier generation similarly shared signs with the artists of the counter culture (Stokes 1986: 372-378), these were picked up by audience members and used as stylistic markers to differentiate their collective identity (Laing 1985, cf. Hebdige 1979). Marketers work hard to instigate such exchanges.

In considering the promotional phase of corporate marketing especially advertising, we strike another of the peculiarities of the culture industry. Unlike the manufacturers of consumer goods generally, a smaller propor-tion of the cultural commodity manufacturer's promotional activity is

---

23  *Contra* textual analysts, the meaning of any cultural object is not simply 'in' the text but is the product of an *interaction* between artist, manufacturer and audi-ence, a symbolic relation mediated by the commodity form (cf. also Frith 1978: 172-3).

24  Again, the sociological point must be made – in contrast to the dominant ten-dency in cultural studies to reify and isolate the aesthetic (e.g. Baudrillard 1975) – the reasons audiences choose particular cultural objects stem not only from specifically aesthetic but also social and psychological foundations. Cul-tural commodities, in fact, commodities generally, must be understood as *ob-jects for appropriation in the social construction of an individual's everyday life(style), and consumption-in-general as a moment of agency performed through a specific mode of appropriation* (cf. Featherstone 1987). Media/cul-tural studies urgently requires an adequate sociological theorisation of con-sumption along these lines, as seems to underpin analyses by Bourdieu (1984), Hebdige (1979) and Morley (1980). Interestingly, if some academic analysts seem blind to this, practitioners are not; recognition of active choices made by consumers – whether rational or irrational – and the difficulties marketers con-front in persuading them away from their existing preferences, is very much part of the practical consciousness of the culture industry.

directed at the final, individual consumer. Most of the advertisements, posters, and display and promotional materials produced are designed to convince the publicity and retail sectors. The reason for this lies in the systematic publicity relation forged between manufacturers and the publicity complex, mainly the media. As we will see in the next chapter, these cultural mediators do much of the display and promotional work needed by manufacturers to make their commodities sell.

But whoever the target audience, the purpose of corporate publicity objects, in the case of name-based marketing, is to promote the artist to a superior position within a hierarchy of cultural value by maximising their significance. The object is to make their artistic greatness obvious but *before* the moment of consumption; to make a pre-emptive transformation of its object – *to make the artist appear as if already a star.* To achieve this goal, the promotional campaign displays and elaborates the artist's idiolect. Its brilliance is presumed to be self-evident from the contents of their work which targeted audiences are given an opportunity to sample. The most revealing fragments are used in making the promotional objects and presented rhetorically to make claims of obvious excellence[25]. In case of a new artist whose idiolect bears traces of earlier stars who influenced them, promotion may reference these through remarks such as 'in the style of..', 'following in the footsteps of..', thus drawing from their reputation. By locating the artist's name inside a structure of signs whose significance is already socially recognised, the artist's reputation grows by association. In case of established artists, new work may be linked to their previous successes; signifiers such as 'from the author of...', 'the latest from...' locate the new work within an a successful repertoire which automatically accords it an already-existing value, thereby indicating that the artist/work is among the most important cultural commodities currently available in that market niche.

Promoting the name of artist and/or work to the highest rung of artistic significance, makes it appear as a horizontally and vertically positioned signifier of stardom, a leader amongst a multitude of competitors. The company attempts to have them recognised as a luminary of the culture industry – not only talented but outstandingly so, not only an artist but a star, the creator not just of artworks but of masterpieces. This is part of the corporate attempt to shape the market in line with its preferred creative policies; to beat the market indeterminacy of what Denisoff (1975: 94)

---

25  They also draw on rhetorical dimensions of transcription practices; e.g. in television or radio advertisements, editing and effects, layout, limiting and compressing voice-overs, and reverberation.

refers to as 'the vinyl crap game' – although whether this is always a successful strategy is an entirely different matter[26].

We can now see a point raised earlier more clearly. The fact that audiences have had their favourites and that entrepreneurs have exploited their popularity is not new. What is, is the manner in which stars are made and the mode of company intervention into the cultural marketplace it represents. Rather than ascription of reputation as a result of audience judgements, corporations employ powerful marketing techniques to impute significance prior to the act of consumption. Like all marketing strategies, *the making of stars is a pre-emptive strategy.* Companies make what is really a claim a reputation but which is made to appear to potential consumers as a given. The market power of the star's name flows from the naturalness of the image constructed, which trades off the obvious signs of the artist, their talents and creativity. Its signifier is used to make the product appear as a positioned value before exchange and consumption. If successful, the result is sustained and high-volume sales.

## 6.3.2 Marketing Form-Based Cultural Commodities: The Making of Styles

As suggested in the previous chapter, name-based creative policies are widely recognised by commentators and analysts, but form-based approaches are not. The same applies to their circulation counterparts. Stars are frequently discussed, but few writers have grasped the importance or functioning of styles as a constituent element of the present-day culture industry.

Particularly from about the 1960s (Denisoff 1975: 124) and under the influence of marketing, the cultural marketplace has been fragmented into numerous taste segments, many of which the corporations themselves have partly created[27]. Manufacturers have a wide range of possibilities

---

26  Not only do audiences sometimes see through and reject artificiality, they not infrequently disagree with the definitions offered by the industry. The case of singer-songwriter Randy Newman is instructive. Thought by many in the industry to be immensely talented, if somewhat idiosyncratic in his art, Warners Bros tried hard to turn him into a star through heavy promotion of his albums. He never, however, rose above cult status, despite one moderately successful single hit, 'Yellow Man' (e.g. Tucker 1986: 511-513).

27  It is not possible to trace here a history of product differentiation and market segmentation in the culture industry. The market has been a complex field of economic, political and cultural forces and possibilities. Within the music business, for example, the advent of corporate production has obviously been im-

they can try to exploit. Their strategies are guided by the information they glean from the market[28] on audience segments and the types of artworks they purchase. Because of its peculiarities and its connections to form-based production/style-based marketing, 'market research' in the culture industry is worth briefly commenting on.

In industry generally, systematic and scientific market research is now

---

portant and was itself made possible, amongst other factors, by the post-war economic boom and probably the baby boom, which provided market conditions for development of rock and roll and its subsequent subdivision (e.g. Denisoff 1975: 16-30). Other forces flowed from artists and artistic institutions themselves (not only musicians), especially those outside the mainstream, generating a proliferation of new movements (e.g. funk, punk, reggae, disco; see Tucker 1986). Denisoff (1975) and Chapple and Garofalo (1977) both weave discussion of the proliferation of styles and audiences into their analysis; see especially chapter 9 in Denisoff for a discussion of bubblegummers, teenyboppers, collegiates and academics. Another contributing factor has been fragmentation within the citizenry as a result of wider social forces which created the foundations for new audiences; e.g. political shifts and the growth in urban social movements, fragmentation in the workplace, and market segmentation in the wider marketplace. Pichaske (1979) is interesting in this regard. From the position of a sub-cultural insider, one of the 1960s generation living in the U.S., he provides an account of the responses and fragmentation of various rock and roll audiences to artists and their development, in a context of intersecting literary movements and their articulation to wider political movements, actors and events (e.g. Nixon, Vietnam, the black movement, the anti-nuclear movement, and so on).

28  Critics frequently argue to the effect that product and audience differentiation is entirely corporation or production (cf. demand) driven; i.e. that products reflect management thinking (e.g. in their aesthetic or ideological contents). As argued shortly, 'research' (broadly: market information, whether formally or informally derived) is much more central to company thinking than is commonly credited; there is, as Frith notes (1988: 101) a market populism in industry thinking. On the other hand, the consumer sovereignty which companies protest, operates only in narrow ways. The research serves to legitimate what Galbraith refers to more generally as "the elaborate myth...of the theory of consumer demand" (1970: 141). As the following discussion suggests, it is either empiricist and/or built around economic categories, or highly selective. The logic of commercial creative strategies could be characterised as 'what can we be sure will be popular' rather than 'what might audiences possibly be interested in'. Nonetheless, whilst heavily mediated, there is still considerable room for 'consumer demand' in corporate thinking; i.e. a significant degree of reciprocity between manufacturer and audience, between creative policies and existing tastes. This is a complex and problematic issue, much more so than is commonly allowed, and warrants more research.

widely used, although whether as much as marketers themselves make out may be questionable (cf. Baker *et al.* 1983). This is much less so in the culture industry, because of the conditions under which it operates. Research tends to be a lengthy process, most valuable as a tool for long-term planning and long-run product lines, stabilities which do not apply to the culture industry. Because of apparent rapid and unpredictable taste changes, corporations must be attuned to staying ahead of audiences and changes in fashion. Equally, scepticism regarding the value of research flows from the belief that success flows from a "combination of luck, timing, hard work and the great man theory" (Denisoff 1975: 180). The tradition of the patron and the impresario with a gift for recognising and developing potential talent and who lives within the artistic milieu, is embedded within the expectations which corporations have of their creative managers[29]. Management tend to eschew formal research in

---

29  Although industry members do not understand their activities in these terms, their informal research activities parallel qualitative research approaches employed in the social sciences. There are two dimensions to this. One is an organic involvement of creative managers with artists and audiences as an insider (cf. participant observer). They are presumed to share their lifestyle and expected to be actively involved in the field by going to concerts, talking with audience members, watching and assessing artists in performance, and discussing their work with them (there are residues here of the master-craftsman out of which modern creative management practice developed). It is regarded as particularly important to keep in touch with developments in the periphery out of which many new stars and styles emerge. Because they believe they share lifestyle, preferences and enjoyments with the audience, creative managers are confident they know and understand what audiences want and can use their perceptions to make creative and marketing judgements and decisions. Involvement in 'the street' is regarded as particularly important for those in the publicity sector such as columnists, reviewers, and presenters (although whether this generates valid understandings of audience preferences seems questionable; their production positions within the culture industry probably influence their perceptions thinking, as would their socio-economic position; cf. also Frith 1978: 191-202). The second dimension is more inward looking. The reference point is industry peers and their collective perceptions. Managers search out trade news, industry gossip, talk 'shop' with other artists and critics, and make observations of competitors (also Denisoff, 1975: 180). The publicity sector plays a particularly important role. It is treated as a reservoir of knowledge and as a determinant of tastes; especially in naming, discussing and assessing significance of emerging types ('what's happening on the street'), which manufacturers pick up and incorporate into their creative and marketing policies. What is created is a closed system of professional reference, built on

preference for what they speak of as 'gut feeling' and 'intuition', with many judgements made by referring to industry peers (Ryan 1981). There is a shift, however, towards a positivist, commercial model of market research – the form of research promoted by marketing management, research, marketing and advertising agencies[30] – which reflects the outcomes of power struggles between marketing and creative management within the corporations of culture (cf. Coser *et al.* 1982: 208).

The result is a management language of 'styles'; empirical classifications of cultural types which are correlated with particular audience segments. In meta-stylistic terms, for example, rock and roll is believed to popular mainly with youth and young adult audiences, soul and rhythm and blues with urban blacks, country and western with rural audiences, and middle-of-the-road music with older adults and mums and dads, but there are also finer stylistic demarcations. Rock and roll, for example, is divided into pop and rock, where the former is said to appeal more to children and younger teenagers, adults and musically-conservative audiences, and the latter to older audiences and the 'music freaks' (Frith 1978: 150) – and within those, for example, disco for young urban upwardly mobile singles, heavy metal for young blue-collar males, soft rock for the post-war baby-boomers now adults and parents, and so on[31]. Conscious use of strategic research to plan a range and volume of releases is not widespread. More commonly, manufacturers adopt a reactive approach to the market and try to exploit whatever style is currently 'hot' (Denisoff 1975: 138-139).

Styles, however, do not pre-exist the marketing process, and the marketing business of 'making styles' as a compliment to 'making stars', is a vital part of the corporate approach to cultural production.

First, we need to distinguish the notion of style from that of cultural form (cf. also Shepherd 1987) – as represented in Figure 6.1. As defined in chapter 5, I take the idea of cultural form to refer to a discursive

---

internal judgements, assessments and assumptions of aesthetic and commercial kinds, and which excludes direct audience input.

30  These include the use of sales figures, occasional surveys, attitudinal research and focus panels (e.g. Coser *et al.* 1982: 201-205); taste preference polls (Denisoff 1975: 180); and product testing (e.g. Tucker 1986: 527). Because of the technical demands of advertisers there is extensive use of ratings and circulation figures in the media.

31  To maximise financial returns and identify major artists/works, companies look for those which have the power to transcend conventional barriers and 'cross-over' into various audiences. Cross-overs are a market mechanism for defining major talents. The industry recognises that artists whose imagination and abilities break the conventional bonds of taste and habit transcend specialised audiences and have broad appeal.

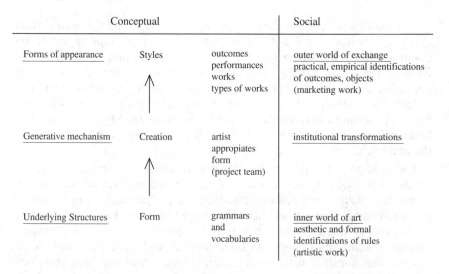

|  | Conceptual |  | Social |
| --- | --- | --- | --- |
| Forms of appearance | Styles | outcomes<br>performances<br>works<br>types of works | outer world of exchange<br>practical, empirical identifications<br>of outcomes, objects<br>(marketing work) |
| Generative mechanism | Creation | artist<br>appropiates<br>form<br>(project team) | institutional transformations |
| Underlying Structures | Form | grammars<br>and<br>vocabularies | inner world of art<br>aesthetic and formal<br>identifications of rules<br>(artistic work) |

Figure 6.1 The Form/Style Relation

account of the underlying structures and mechanisms, the grammars and vocabularies, which generate various types of artwork. Industry talk of 'styles'[32], however, seems to refer the objects these structuring principles create. It is a practical language, concerned less with how these objects are made than the obvious facts of their appearance. Saussure's (1974) distinction seems to make sense of this: we can say that *cultural form* is to *style*, what *langue* is to *parole* (cf. also Marx on real (essential) relations and phenomenal forms – Sayer 1983: 113-115). The underlying rules of form generate several styles of objects through the transformative, creative work of many artists. From the range of works created, market researchers identity the observable features of each, classify them accord-

---

32  There is also an unresolved ambiguity in the way in which this word is used in discussions of cultural production. One usage refers to the idea of a 'personal style' (idiolect) which identifies a particular artist; the second, the idea of a 'style' in the sense of an objective type of artwork. By far the most common usage I met in field work reflected the second of these. Presuming that this usage is of recent currency, and given the validity of the following discussion (especially my account of the relation between stars and styles), it seems likely that the objectification of styles is fundamentally connected to the development of the corporate era of the culture industry.

ing to various criteria, and name the resulting types as the styles which make up their cultural field. This represents an attempt to order the cultural objects for which there is demand. On the one hand, therefore, forms refer to underlying structures, and styles to the forms of their appearance. On the other, in a social rather than formal sense, form also reflects the aesthetic interests of artists, the members of the project team, and their orientation towards the 'inner' world of art. Styles, on the other hand, reflect interests in the 'outer' world of exchange, more like those of the marketer.

The tendency throughout the industry to talk in the language of styles, needs to be seen as an indicator of the impact marketing has had on corporate cultural production. Marketers are not particularly interested in cultural commodities as aesthetic or artistic objects; they focus on their appearance of market value, their practical concerns are oriented towards making commodities look saleable. Market research, therefore, tends towards the empirical features of cultural objects, treating them as stylistic signs. When marketing new commodities, these are repeated and high-lighted. This is the first step in 'making styles'. Something of this can be seen in the emergence of disco music:

Early disco music owed very little to rock and roll in its direct antecedents, country music and rural blues. Instead, disco found its paradigms in the suave, polished [soft soul] music of Kenneth Gamble and Leon Huff's Philadelphia International Records production style; in the most elaborate ballads of Stevie Wonder, post-Temptations Eddie Kendricks, and Marvin Gaye; in the lush and often campy orchestrations of Barry White; in the cool makeout music of Jerry 'The Ice Man' Butler and Issac 'Hot Buttered Soul' Hayes (Tucker 1986: 524-525).

Elements of these idiolects were imitated extended in recordings by artists such as the Hues Corporation, George McRae, KC and the Sunshine Band (Tucker 1986: 524-525). From these, a driving dance beat, prominent percussion and extensive use of the synthesiser became some of its principal trademarks. A crucial stage in the marketer's work of making styles – of collecting together otherwise arbitrary characteristics, conven-tionalising their association and giving them unity and coherence – is giving it a name: in this case, it developed as a contraction of *discotheque*, the upmarket dancing venues where live disc jockeys would play long, loud sequences of these recordings (Tucker 1986: 524). Once named, a style attains a new level of objectivity, it begins to exist as a cultural fact and can be materialised in packaging and publicity.

We are now in a position to grasp the function and dynamics of style-based marketing. To fulfil annual production quotas, corporations set out to release works which fit into or can be made to fit into currently fashionable styles. Their attention is attracted by artists whose work is consistent with and competent within them; as, for example, companies signed 'folkies' during the folk-protest period of the late 1950s and early 1960s, and outlandishly dressed bands with spectacular stage acts during the 'glam rock' craze of the 1970s (Tucker 1986: 487-496). Artists whose work is typical of a style and have some small sign of originality (such as a repertoire of originals in a popular style, or a suitable voice for a popular type of song), are signed to short-term contracts. While the original thereby created has commercial potential, it still has to be realised via marketing. In terms of their cultural workings, style-based and star-based marketing are similar; thus many of the points discussed in the previous section need not be repeated. An image must be assembled for the work and/or artist; it should bear some recognisable relation to the natural meaning and importance of the commodity; the signs which constitute it must be significant to the targeted audience; and it should offer a fantasy of satisfaction. The difference in style-based marketing is that the focus is on *signs of conventionality*.

This needs explanation. The appeal of form-based works lies in their typicality, and their continuing sales on the habit of buying according to taste. Style-based marketing can be successful as long as the packaging evidences signs drawn from the cultural, social and affective languages conventionally associated by targeted audiences with that type. The product is positioned by surrounding it with the conventional signifiers of the style it purports to represent[33].

This strategy is clear in the most explicit examples of style-based marketing as occurs with, for example, compilation recordings. Packaging is built around a title which signifies its referent's conventionality; for example, *Australian Country Jamboree, Great Moments in Opera, Let's Dance – Disco Time!, The Worlds Greatest Tenors,* and *No. 1 Hit Love Songs.* Their covers, sleeve and publicity material feature the familiar icons of each style and/or the mood and/or consumers conventionally associated with their consumption. The cover of *Australian Country Jamboree,* for example, features photographs of horseriders in jeans, boots and bushshirts and mustering stock, and various country icons such as saddles, akubra hats, and country and western guitars. *The World's Greatest Classics*-type compilations might have more serious and high-quality but equally iconic packaging based on photographs or paintings of

---

33 All cultural goods are a mixture of convention (form) and the innovation (creativity, idiolect), and marketing operates within this nexus. Analytically, the issue is one of emphasis. Style-based marketing focuses on the former, star-based on the latter.

orchestral concerts or operatic performances, or symbolic representations of the uplift or inner peace some listeners are thought to seek from this type of music.

If these are explicit cases of style-based marketing, what is not so obvious is that it also enters into a large proportion of releases which seem at first glance to be star-based. It seems to be most common in arenas where the type is a big seller such as in rock music, where there is overproduction by competing companies and large numbers of lesser or second-level stars. Many releases are dominated by their signs of conventionality. Again, disco offer good illustrations, as in the case of the group Chic. Musical and extra-musical codes were invoked in all aspects of the packaging from the name to their physical appearance to album covers. In line with the fashionable dress codes associated with the style, Chic came on like the snappiest dressers around (note also the connotations of the French *chic*). Tucker's description captures the iconography of their identity, a total package in which every detail signified the style and its context of consumption:

'Dance, Dance, Dance' was a solid hit, but a derivative one – it was just an exceptionally well played version of Philadelphia International-style disco. It was Chic's next hit, 'Le Freak" (1978), that expressed Edwards and Rodgers [bassist and guitarist respectively, the group songwriters, and producers of their own recording] originality. A cool, stark guitar-plus-bass riff, coupled with the female voices' frosty declamation of the chorus 'Le freak, c'est chic' exerted a fascinating, erotic allure to listeners.

The members of Chic, attired on their album covers in tuxedos and evening gowns, represented disco's most idealised dreams of upward mobility. Chic's image was minimalist elegance; their music was high-tech pop – glistening, calm and functional. Critic Stephen Holden described Edwards and Rodgers as "minimalistic aural interior decorators"...If, as its detractors said, disco was wallpaper for the ears, Chic manufactured the most refined and minutely detailed wallpaper of all (1986: 529).

A similarly comprehensive marketing and merchandising logic is evident in the creation and marketing of the group the Village People, a pop concept invented by producer Jacques Morali. Six beefy male singers were presented as cartoon homosexual pinups; as a cowboy, a construction worker, a 'leather' man, an American Indian, a military man and a policeman. Their music and appearance utilised nothing but conventional disco signs; sharply dressed singer-dancers and sleekly-polished, intricately-arranged songs. Every publicity shot, every film and video clip, every recording cover, presented the same image. Their stage performances were built upon the same codes: "As a live act, the Village People were even more outrageously artificial – they lip-synched their songs to prerecorded music, changed costumes onstage and wiggling to please like male strippers" (Tucker 1986: 532-533)[34].

---

34 Style-based marketing occurs not only in the explicitly commercial arenas of the culture industry (cf. arguments about 'serious' and 'popular' art in previous chapter). The packaging of classical recordings also seems to illustrate the point. For example, the cover of I Musici's recording of Vivaldi's *The Four Seasons* is built around a photograph of Jean van Blarenberghe's (otherwise inconsequential?) elaborately framed, four-panelled painting of the seasons; Respighi's *Ancient Airs and Dances* (a 20th century orchestration of 16-17th century lute pieces) recorded by Neville Mariner conducting the Los Angeles Chamber Orchestra, features an (unidentified) late-mediaeval painting of three courtesans in a gentle dance; the Concertegebouw Orchestra's recording of Shostakovitch's 5th Symphony conducted by Bernard Haitink, features an angry, abstract-expressionist painting (standing for the ambiguity of life under totalitarian, bureaucratic states) commissioned from Aubrey Williams, titled *Shostakovitch's Symphony No 5*. Compare these with star-based packaging, focused on the artist; e.g. albums by Joan Sutherland, Placido Domingo, orchestras conducted by Herbert von Karajan. Behind the literal and iconic connections between packaging and contents in these examples, the use of paintings signals that the objects are to be understood within the broader conventions of 'high culture'. It declares that this is serious music, music to be contemplated, substantial and high-minded music, for cultured and refined listeners; i.e. classical music (cf. country, rock, ethnic – or even light classical). This effect is amplified by the liner notes, usually a lengthy and detailed musicological and contextual discussion (often in several languages) of the work and/or composer, and/or performer.

Jazz releases seem to show similar types of patterns. The traditional approach to covers (perhaps also associated with traditional styles of jazz) is based on photographs or drawings of artist plus instrument in performance or a performance setting such as a club or studio; e.g. various recordings by Stan Getz, Maynard Fergusson, Parker, Hodges, and Ella Fitzgerald. Settings (club, studio, cabaret) instruments (saxophone, brass, f-holed guitars, grand piano), clothes (relatively conservative, casual) and behaviour (natural, casual, cheerful, engrossed in performance, sometimes sweating heavily with the intensity) and extensive liner notes, reflect conventional images of jazz; less serious and formal than classical, but more substantive, less frivolous than rock/pop. Progressive styles, jazz-rock fusion, and so on, such as works by Billy Cobham, Chick Corea, like earlier work of Brubeck, Coltrane etc., differentiate these recordings from more traditional approaches with more consciously composed and artistic covers which are built around abstract or symbolic themes to signify their seriousness, their intellectual dimensions, their innovation.

Rock/pop releases seem more diverse and hence harder to classify without systematic content analysis. But certainly, a conventional approach to covers

Style-based marketing proclaims the identity of the commodity to potential purchasers in easily recognisable terms. These are founded upon sets of aesthetic, social and psychological languages which link artist, work and audience through the commodity in a framework of common understandings, where the meaning of the commodity is an effect of their mediated relations (cf. Frith 1978: 195). While the dominant impression of style-based marketing is representativeness, it must also present the commodity as a variation on that theme, as "one of a kind with marginally different credentials" (Stokes 1986: 426). For the reasons outlined in previous chapters, to have value as a *cultural* commodity, it must signify its relative originality. Accordingly, pasted over its fundamental conventionality are a few tell-tale signs of variance to make it seem interesting and thereby warrant purchase. In the case of form-based musical recordings, an individual title is sufficient to identify a particular performance and a unique commodity[35], to establish and confirm its status as an artistic object.

Turning to the promotion phase of style-based marketing, we find that it differs significantly from the star-based approach – not in its functioning but in its organisation. Only limited efforts are put in by the manufacturer, not out of neglect, but related to its anticipated sales pattern and the role of the publicity complex. As will be seen in the next chapter, manufacturers are reliant on publicists to display and promote the styles of work currently available and are more inclined to release the material and wait and see. The work of many competent and interesting second-level artists is released on this passive 'buckshot' principle: since the style of work is known to be popular (and because there are limits to the numbers of releases which can be publicised at any time), it might strike a chord and

---

for more-or-less conventional, second-level artists (Australian examples might include Hoodoo Gurus, Mental As Anything, Australian Crawl, regarded as competent pub and concert performers) features a realistic or post-modernist layout, representations of the artist, where the telling signs of typicality flow from settings (concerts, performances, street scenes, posed shots to display signs), clothing (street gear, jeans, t-shirts, fashion), posture, facial expressions and gestures (jiving, 'cool'), hairstyle (long, close-cropped, depending on the style), facial expression, and instruments (electric guitars, drum kits), and a general sense of youthful fun and good times which are presumed to pervade the entire rock 'n roll sub-culture.

35  Empirically, the positioning and prominence of the title on the cover seems to be a tell-tale sign of style-based marketing. In star-based marketing, the title or name is made the centre of attention. In style-based marketing, the artist's name is subordinated to the title and/or its signs of conventionality, as in the case of titles dreamed up for compilation albums.

take off, at which point the company will get behind it with a substantial promotional budget (this approach explains the sparse publicity received by some artists, which they complain about vociferously; e.g. Denisoff 1975: 97-99). The low level of marketing effort is also connected to anticipated sales patterns. Because form-based works tend to be steady sellers where sales build up slowly and sustain longer, there is not the same compulsion to achieve immediate impact upon release – although since form-based works often experience seasonal peaks and troughs associated with holidays and special occasions, manufacturers may allocate a promotional budget just prior to these periods.

Style-based marketing is part of the corporate attempt to control the cultural marketplace, what Frith speaks of as:

> a continued effort to freeze the rock audience into a series of market tastes. Record companies themselves, radio programmers, music papers, DJs, critics, all attempt to control musical demands and so ease the process of meeting them. If audiences can be persuaded that a precise style, genre, artist or image meets their needs, expresses the solution to their particular leisure problem, then...their commercial exploitation [is] made easier (1978: 208).

While generally correct, what he does not seem to sufficiently grasp is the increasing importance of making styles as a vital part of corporate strategies to build and maintain a predictable market environment. In that sense it is a central and characteristic feature of the corporate form.

## 6.3.3 The Rationalisation of Circulation: Stars and Styles as Brands

We are now in a position to see more clearly the rationalisation effect generated in circulation by the application of marketing techniques in the culture industry. From the point of view of the corporations of culture, the stars and styles they make *come to function as approximations to brands*[36].

In star-based marketing, the name becomes the signifier which announces the value of the commodity. It becomes the brand which guarantees the artist's repertoire and represents the commodities which carry it as objects of recognisable utility and worth. Because of the name's

---

36 Since cultural commodities are purchased for the work of the artist, there is little point in manufacturers developing company-based brands – although, for example, Deutsche Grammophon and Blue Note recording labels indicate instances where this has been successfully achieved. Note the position of the logo on covers released under these labels – but these play a subordinate role in marketing.

accumulated market reputation, it becomes a valuable asset to the manufacturer. Making stars through the marketing process, the pre-emptive dressing up of artists with the signs of stardom and promoting their names, promises to make success of their works more predictable. In that sense it introduces a degree of order into the circulation of their cultural commodities.

Styles function similarly and serve the same purpose. Popular styles become the framework through which particular commodities are pre-sented to the market. As signified through the packaging, the recognisabil-ity of commodity becomes both the measure and guarantee of its value. As the circulation counterpart of form-based production, it compliments name-based production/star-based marketing and is equally important in understanding the operations of the corporations of culture: it is a crucial tactic in building market share – in fact, since styles are generally more enduring than stars who tend to come and go, they may be more important over the longer term.

There is actually a systematic relationship between stars and styles which is the real secret to the continuum between star and style-based marketing. This is hinted at by music critic Robert Christgan in defining the 'rock' as opposed to 'rock and roll' developing in the 1960s and 1970s, as "something like 'all music deriving primarily from the energy and influence of the Beatles – and maybe Bob Dylan'" (in Stokes 1986: 244). Chapple and Garofalo (1977) provide a chart of 'Marketing Trends and Stylistic Patterns in the Development of Pop/Rock Music' (see also Gillette 1971) which traces seminal influences in the development of various styles: how rock and roll itself flowed out of white versions of various black forms, recorded by Bill Haley and the Comets and Elvis Presley; rhythm and blues out of Fats Domino, Little Richard, Sam Cooke and Chuck Berry; and how later, for example, country rock grew out of late-1960s work of Bob Dylan and the Band; soft rock from Simon and Garfunkle, the Mamas and the Papas and Buffalo Springfield; and so on[37].

The stars-into-styles transformation proceeds in a series of steps. In packaging and publicising their artists, companies constitute their idiolect, thereby making it available to others as a vocabulary of signs which can be appropriated in part or in whole – as indicated by the genesis of disco, where "the genre was breeding...like flies" (Tucker 1986: 528). As artists are influenced by their predecessors, whether voluntarily or as directed by

---

37  Wellek and Warren (1963: 235) make the same point in relation to writing:
    "For the definition of modern genres one probably does best to start with a
    specific highly influential book or author and look for the reverberations: the
    literary effect of Eliot and Auden, Proust and Kafka".

companies, it is not long before the personal style of a star, through imitation, is transformed into a public style (much of this work is dependent on the publicity complex, but discussion of this is being saved for the following chapter). As this occurs, its appearances are convention-alised as a style, and its underlying structures and mechanisms, its grammars and vocabularies, are represented as a identifiable form, available for artists and companies to adopt in the search for popularity.

The corporations of culture benefit both ways. Their stars function like brands and in the most successful cases, give rise to styles which function the same way. This lesson has not been lost on culture companies over the course of the 20th century. Competition through the making of stars and styles as the foundations of product specialisation and market segmenta-tion, and with it, the search for relative originality as style-based market-ing has come to play a more and more important role in sustaining corporate dominance, has led to a proliferation of artistic types. Here we see the structural reasons behind the diversity of the cultural marketplace to which so many authors refer. Yet we should not be mislead by the surface plurality. More often than not, it is stylistic innovation which, through the efforts of marketers, is drawn to our attention. Stylistic innovation is no less real than path-breaking creativity, but it is marginal innovation over institutionalised form, driven by corporate marketers in their efforts to position their releases as leaders within different market niches and make them the fashions of the moment.

Note that for this to work, corporations must allow their stars the independence to create relatively freely: this is why, as Frith (1978: 189) notes, record companies "are happy to accept the concept of rock 'progress'". While it reintroduces problematic indeterminacies into cre-ation, they can take advantage of the results by riding the waves of fashion their stars create for them. It is still a gamble for a business concerned with control and prediction (Frith 1978: 189): the star might introduce innova-tions which the audience is totally unprepared for and their work be a total market failure, but since they are engaged on contract, to survive financially, they operate within the dictates of commercialism, working around rather than outside the perimeters of existing styles. With commer-cially successful innovation by stars, new, popular and fashionable styles can be created, which makes sales of form-based work not only more predictable but more likely. There is security for the corporations in this system.

## 6.4 The Determinant Effects in Production of Marketing Cultural Commodities: Commercialism and Formatting

The fact that stars and styles have been made to function like brands has determinant effects back in the creative stage of production. For marketing to work, the constituent signs of stardom and stylishness must be used again and again in new originals. Given the importance of marketing to corporate operation, this makes the management-backed rule of repetition a condition of commercial success and a powerful force working on the project team. It represents an important historical development in the culture industry and a further dimension of the corporate form of cultural production; the location of the marketer within its constituent structure of relations, as a sign of the *institutionalised* penetration of the market into production. As such, making stars and styles as a condition of circulation is a decisive influence underpining the shift towards formatting the creative stage of production.

To elaborate: Marketers need predictable commodities to work their magic on. To create successful marketing campaigns through packaging and publicity, they believe that the objects they work on must already bear conventional signs which have proved their worth so that the value of the commodity can be recognised by potential purchasers[38]. Marketing imperatives thereby enter directly into the design process as a demand for works with these signs – and as we saw in the previous chapter, commercialism has been assimilated as part of professional creative management (cf. Frith 1978: 79). The plan created by producers is expected to possess familiar signs of stardom and/or stylishness. Combine this with the pressures of deadlines and we can see some of the conditions encouraging the repetition in creation of previously successful approaches; more than that, of turning signs and texts into formulas and directing executants in their reproduction. To create formats which generate appealing works,

---

38  To that extent, marketing operates with a conception of audiences which takes human enjoyment of familiarity to an extreme: as their *only* motivation for cultural consumption. It is not clear to why this is so, other than acknowledging their difficulties in changing consumer habits. Generally speaking, audiences show considerable loyalty to favoured stars and styles. Why, makes an interesting sociological question, which may be associated with the modern search for 'ontological security' (cf. Giddens 1984: 375).

they borrow stylistic markers from the present crop of fashionable stars[39]. In the corporate model, in other words, there are structural necessities connecting marketing and creative management, such that the star/style-format nexus is part of the corporate form of labour organisation. We can return to the development of disco music to illustrate the point. Tucker, for example, notes that:

Most disco artists were anonymous acts, puppets of the producer – the true disco auteur – who usually had one big hit and then disappeared as quickly as they had surfaced (1986: 529).

For example, Gamble and Huff, the creative managers at Philadelphia International Records, and the creators of many of the early disco hits, were the creative managers of corporate project teams – in fact, they were named artist-managers, simultaneously its managers and stars[40], whose production style (orchestration, arrangements, transcription techniques) contributed enormously to its development. As disco became a recognisable style, creative managers such as independent producer Giorgio Moroder collaborated with Neil Bogart of Casablanca Records in Los Angeles, to exploit it. They initiated and directed each original through to completion, the performers they hired were unknowns and employed as professional creatives. A known, marketable outcome was anticipated, and executants were subject to a matrix of directions personified by creative management. Moroder's most notable success was with singer, Donna Summer. He incorporated the basic stylistic elements of disco into an 8-minute recording ("insistent beat...soaring synthesiser line" etc.;

---

39  PWL records, referred to earlier, are known to engage in 'sampling'; i.e. lifting ideas, sounds or chord progressions from other people's material and remixing them as its own (*The Sydney Morning Herald* 19 August 1989: 73). This seems to represent a kind of post-modernist practice in its tendency towards echoing and repetition. See also the earlier footnote.

40  This and the following case study, likewise PWL, make excellent illustrations of arguments presented in chapter 4 of the structure and operation of the corporate project team. It also demonstrates the importance of seeing the production system as *a structure of relations* which underlies the technical or organisational division of labour, hence seeing positions filled by strata of workers. In the case of both Philadelphia International and Motown, the individual people do not empirically coincide exactly with my account of its structure, especially in creative management where some individuals incorporate several or parts of several positions (although the artists employed almost exactly fit the executant positions I described, especially in the Motown case). Despite this variation, the collective activities in which these strata engage, fit exactly with the account provided.

Tucker 1986: 525) and over the "churning, urgent instrumentation" guided
Summer in providing a "searching, sexy vocal" composed mainly of the
title repeated over and over linked by orgasmic moaning (Tucker 1986:
527). The result, 'Love To Love You Baby', was an enormous international hit. Although, according to Tucker, Summer later demonstrated
that she was artistically much more than her producer's 'puppet'[41], her
initial recordings were designed and directed to the same formula:
"Summer followed up 'Love To Love You Baby' with the predictable
rip-off sequels, an album of variations bearing the same name as the
single, as well as 'Love Trilogy', a seemingly endless bit of vocal moaning
and synthesiser noodling" (Tucker 1986: 528). The companies and artists
attempting to ride the disco wave organised production around the same
rules. The style had been transformed into a format through the corporate
form of organisation wherein each original was created, all of which
flowed from logics of marketing and merchandising.

An even more explicit illustration is provided by the international
conglomerate Motown Industries (e.g. Chapple and Garofalo 1977: 88,
258-261, Stokes 1986: 294-300), set up as a record label in the early 1960s
by middle-class record salesman Berry Gordy (and interestingly, the
organisational model around which PWL records discussed earlier in this
chapter was explicitly organised; see *The Sydney Morning Herald* 19
August 1989: 73). Gordy realised that urban black audiences preferred
rhythm and blues-styled music but that large-scale financial success
demanded marketing the company's products also to white audiences. He
himself retained control of marketing and turned his marketing strategies
into a creative production policy. He built what became known as 'the
Motown sound'[42]; its most obvious features being a foundation in rhythm

---

41  It is worth noting how Summer's subsequent career confirms other aspects of
    the arguments presented in chapter 4. Initially employed as an unknown singer
    to complete Moroder's design, as her work won enormous popularity, she ac-
    quired sufficient personal reputation to demand greater creative freedom from
    her producer-director. Thus, her later recordings moved away from disco to-
    wards more sophisticated ballads and cabaret songs which, according to
    Tucker, "broadened her audience beyond the disco crowd and established her
    as a pop artist of some distinction" (1986: 529). In my terms, employed initially
    as a creative professional, as a pure executant subject to the direction of cre-
    ative management (in this case, producer and director personified in the one
    individual), Summer's name accumulated considerable reputation which she
    was able to transform into organisational and economic terms and reposition
    herself as a star, a contracted artist.
42  This is a classic case of a corporation making a form its own (see chapter 5) and

and blues, with "rich gospel harmonies over lavish studio work...clearly black but not threatening, and very danceable"; each "designed and mastered for three-minute radio exposure" (Chapple and Garofalo 1977: 259, 288). Each recording was built around a heavy backbeat (second and fourth beat), with horns and strings added in the final mix, and "vocal sweetening to fatten the tracks" – the method included a specific recording sequence with extensive overdubbing (Stokes 1986: 297). Production was tightly policed and organised, in Gordy's words, as "a factory-type operation" (in Chapple and Garofalo 1977: 88). Everything had to fit. Planning was highly detailed. Writer-producers Brian Holland, Lamont Dozier and Eddie Holland were employed to train the singers Gordy contracted, to write songs and to produce the label's recordings. Earl van Dyke's studio band was contracted exclusively to provide the backing, and Cholly Atkins to choreograph each stage act. Artists such as the Supremes, the Four Tops, Stevie Wonder, the Temptations, Martha Reeves and the Vandellas, like executants in every corporate project team, were moulded to the requirements of the label's format, which many, Martha Reeves, for example, bitterly resented. All the Motown products, the recordings, live performances and appearances, the artists themselves, were made similar in style, conforming to a 'corporate black' identity, but with the natural features of each as stylistic markers (e.g. the wispy sentimentalism and sexiness of Diana Ross's voice, highlighted by scoring the music too low for her register). With this tight artistic control, Motown had a remarkably successful string of hits throughout the 1960s and 1970s; "The artists, producers, promotion and training added up to the Motown system, a system that might occasionally have held back performers who didn't fit in smoothly but finally made the company the era's most dependable hit factory" (Stokes 1986: 299). Motown is a classic case of corporate cultural production; how the star/style is to marketing strategies what the format is to creative policies, and how through their articulation, the corporate form of cultural organisation has been forged.

Not only do marketing imperatives shape the moment of creation, but also the pre-production development of new artists, especially for those wanting to become mainstream stars – in this we see the pressures placed upon stars by the corporate form of production from another angle and in more detail. According to the conventions of art, developing artists should learn ways of expressing their own voice, of developing their idiolect, of 'doing their own thing'. However, the more they do so, the more idiosyncratic their creativity, the less likely they are to be signed by the

---

transforming it into a private asset, by devising a distinctive stylistic variation – 'the Motown sound'.

majors. To be successfully marketed, it is not enough to be talented. The conservative bias in marketing is based on repetition of what is already recognisable. It pressures artists to temper the type and degree of their originality, to create upon themselves and in their work, signs drawn from the languages of style already spoken in the market; i.e. to develop a *commercial* idiolect. This pressure might come from creative management in the person of a personal manager, casting agency, or a talent scout for a major company, but equally, those aspiring to stardom know that if they are to be noticed, since commercialism demands they treat themselves as objects to be marketed, their signs of talent must be drawn from fashionable codes. Because the rules of the game dictate it, they cooperate in the commercialism of their career. In the words of English composer/producer Tony Hatch:

Whether you're a performer or writer, you're the designer, manufacturer and salesman of your own product. Just like a company producing a new line in household goods, you must put time and effort into the initial development. Furthermore, you will have to invest money in the promotion and presentation of your product (in Frith 1978: 76).

Once an artist's image is established, as either a star or type, the rules of the game demand them that their idiolect be endlessly repeated. The commercialism presumed by contracted artist production relations leads stars to live up to and preserve the identity that has been built up around them whether by their own or others' efforts. They are condemned to a life of repeating the same live show, the same songs, presenting themselves the same way. Their market identity becomes a cage which restricts their artistic development. John Lennon, for example, recalled that in relation to his songwriting for the Beatles:

I had a sort of professional songwriter's attitude to writing pop songs; we would turn out a certain style of song for a single and we would do a certain style of thing for this and the other thing. I was already a stylised songwriter on the first album (in Frith 1978: 166).

The consequences can be significant, both artistically and emotionally. Some artists refuse the categorisation and take the risk of regularly breaking the mould they are being cast into, but most do not. Pichaske claims, for example, that:

The Stones fought absorption with self-parody. The Beatles fought it with dissolution, but only after the myth itself became hollow, only after the dream had turned into a nightmare. Janis Joplin, Jim Morrison, and Jimi Hendrix fought it by living themselves to death. But Bob Dylan was willing to walk away at the moment of triumph to remain his own man (1979: 177).

The impact of marketing also has consequences for those aiming or forced to aim by lack of talent or opportunity, at a professional career[43]. Their task is demonstrate their typicality, their representativeness, by acquiring company-preferred skills and demonstrating their increasing professionalism in small-time jobs. Motown musicians such as the Four Tops were a case in point. Gordy insisted they constantly attend the studios, to sing back-up for others and do demonstration tapes; in other words, to learn the Motown format till they were ready for their first solo effort (Stokes 1986: 297-8). Prospective professional creatives have to pattern their work after a successful prototype or style (Denisoff 1975: 58), by cooperating in their 'absorption' (Pichaske 1979: 153-177), by dressing themselves in the conventional signs of the format adopted by the company. As their professional reputation grows, their competence-within-a-style – and in an age of product specialisation this is likely to be an increasingly narrow style – they are stuck with reproducing the same type of work over the length of their career. For some, the life of a professional creative is a safe option. For others, versatility, proficiency across many styles, is one avenue of escape to a freelance working life, but like stars, they too must contend with the pressures of commercialism.

Marketing imperatives, therefore, have had a decisive impact on the conditions of creation. They influence the organisation of work; what can be created – or rather, what will be reproduced – the forms of labour to be engaged, and to a lesser extent, which tastes will be fulfilled and which left dormant. The overall effect has been a tendency towards commercial cliché, formula and creative stagnation. Thus, in the rock and roll business, by the mid-1970s:

As the big bucks were rolling in, much of the Big-Time establishment rock was proving efficient, ingratiating and dull...faceless rock – crisply recorded, eminently catchy, anonymous hits by bands such as Styx, REO Speedwagon and Journey (Tucker 1986: 521).

Despite the complaints of artists and critics, this tendency is not absolute. Rather, this analysis suggests there is a countervailing tendency. For reasons to be demonstrated in the following chapter, styles too come and go. Despite a cautious desire for their stars to immediately repeat their previous best seller, the corporations of culture have a contradictory

---

43  This further illustrates the point made in chapter 5 that rationalisation of the cultural marketplace is a determinant condition in the development of formatting, and in concert, providing the scale of corporate operation and financial stability which enabled the construction of professional creative working conditions.

longer-term reliance on them to create innovative works which initiate the new styles they can exploit through form-based production. The traditional autonomies associated with the artist remain fundamental to the structural position held by the highest level stars, albeit mediated by commercialism. CBS, for example, allowed Bob Dylan a remarkable degree of autonomy (Stokes 1986: 311-313) for precisely that reason. Thus, even with the strictures of marketing and formatting, top-level stars can still be innovative, although second level stars and professional creatives have few such opportunities – unless they are lucky. Rather than a simple model of corporate cultural production driving everything towards cliché and formula, or the cultural marketplace as a site of infinite diversity and little order, the truth is much more complex[44]. The social region wherein cultural commodities are manufactured and circulated by the corporations of culture may seem like a maze, but is, in fact, systematically structured and underpined by contradictions. There are powerful forces pushing towards rationalisation and control, but unequally powerful although possibly fading forces pushing in the opposite direction. Within their articulation, there are many cracks and fissures wherein agents can exercise their agency both inside and outside the corporations, whether to free up or consolidate these structures and their logics, depending on their interests and motivations.

# 6.5 Conclusion

It seems then that like their counterparts in other industries, the corporations of culture have developed in part by learning to market their output in an attempt to organise the cultural marketplace and give it a degree of predictability. The particular form this has taken is the making of stars and styles. These are created through the systematic packaging and publicity activities undertaken by companies and artists, the effect of which is to make them function as something like short-run brands. When cultural commodities are presented to the market bearing the conventionalised signs of stardom and/or stylishness, they appear as repositories of value;

---

44  This argument also challenges the often-made claim noted earlier that experimentation can only take place in the periphery. While independents and amateurs do not face the same commercial pressures and can afford to experiment, major artists engaged by the corporations of culture – because they require periodic stylistic innovation – also have opportunities which they can exploit.

they seem to offer promises of outstanding satisfaction, hence possess a competitive capacity to attract potential purchasers in an overstocked market niche. As such, they provide a foundation for longer-term patterns of sales than offered by single releases, and a corresponding capacity in circulation to match the expanded production capacity of the majors which dominate the present-day culture industry. What is more, these attempts to regulate the market seem, in effect, to be part of the structural and historical conditions which enabled the formatting of the creative stage of production. To that extent, the making of stars and styles, as an historically specific mode of strategic intervention in the mechanisms of the market, have become part of the general conditions for rationalisation of cultural production and circulation which characterises the corporate form of cultural production.

One of the greatest problems confronting the corporations is an important feature of the present-day culture industry and one which has so far been ignored in this analysis: the cycles of fashion which periodically flow through the market. Companies set up their production and marketing systems, and the next moment the popular stars and styles they have planned their production around, change. This suggests, that despite the tendencies discussed in this chapter, the market is not as rational or organised as the corporations would like it to be. This constant turnover in popular styles is systematically linked to the marketing work done by the publicity complex which manufacturers make considerable use of. Paradoxically, cycles of fashion are an effect of these systematic relations. The rationalisation effect of marketing is undone by the operations of the publicist who manufacturers need to promote their products. This is a major contradiction within the culture industry and will be the focus of the following chapter.

# Chapter 7
# Rationalising the Cultural Marketplace: The Publicity Complex and the Cycles of Fashion

## 7.1 Introduction

Throughout the 20th century, the corporations of culture have adopted marketing techniques in an attempt to regulate the cultural marketplace. Yet corporate managers and marketers complain of the continuing intractability of their markets: according to a former business manager of CBS, for example: "Our industry is a classic example of crap shooting. When you win you win big. But you have to take a 70% stiff ratio" (in Denisoff 1975: 36). Analysts such as Denisoff (e.g. 1975: 36-37) argue from evidence such as this that the manufacturers of cultural commodities lack the market power of their corporate counterparts in industry generally. This suggests that despite the considerable marketing efforts put in, attempts at control have been none too successful. Is this the case, and if so, why? These questions are the focus of this chapter.

In outline, my argument runs thus. Because of the contradictions which constitute the cultural commodity, they have a particular need for rapid and intensive 'publicity' upon release. They need to make an 'impact' in the crowded and competitive marketplace. Hence, the culture industry has developed in part around a series of mechanisms intended to play upon audience tastes and create the conditions for exchange. These go beyond the 'paid advertising' discussed in both this and the previous chapters. A systematic relation has been forged between two of the sectors described in chapter 3; the producers of private goods (the manufacturing sector) and the producers of public goods (the publicity sector, mainly the media). The publicity sector is first and foremost a centre of cultural commodity production, yet it simultaneously creates extensive 'free advertising' for the products of the culture industry. This duality is a central concern of the discussion. When public goods producers create their own commodities, they make extensive use of those released by the manufacturing sector.

The consumption of the public goods they create has the effect of generating publicity for the items and objects used in their making. In this sense, the public goods sector also functions as 'the publicity complex', as a dual producer/publicist. Manufacturers benefit from the publicity effect in that it helps create the stars and styles they individually and collectively need to maintain market share, a process which proceeds through their 'display and promotion', and the construction of various 'orders of cultural things'.

However, as quickly as one order of stars and styles is put in place to stabilise patterns of demand, the ongoing activities of the publicity complex undermine it. Their work determines which objects are fashionable, yet just as quickly they devalue their popularity and replace them with something else. The result is 'cycles of fashion'. The systemic character of the manufacturer and producer/publicist relation has, by its effects, replaced the 'truncated *product* cycle' with a 'truncated *star/style* cycle' and maintained the instabilities of the cultural marketplace. Overall, we see that corporate attempts to create the long-term market trends needed to expand production are undercut by the normal operations of the publicity sector which is crucial to the circulation of its products.

## 7.2 Publicising Stars and Styles: The Circulation of Cultural Commodities and the Publicity Complex

As previously argued, under conditions of expanded production, the contradictions of the cultural commodity require the corporations of culture to organise creation around constant production cycles. Further, the inexplicability of the market encourages the overproduction of titles relative to effective demand. Consequently, the cultural marketplace is typically cluttered and competitive. Equally, the use-value of cultural commodities declines rapidly upon release. These factors combined mean that cultural commodities need to make an immediate impact upon the market in order to attract sales. The appearance of each new release has to be managed so that its promises of cultural utility and commercial worth are made to appear factual and significant. Accordingly, they are extensively 'publicised'; displayed in public and promoted to a position of reputation in a hierarchy of cultural value.

## 7.2.1 Paid Publicity: The Costly Case of Advertising

One mechanism for achieving publicity is advertising. In the simplest case, this involves the cultural commodity manufacturer[1] commissioning an advertising agency to create one or several advertisements for the commodity and organising a campaign using appropriate media. An agency is chosen on their reputation for creating and placing fresh and innovative campaigns which are effective at conveying the message to the targeted audience; their expertise lies in the business of 'communication'[2]. The

---

1    It is occasionally the retailer who organises the advertising campaign. Only rarely do manufacturers of cultural commodities have their own advertising department. For a number of reasons, advertising agencies have managed to monopolise this form of work; these include the fact that the fixed and human costs of maintaining advertising departments (especially those associated with creative staff) are too high for manufacturers to maintain; that the economic and creative demands of advertising encourage a system based on sub-contracting of independents who have the time, space and motivation to generate new ideas, hence agencies commonly sub-contract work to independent creatives and production (transcription) crews or houses; agencies are better placed by virtue of their on-going relations with the media to purchase time and/or space at negotiated rather than more expensive rate-card rates, a benefit which flows back to the advertiser; and agencies have been successful in convincing the market that 'communication' is a specialist area of expertise and that they are the primary repository of such skills.

2    Of the many terms in the media/cultural studies area with ambiguous status, 'communication' most of all requires substantial sociological theorising. I cannot do so here, but the direction it should take is suggested by these and later points; note too my later discussion of 'the publicist'. The beginning point must be, using Sayer's (1983) terminology, that understood sociologically, 'communication' is not a transhistorical but an *historical* category: it represents an historically specific mode of cultural interaction and not an abstract, ahistorical, much less prescriptive label for any kind of cultural relation (cf. for example, the 'Editor's Introduction' from Davis and Walton in their *Language, Image, Media* (1983), and my review in *Australia and New Zealand Journal of Sociology* Vol 21 No 3: 498-501). Paradoxically, the *ontology* of communication was unreflexively captured years ago in the classical models with their source-medium-message-receiver sequence (for summaries of several versions, see e.g. Fiske 1982: 6-41). Its immanent relations of power and the specificity of its constituent positions, however, is usually ignored. Positions in the communication relation are institutionally separated and unequally powerful, and the message pre-defined and privileged (cf. Bonney and Wilson 1983, McQuail 1983). The advertising relation constituted upon display and promotion is one form of its appearance (historically, it may even represent its *essential* form, although I cannot consider this here). An expert, authoritative source constructs a mes-

agency is briefed by the marketer on sales targets and the identity of the commodity as understood by the manufacturer, and a campaign is designed with these goals in mind.

The organisation of work in making the advertisement is corporate in form, as illustrated by a model of advertising agency operation which can be called 'The Advertising Agency'[3]. The advertisement is produced in a number of stages, conception and execution, then transcription and duplication, each carried out by different types of workers and sometimes by different firms, crews or individuals[4], but all overseen and directed by the agency through the creative director. Creatives are organised in a project team, headed by creative management (executive status creative director, production director) who direct executants (writers, graphic artists, musicians, announcers, and so on) to perform to their plan. Creation is formatted; i.e. the conventions underpining different types of advertisements are appropriated and inflected through the agency 'house

---

sage designed to privilege a desired, pre-emptive set of meanings, which are objectified and naturalised by the medium. The receiver is a distanced, privatised individual, lacking the power to contradict its propositions; consumption-as-appropriation certainly offers the possibility of adapting its value to private purposes, but in itself, this has no social consequences. In this sense, the practice of communication represents the changing structures of cultural life: it is predicated on the practice and structure of monologue not dialogue, is closer to selling than sharing, and is probably associated with the corporate era of cultural production (see also footnote 24 below). As the culture industry penetrates into so many arenas of cultural life, this mode of cultural interaction is being generalised. This is particularly noticeable in modern political practice, where the packaging and selling of governments, politicians and policies is becoming a widely-accepted cultural fact (e.g. Mills 1986, also the article entitled 'Turning politicians into packaged goods', *Marketing* May 1989: 56-59).

3    This model is based on two Australian agencies, one a subsidiary of a transnational agency and part of its large international network (with a minority local shareholding); the other, a majority Australian-owned agency with subsidiaries/partners in all Australian states. Observations and interviews were conducted with corporate, sales and creative management, account executives, media buyers and creatives.

4    I am treating this as work performed in the agency. In fact, frequently, much of it, for example, recording, transcription and duplication, is carried out outside the agency itself by independents such as production houses, freelance film crews, freelance directors, actors, writers, musicians. In all cases this is dependent, sub-contracted or casual production (see chapter 4); i.e. while there is formal independence between the parties, the agency has firm creative control through the person of the creative director. In other words, in spite of the juridical relation, they are directed 'as if' they were agency employees.

style', and presented to executants as a set of creative rules. Yet the project team has to find that 'spark of creativity' which makes the advertisement stand out as unique and worth taking notice of.

The purpose of the advertisement is to display and promote its referent, the cultural commodity – or more precisely, the significance-of-the-commodity-in-its-context-of-use. Based upon the identity and reputation of the commodity as posited in its packaging, cultural workers stitch together a text by appropriating signs from the forms of life in which the commodity is being positioned. If the commodity is represented as the work of a named artist, the advertisement focuses on the artist's idiolect and creativity as revealed in that particular work; this is the key element of its message. If the marketing strategy is style-based, the advertisement highlights its signs of typicality. Because the price mechanism for realising market value is stratified, the commodity is credited with a certain type and quantity of significance; it is allocated to a position of leadership in a specific hierarchy of value through signifiers such as 'the latest from...'; 'the best of...'; 'The greatest operatic tenor since...', 'Introducing an outstanding new author...'; 'If you enjoyed...wait till you see...', and so on. These signify and differentiate its superior specificity as use and exchange value compared to competing products.

Of course, the advertisement cannot do its signifying work until it is circulated through a medium to its intended consumer. More than that, from the advertiser's point of view, the medium must offer cost-effective access to the targeted audiences. Much work goes into the scheduling of the campaign in order to achieve the desired level of impact. As the advertisement is being created, research data supplied by the medium or research agencies, such as ratings, circulation breakdowns and attitudinal data, are used by the agency media department to book a campaign schedule on the target audience's favourite media. Copies of the advertisement are then supplied to each medium participating in the campaign, whose staff combine it with other items to make an edition (press) or programme (broadcasting) according to the agreed schedule.

As in the case of advertising generally, the putative value ascribed to the commodity flows from several sources and functions through the semiotics of the advertising process as a whole. Most important is the recognisable significance of the signs used in the advertisement's making; the greater their reputation, the greater the value accorded the object on whose behalf they speak. Some flows from the creativity of the advertisement itself, from its significance as a cultural commodity. Some derives from the campaign's intensity and placement; saturation campaigns imply an important commodity, and placement on a popular media outlet means that it lends its reputation to the commodity, especially if the advertisement is placed alongside significant items, such as popular programmes, special events and premiers, top stories, 'big game' telecasts and so on. The result of this publicity, the planned effect of the advertising campaign, is a *circle of significance* surrounding the commodity.

For its semiotics to work, the publicity campaign must also meet certain technical conditions. Given product specialisation, an effective campaign must be directed at the *specific target audience*, not just an undifferentiated mass audience. It must also be scheduled to reach a *high proportion of individuals* within the target audience, and with sufficient *frequency* for them to become familiar with its message (Fowles and Mills 1982: 63-78).

Like all publicity, advertising is part of the circulation of cultural commodities, but as paid publicity for a cultural commodity, it entails the work of a cultural commodity producer (the agency plus sub-contractors), and a medium for its distribution – collectively, 'the publicist'. It is a complex combination of activities involving the production and circulation of a further cultural commodity which has its own circuits of value production and circulation, understood in both the economic (money) and cultural (reputation) senses. As argued in chapter 3, in economic terms, the manufacturer/marketer pays for the production of the advertisement and rents the distributive capacities of the medium. While the advertisement as a public good is supplied free to its intended cultural consumer – the targeted audience – a proportion of the costs of paid publicity are added to the overall cost of the commodity. Parallelling these money flows, the agency and the medium create the cultural value of the advertisement and the campaign, most of which is transferred to the advertisement's referent. With these various companies to pay, advertising is an expensive business for the manufacturer. Production costs can be considerable, especially for a spectacular concept; similarly for placement costs, particularly if the corporation wants impact with a saturation campaign on a popular medium. Historically, this encouraged manufacturers of cultural commodities to look for an alternative to paid advertising – hence the development of institutional arrangements within the culture industry I will refer to as 'the publicity complex'.

## 7.2.2 The General Tendency Towards 'Free Advertising': The Publicity Complex

The culture industry reveals a tendency towards publicity in a manner which goes beyond the paid relations of advertising. It has developed an immanent structural connection between its production and circulation systems which generates the same effects of display and promotion. In the corporate era of capital generally, all types of commodities are marketed and merchandised, but the level of publicity given cultural commodities far outweighs that given any other kind. They receive an enormous amount of 'free advertising' (Smythe 1977, also McQueen 1977[5]), an effect generated through the work of 'the publicity complex'. In using this term I am referring to the collective efforts of various kinds of advertising agencies and the freelancers and independents they sub-contract to, promotion and publicity agents, personal management agents and tour promoters[6], and the media, consumer, trade and specialist newspapers, magazines and newsletters and radio and television stations, which carry the messages they place (e.g. Chapple and Garofalo 1977: 123-170, Coser *et al.* 1982: 285-361)

To illustrate the general outline of the role of publicity complex and its effects, we can look briefly at examples of product launches. To cash in on the late-1960s revival of 1950s-styled rock and roll in the United States, Buddah Records signed a satirical group called Sha Na Na. Company manager Neil Bogart's description demonstrates the recording company's reliance on the publicity complex in introducing the group to the market:

---

5    Both these authors seem to have picked up elements of the duality of parts of the publicity sector. The critical spirit motivating both these accounts is important, although both, in my view, are too polemical and in some cases wildly incorrect in their assertions (see also chapter 3). Smythe (1977: 5) talks about the "free lunch" offered by mass media as the "materials which whet the prospective audience member's appetites" to attract and ready them for advertising messages. This is simplistic: there is no understanding here of the complex interplay of the dualities and specificities of public goods production, or of consumption-as-agency. McQueen (1977: 33) comments, "The values of advertising are those of capitalism and every time there is an advertisement for a particular product, capitalism gets a free plug as well". As is clear from the detailed, step-by-step approach I have taken in this work, while the general outline of McQueen's arguments seems similar to mine, I think the intermediate steps have to be worked through and the mechanisms revealed before highly generalised statements such as this can be accepted.

6    Tour promoters are an important part of the publicity system in the performing arts; in the music business, for example, their role is crucial in building an artist's career (e.g. Frith 1978: 93-94). Throughout this discussion, however, I concentrate on the role of general consumer, trade and specialist press (including 'fanzines'), radio and television, since they are at the core of the publicity sector. The agents and promoters who make up the secondary layers of 'the expanded industry' (Chapple and Garofalo 1977: 123-170) tend to play a secondary role.

With slogans, stickers, buttons, industry and consumer contests, and even black
leather jackets for our promotion staff, we brought back the fifties...We trans-
ported the group from coast-to-coast, making sure they were seen by their
audience and their potential record-buying public. We flew in radio men, promotion men, and distributors into New York and San Fransisco to see the group.

In all, our promotion went on for five months before the group's first album was
released. Before that first record hit the stores, the entire country was aware of Sha
Na Na...Before the album they had appeared on the *Merv Griffin Show* and had
been the subject of a feature in *Rolling Stone*, all of which led to their being invited
to appear at Woodstock.

After initial development of the act by getting them seen and talked about, we
began to concentrate on packaging the album...With the LP ready, we prepared
radio promotion stickers, information on the group and the music they were
singing, as well as a press kit that contained everything from Sen-Sen to a black
plastic comb.

Today an artist isn't developed overnight. With Sha Na Na we spent five months
paving the way for their arrival. Some artists take even *longer* (in Chapple and
Garofalo 1977: 180).

Another recent example (the following from *The Weekend Australian* 6-7
July 1985: Magazine 4-5, 22-23 November 1986: 19, *National Times on
Sunday* 7 December 1986: 19, *The Sunday Mail* 8 May 1988: 3-4) was
masterminded by Australian entrepreneur and promoter John Cornell,
the long-time business partner of comedian Paul Hogan and "the money
man and promotional brains" behind the immensely successful Australian
film *Crocodile Dundee*. While the film was in pre-production development, Hogan offered his services to the Australian Tourist Corporation to
front an intensive U.S. television campaign promoting the country as a
tourist destination. The idea, according to Cornell was to "familiarise
American audiences with Hoge's [Hogan's comic character] particular
charm". This, by all accounts, was highly successful. The actor became a
household name, with "the cute blond guy with the shrimps on the barbie"
becoming a favourite with American females. The film itself, in which
Hogan plays the main character, was "aimed fair and square at the
lucrative U.S. market" and designed to capitalise on his popularity. With
release approaching, he undertook a whistlestop all-states tour, appearing
on as many radio and television shows as would accept him, including a
segment in the television public affairs programme, *Sixty Minutes*. Coupled with Paramount's $9 million launch budget, this intensive publicity
helped turn the first *Crocodile Dundee* into a box-office smash, notching
up $141.5 million in its first 66 days. Such was the impact of both film and
character that a sequel, *Crocodile Dundee II*, was quickly prepared. This
time, however, the publicity strategy was restricted to substantial profiles

in high circulation media, including *Playboy* magazine, *Time* and *Life*, and *Ladies Home Journal* - although undoubtedly helped by interest in the daily media in his relationship with co-star Linda Kazlowski whom he later married. What we see in these two cases is careful exploitation of the publicity complex, one style, the other one star-based. The media were invited to use the commodity and the artist behind it in interviews, news, gossip columns, advertisements, chat shows, magazine segments, film and album review columns and programmes, and the like – in the items which comprise the commodity they themselves are producing – the effect of which was to publicise both product and artist.

Unlike advertising, this publicity was provided 'freely' by the media. Most writers on the culture industry recognise the importance of the media in providing publicity in this manner (e.g. Coser *et al*. 1982, Frith 1978), but few deal with its systematic underpinings or the mechanisms whereby it is realised. My argument is that publicity is an effect generated by the normal operations of the makers of public goods. By using private goods produced by the manufacturing sector in making their *own* commodities, the public goods sector serves to publicise them. This reveals the complex *duality* of the public goods sector: it is simultaneously the industry's publicity complex – a duality I will refer to as the public goods producer/publicist sector. Further, this free advertising is no hit-or-miss affair. It is commercially both *efficient* and *effective* in achieving an impact for the commodities it publicises.

In general terms, the duality of public goods producer/publicist sector is not difficult to demonstrate[7]. For example, television stations use the products made by film and television production companies in their programmes; advertising agencies use popular stars and styles in advertisements; radio stations not only use recordings manufactured for the consumer market to make up their programmes, they also build their music formats around popular styles of music and highlight the work of stars; newspapers and magazines review books, films, theatrical performances, recordings, and the like, to provide copy for their arts and entertainment pages; specialist magazines cover the music business, others

---

7   As indicated in chapter 3, the press have an ambiguous position in this discussion. In principle, they are private goods in physical or technical form, yet are public goods in cultural form. Because of difficulties of realisation in recent years associated with rising production costs (newsprint, labour) and downwards pressures on cover prices, they have increasingly organised their production around the principles of public goods production. They are now heavily reliant on advertising for income. To simplify this analysis, I treat them here simply as public goods.

film, and others, the entertainment industry generally; and all media interview and profile authors, film and television and radio stars, singers, groups, and artists of all kinds in their news and arts/entertainment coverage. A new dimension of this, and an important one in an era of global marketing, is the 'tie-in', where one cultural commodity is derived from or associated with another, as in cases of the soundtrack recording of a film, a film or video release of a rock group concert or tour, and novelisations of a film, or films adapted from successful novels (Coser *et al.* 1982: 200-223, especially their discussion of the 'Hollywood-TV-Publishing Complex'[8]). Each commodity, in effect, publicises the other, and the work done around them by the publicity sector, expands the reputations of both.

The detail of this duality, however, is more complex. Take, for example, the ways that television channels use films and film stars in their normal programming – as in the case of 'Channel One – *Still No 1*', a model I have constructed to demonstrate their organisation[9] (cf. also Williams 1976b). To show the realisation of the publicity effect, I need to outline how Channel One's programme production is organised. The commodity is produced through a corporate organisational framework; the project team comprises a creative management stratum of producer and director (network and station programme managers, and various specialist producers/directors respectively) and executants (leading performers including named presenters, and supporting performers including 'backroom' programme/studio employees). Creation is geared towards the daily production of a continuous flow of items, which in their combination appear as a

---

8    This is a useful formulation. My interests are wider than just publishing, hence my preference for the more general term 'the publicity complex'. Nor do Coser *et al.* include relations between publishers and "key *outsiders* in the book trade" (1982: 285-361 – emphasis added) including middlemen and book reviewers, within their Hollywood-TV-Publishing Complex. My point is precisely that the publicist, understood as a structural position incorporating these forms of cultural work, is now part of and integral to the corporate form of cultural commodity production.

9    This model of is based on the operations of three Australian capital city stations studied in the course of field work, one from each of the three largest Australian markets, Sydney, Melbourne and Brisbane. Each represented one of the three major networks. All were subsidiaries of major multi-media corporations and each held major shareholding in at least one other metropolitan channel and several regional channels (and in one case, several radio stations). Data collection was based on observations and interviews, primarily with general, creative and marketing management. This case study amalgamates data from these various sources.

programme, Because of the character of public goods production, only a proportion of items are objects created on-station; Channel One does some local and network production such as a long-running, nationally distributed children's programme, news, special events and sports telecasts[10]. In these cases, specific purpose, short-term project teams are set up, but these function as cells within the larger project team. Most items, however, are purchased or leased from manufacturers. The most important creative work done at Channel One, the work of programming, can be characterised as *collection* and *scheduling*[11], both of which are oriented towards the dualities of public good/publicist production.

Collection is the task of creative management. In the case of Channel One, the network and station programme managers (the collective producer) select items from the range of goods available from various corporate and independent, local, national and international film and television production companies and their agents and distributors[12]. To

---

10   By way of comparison, newspapers such as *The Daily Courier* and magazines do proportionally much more in-house production; there is therefore a substantial staff of journalists, writers and sub-editors. Music-based radio stations like FM-RADIO, except for specials and news, do almost none.

11   These terms also stand metaphorically for journalistic work. Much reporting is little more than collection of information from agencies such as governments, cabinet ministers, departments, and from corporate bodies such as employer groups, unions, and interest groups, to say nothing of newsfeeds from news agencies, other outlets in the corporate group, and syndication services. Scheduling as discussed here, corresponds to the work of sub-editing and layout.

12   Based on the comments of Channel One creative management, the selection process seems to be based on at least three important cultural criteria (I am ignoring important economic considerations in selection decisions such as the possibility of selling subsidiary or network or regional rights to other stations). Selections are made on the basis of the existing hierarchy of cultural value, on the reputation or potential reputation of existing stars and styles. An evaluation is made of their relative appeal. If they are likely to be popular with the medium's audience and achieve strong penetration into target audiences, they are strongly sought after; blockbuster films such as the *Star Wars* films with their human and not-so-human stars are obvious examples. Second, selection is made on the basis of the format, whether or not the available objects are consistent with the types of items the station wants to combine into a programme. For example, Channel One is big on sport and searches for major events to cover and shorter magazine items to include in its Saturday afternoon sports programme. Third, selection is made on the basis of stylistic innovation; that is, the creative quality needed to add cultural significance to the medium's own

maximise the appeal of their own commodity, management look particularly for objects with superior reputations, the works of popular stars and
styles. Once items have been selected and consolidated as a library,
creative management draw up a programme schedule. Items are programmed at appropriate times for the audiences they are intended to
attract; the most popular at peak times with others allocated elsewhere,
and those of least significance away in 'the graveyard' (late evening or
mid-dawn). As the time of telecast approaches, programme staff prepare
the items (e.g. editing for commercial breaks) for assembly into a flow.
Presenters assemble them in the studio as they are being recorded or
transmitted. The schedule drawn up reflects the channel's format. According to the general and programme managers, Channel One's is:

aimed at attracting families. Families of all ages...For some reason we do best with
white collar more than blue collar suburbs. We didn't design it that way, it's just
what happens. It's because we've been around a long time, and we've stuck to our
guns by offering quality entertainment...We rate well in the older demographics.
With the population ageing, and product manufacturers eyeing off the older
demographics more, that doesn't do us any harm. But we have a problem in the
15-24 male and female groups. We're thinking about a nightly rock feature to deal
with that...Television is about entertainment. We try to offer a mix of programmes,
not too serious, we leave that to the ABC [Australian Broadcasting Corpora-
tion]...We're strong on films, Australian series and sports; they're the ones we do
best with.

As can be seen in Figure 7.1, Channel One runs a more-or-less standardised schedule across the week[13]. The basic pattern is maintained Monday

---

product. If innovative items cannot be found they can be scheduled in an innovative manner, which has the same effect.

13  It is worth noting that a degree of 'massness' still enters into television programming, not unlike the creative policies developed by daily newspapers.
Each attempts to combine several target audiences and attract all to a single
day's programme or edition by providing a collection of discrete content types
(see Figure 7.1). By way of comparison, *The Daily Courier*, depending on the
day of the week, divides each edition into separate sections; including local and
national news, international news, editorial-comment-features, real estate, financial and business, sport, women's pages, arts and entertainment, motoring,
and so on. Reflecting the fact that radio stations have adopted 24-hour and
highly specialised formats aimed at specific audiences, station FM-RADIO has
a combination top 40-album-oldie format aimed at a primary target audience
of 15-24 years and a secondary target of 18-35 years which comes into play
especially in the breakfast and morning zones; that is, programming is 'day-
parted' to account for work and domestic cycles of activity and the potential

| Zone | Target | Type |
|------|--------|------|
| 6.00 am Breakfast | Family | New & current affairs magazine programs |
| 9.00 Morning | Children Housewives | Childrens programs Serials, soaps |
| 12.00 Afternoon | Housewives | Chat shows, studio programs films, soaps |
| 4.00 Late Afternoon | Children Teenagers | Cartoons, childrens programs game shows |
| 6.00 Early Evening | Family | News, public affairs comedy Australian series |
| 8.30 Evening | Adults | Mini series, News updates Quality Australian series & drama series |
| 12.00 Mid-Dawn | Adults | Films, serials, magazine programs |
| Saturday - Sunday 12 midday | Males | Sports programs |

Figure 7.1  Channel One Program Schedule Monday - Friday

to Friday but modified on Saturday and Sunday to include sports coverage in order to build up weekly male audiences. Note the shifting focus on different target audiences throughout the day: the family as a whole during breakfast, then pre-school children and housewives throughout the morning and early afternoon, returning to a family orientation later in the

available audiences. The purpose of these schedules is the same as that of Channel One.

day. According to the programme manager, this is intended to match "the cycles that a family goes through in its daily routines. We try and catch them as they come and go". Management pays particular attention to its programming following the 6.00pm news/current affairs items, in the belief that "if you've got them for the news, and follow it with a ball-tearer, then you've got them for the night". Most importantly, given the media's dual producer/publicist activities, in addition to running regular advertising on local radio stations, in the local press, and in specialist television magazines, part of Channel One's publicity department creates on-air campaigns in an attempt to attract target audiences to other programmes. There are nightly 'promos', for example, previewing the following week's episode of popular programmes and other programmes coming up later in the week, especially new mini series, new films, Saturday's 'big game' and so on; 'trailers' aimed at housewives for items scheduled in the morning and afternoon zones are run in the breakfast programme; and there is extensive promotion in prime time (roughly, 5.00pm-10.00pm, especially 6.00pm-8.30pm) of feature items in other zones. As given by the duality of the public goods producer/publicist, their purpose is to maximise penetration into various commercially-desirable audiences, and by patterning the channel's programming, moulding the habit of extended viewing. The channel thereby attracts a collection of sizeable, precisely-defined audiences, and carries them across different zones and days of the week to boost its total share of viewing. This viewing profile, its share of viewing together with the reach and frequency it offers, is the foundation of the distributive efficiency the station needs to attract advertisers. These same efficiencies become part of the benefit offered to the recipients of the free advertising effect; it accrues automatically to the manufacturers whose products are used in the programme.

We are now in a position to grasp both the complexity and economic efficiency of the relationship between public goods production and their publicity effects. This can be illustrated with a special feature Channel One decided to run. It had won the Australian rights to telecast the second of George Lucas's immensely popular *Star Wars* series of films, *The Empire Strikes Back*. The channel already had the first of these in its library, as well as a documentary called *The Making of Star Wars* dealing with the innovative animation techniques developed for them. The recognisable significance of these films made them outstanding programme items in the eyes of creative management. The initial intention had been to use *Empire* later in the year to coincide with school holidays. At the time, however, local newspapers and other media were full of the impending cinema theatre release of the third in the Lucas trilogy, *Return of the Jedi*. Because of the obvious tie-ins, and the fact that these films, according to the programme manager, were, at the time, "occupying a significant slice of the audience mind...the opportunity was too good to miss". He decided to schedule the three items, documentary first, followed in order by the first and second of the films, at a special Friday evening family-viewing time of 7.30pm, even though it meant temporarily displacing a popular American comedy series. The topicality and popularity of these films guaranteed the channel sizeable audiences across a number of audience segments; young families, adults, children and teenagers across several socio-economic groups. From the point of view of the manufacturer, distributor and exhibitor of the films, especially *Return of the Jedi*, and the makers, licensees and retailers of the toys, dolls, books and other promotional paraphernalia associated with them, they received what was, in effect, a total of something like 6 hours prime-time publicity for their products – free. Furthermore, it was highly efficient publicity, aimed precisely at the target audience for the film and associated products and transmitted in a manner which served to maximise the significance of all. By any measure, this is saturation publicity of enormous impact, and demonstrates something of the quantity and quality of the publicity effect generated by the production and circulation of public goods[14].

## 7.2.3 Publicity: The Objectification of Stars/Styles

I want to look more closely at the socio-cultural mechanisms which create the publicity effect. In outline, publicity work is crucial in making the stars and styles corporations depend on for their long-term profitability. When public goods producers use cultural objects in their own production processes, they serve to give them a public existence. By displaying the object's characteristics and associating these with a name, they give it objectivity, thereby making it appear as a cultural fact. As a recognisable object, it can be promoted, given a horizontal position as a definite cultural object and a vertical position in a hierarchy of value. Promoting the many objects in a cultural arena serves to create an objective order of significance, a naturalised, taken-for-granted order of cultural things, stratified according to value, whose influence spreads across the market

---

14 The power and value of this publicity is also demonstrated by the case of Kylie Minogue (see also chapter 6), who starred in the popular Australian soap *Neighbours*, which Channel One, like other stations in the network, had scheduled in prime time. At the time of fieldwork, she and her recording company were exploiting the intensive publicity gained through this television exposure as a springboard to an internationally successful career as a pop singer.

and acts as a point of reference for manufacturers, marketers and publicists (and retailers and audiences, but I will not deal with these here).

The publicity work done on stars differs slightly from that done on styles and is worth discussing separately. When publicising works created by artists, the focus is their idiolect. There is a continuing debate about its specificities; the nature of their individual talents, their techniques, the particular ways they handle a form of work, their influences, personality, and its relation to their work, and so on. The outcome is a conventionalised picture of the artist and work, expressed as a socially recognisable combination of name and image. The persona, talents and repertoire are turned into a definite and unique object positioned within a specific cultural arena. Examples can be found everywhere, most explicitly in the reviews and profiles published in newspapers, consumer, specialist and trade magazines and newsletters; an instance is an article on actress Meryl Streep from American film writer Jenny Cullen published in the arts section of *The Weekend Australian* (2-3 April 1988: Magazine 3-4) prior to the release of her film, *Ironweed*. The profile was headed "'Now *t-h-a-t's* an actress...'", a title based on a remark made by the film's director Oscar Babenco. Note how Cullen makes various aspects of acting – versatility and professionalism, the ability to bring characters to life, sensitivity to the character, and the chameleon-like capacity to submerge real-life personality beneath the character's, and so on – cohere around the individual's name, to create a sign of unique talent:

*Ironweed* is a film in which Meryl Streep once again proves why she is called the undisputed film actress of the century. It is a performance without equal, culled from the depth and range of this extraordinary woman who, chameleon-like, takes on other characters and becomes them. Streep says, "I have no Method. I've never read Stanislavsky."...Streep says that a flash of intuition taught her about Helen. "I heard a melody in Helen's life and instantly transformed it into a symbol, a treble clef. It expressed for me her passion for music, her inner grace, and it gave me the sad, dropping line of her body. I built up Helen pore by pore".

When Meryl Streep, the 37-year old character actress plays a character it is not enough to slip on the outer layers for a performance. She instead becomes that character for the duration of the film, seldom slipping out of character, soaking up her role until to her it is real. She takes over not only the outer layers and the costumes but the inner life of the character, including secrets and dreams that even director Babenco is unaware of and William Kennedy, who created Helen, has not imagined...

Streep, however, is an Academy favourite and of all today's actresses continues to prove time after time her versatility, range and depth that to date is unequalled in Oscar history. Whether *Ironweed* becomes a box office success remains to be seen. Despite the huge big-name pulling power of Streep and [co-star Jack] Nicholson, some audiences have already voted it too down-beat and depressing. They argue that Streep is too real. Her portrayal of Helen leaves the audience feeling sympathy for the kind of person that on the streets they would avoid. It is the kind of criticism Streep would probably be pleased to get. It means she has succeeded in shedding Streep as she did in playing Lindy Chamberlain with Australian-New Zealand accent in dark wig and print dresses in Fred Schepisi's *Evil Angels*, or with a Polish accent playing the tortured Sophie of William Styron's *Sophie's Choice* or playing the aristocratic Danish-born Isak Dinsen in *Out Of Africa* - she is always totally believable and compelling...

Each role challenges her and excites her and that is what she finds fulfilling. It is the chance to be a chameleon, not just in her looks and voice, but in her attitude, her perceptions.

There is little doubt left here as to Streep's objective status as an artist (and as a star, but I will turn to the allocation of significance shortly).

Publicity plays an even more central role in constituting styles and giving them a social existence. Nowhere is the interdependency between manufacturer/marketer and publicist clearer. A star can be created through a single work – although the comments of Buddah Records management cited earlier suggest that even gaining public recognition of stars can be a lengthy process. A style, however, is stitched together, named, and given public form, over a longer time-span. Rarely does it crystalise instantly. More single events, items, and people, are involved, and is more like a gradual 'making', until a moment of precipitation when it suddenly takes shape as a definite object, a cultural fact, its characteristics and genesis appearing natural and coercive to those involved in its constitution.

It is difficult to provide a single concise illustration of this process. There are multitudes of inputs, fragments spoken here and there, spread over time and across many sites. In film, for example, publicity involves critics and reviewers in a range of consumer and industry media. A style is discussed in their news and review columns and occasional feature articles. In Australia, for example, this might include film reviewers in local daily newspapers and especially critics in the more substantive national or regional dailies, such as Evan Williams in *The Australian*, and Sandra Hall in weekly newsmagazines such as the *Bulletin*; John Hinde, Margaret Pomeranz and David Stratton in their news and review programmes on ABC and SBS television and radio; in specialist trade and consumer periodicals such as *Cinema Papers* and *TV Week*; and academic journals such as *Meanjin* and the *Australian Journal of Cultural Studies*. With the resurgence of the Australian film industry in the 1970s, for example, these outlets were directly and indirectly involved in a debate over the character of 'Australian' film-making, whether it was derivative, or represented a categorical and original cinematic style[15]. By the early 1980s, consolidation had occurred to such a degree that *Time* magazine (28 September 1981: 36-44) felt it possible to run a cover story discussing the arrival of "the Australian genre both artistically and intellectually", based on "the latest of the 'new wave' movies that have been coming out of Australia since the mid-'70s, movies such as *Gallipoli, Breaker Morant, Picnic At Hanging Rock, My Brilliant Career*", and the work of directors and producers such as Peter Weir, Fred Schepisi, Bruce Beresford and Gillian Armstrong – the stars upon whose work the style was taken to be based. These elements were projected as the foundations of the style, a specifically Australian style, identifiable:

not by technical innovation...but a classical elegance of image, plot and character, of stories well told against the spectacular backdrop of a continent that even Australians hardly know...Many of the films – *Picnic, Morant, Gallipoli* – are about looking to the past, about finding and understanding Australia's historical roots.

These reviews and features were produced as items within public goods such as newspapers, magazines and journals, and radio and television programmes, but their publicity effect contributes to the constitution of the now-evident object they claimed to discover.

As noted elsewhere, a crucial part of objectifying a style is conventionalising a name with the collection of fragments thought to constitute it: note, for example, how the *Time* article unifies the films of Armstrong, Weir and Schepisi under the label of an Australian style, which is explicated through the characteristics of their works. Their idiolects are collectively transformed into a style, which in turn, is made to appear as a cultural fact. Another example appears in a review of the film *Blue Velvet* published in *Cinema Papers* (March 1987: 51) which begins:

Let us assume there is a group of directors we can call 'post-modernists'. They would be characterised by their self-conscious eclectic aestheticism and the distance they are able to place between the spectators and the universe represented on the screen. David Lynch would be a charter member of the group and *Eraserhead* one of the touchstones of the style...his films have been collections of

---

15  Note how cultural form and style are mixed here with the search for a national identity, a stage that white Anglo-Saxon Australia has been going through especially since post-war period; see, for example, Dermody and Jacka (1987) and Tulloch (1982).

memorable noises and images, errily still, bordered in black and silence. Tottering in and about these moments there are often some shreds of story (big lumps of it in *The Elephant Man*), bemused and out-of-place...We are pleased to report that not all of *Blue Velvet's* plot riddles are solved by the end, as befits a post-modernist pastiche.

The identity of 'post-modern' cultural commodities, according to this account, is not yet clear, other than as objects marked by a taste for quotation and repetition (cf. also Jameson, 1984, Featherstone 1988). In this extract we see an object-in-the-making, as it stitches together and associates particular characteristics with the name, slowly constructing the conventional framework which identifies the style. The outcome is illustrated by Tucker's (1986: 399) account of the emergence of 'heavy metal' rock music in the mid-1970s. The American band Blue Cheer were enjoying some success, "but there was still no name for what Blue Cheer did – unless you count playing-repetitive-chords-as-loud-as-you-can-on-acid-which-makes-almost-anything-sound-interesting". Steppenwolf then recorded 'Born to Be Wild', which included the phrase 'heavy metal thunder'. The media seized upon it and applied it as a descriptive label to the work of similar-sounding artists such as Blue Cheer, Steppenwolf, Iron Butterfly, even retrospectively to 'hard rock' groups like Deep Purple and the Who.

So in the first phase of the publicity process, stars-and-styles-in-the-making emerge in the debate which appears as an effect of public goods producers/publicists doing their work. They come to acquire a facticity, as a socially recognisable objects with conventional, naturalised meanings[16],

---

16  Whilst I have avoided issues relating to ideology in this work, there are obvious connections in my arguments here with those presented by Hall. He argues (1977: 340-342) that there are three basic functions of the media; first, the selective construction of social knowledge; second, to reflect on the plurality of forms of social life and to provide a constant lexicon of its objects; and third, to organise, orchestrate and bring together that which has been selectively represented and selectively classified, whence "what has been made visible and classified begins to shake into *an acknowledged order*". Clearly, while approaching the activities of the media from a quite different perspective, my conclusions parallel Hall's. It is notable, however, that he goes on to ask "what are the actual *mechanisms* which enable the media to perform this 'ideological work'?" (1977: 342), and continues in abstract semiological vein to offer an answer, which builds upon his earlier work on encoding/decoding. While I have no real argument with him in terms of the functioning of language, I believe that my analysis offers more concrete understandings of some of the structured political-economic contexts of these mechanisms and would probably inform a more specific grasp of the "field of meanings...which are universalised and

available to artists, manufacturers and marketers as a point of cultural reference, to appropriate in the course of making their originals, packaging and advertisements.

## 7.2.4 Publicity: The Ordering of Cultural Things

Once objectified, stars/styles can become subjects of promotion. This is the second phase of publicity. Through the explicit and implicit assessments made of each object used in public goods production, the value of each star and style is assessed and a relative measure of significance allocated to each. As a result, these objects are positioned in a *hierarchy of cultural value*, and the result of positioning many objects is an *order of cultural things*.

This notion of a 'hierarchy of cultural value' needs explanation. Each separate arena or field in the sphere of culture is comprised of a collection of cultural objects (forms, techniques, stars, styles, works) and relative evaluations of each. Each object exists within a recognisable order of significance. No hierarchy is entirely coherent or unified, but is a framework which publicists are always constructing, as objects collected around some principle. Since publicity is a complex practice with many competing players, it is a site of debate and conflict and no hierarchy is ever settled. Nor is significance created and allocated only in aesthetic terms. The market is also an important influence. Commercial criteria of sales or potential sales are taken as a fundamental measure of reputation and contribute to considerations of value[17]. The promotion effect creates a hierarchy of (commercial plus cultural) value for each arena, giving it a structured facticity as a stratified order of cultural things. This order becomes a coercive principle operating across the field and perhaps across the whole industry, as a measure of value, a point of reference for manufacturers, marketers, creative management, and artists in the main-

---

naturalised" (1977: 343) which could be usefully investigated further by cultural studies analysts. This could be a particularly important point when we remember that the media are the core of the publicity complex, and that beyond the restricted area of cultural commodities, publicity is accorded to many aspects of social life, especially economic and political. The effects on these objects are the same.

17   It should be remembered that in discussing publicity, we are dealing with the *imputation* of value prior to exchange and consumption. The claims made for a cultural object, and the putative order of cultural things, awaits the final jurisdiction of exchange.

stream and periphery involved in the production and circulation of cultural commodities.

This process is explicit in the profile of Meryl Streep cited earlier. Statements such as 'the undisputed film actress of the century', and 'she continues to prove time after time her versatility, range and depth that to date is unequalled in Oscar history', proclaim her significance compared to others, based on the apparent obviousness of her talent. Virtually every review of a cultural object, for example, does similar work. For example, in reviewing Steven Spielberg's film *Empire of the Sun* for *The Weekend Australian Magazine* (19-20 March 1988: 12), critic Evan Williams proclaims Spielberg to be "an incomparable weaver of spells, one of the great cinematic magicians". *Empire of the Sun* does not, however, according to this essay, measure up to its maker's talents.

Something strange has been happening to Steven Spielberg. Not content with being the world's most popular film-maker, tired of his reputation as the most successful producer of box-office triumphs in the history of the cinema, he wants to make serious films...one genuine masterpiece to secure his place in history...*Empire of the Sun* is inflated, pretentious, beautiful and essentially rather dull. I wish Spielberg would settle down, forget about Academy Awards, and return to his familiar world of fantasy. He was good at it.

Explicitly, Spielberg himself is located as a meritorious object at the top of a hierarchy of cinematic value. So are his earlier fantasy movies such as *E.T.* and *Poltergeist*, whereas *Empire of the Sun* is positioned well down[18].

A (meta)hierarchy of value both underlies and is a product of encyclopedias, guides and handbooks which survey a particular field. They position the objects in the field by naming, differentiating and evaluating each. The *New Musical Express Book of Rock* (Logan and Woffinden 1973), for example, provides an alphabetical listing of artists and styles, promoting some above others. The entry for the Rolling Stones, for example, covers the biographies and careers of the group and its members, their collective and individual styles, musical influences, and the group's music and image. There is also a comprehensive discography, acknowledgement of the position each single and album attained on the British and U.S. charts, with an aesthetic and commercial evaluation of each woven into the narrative; for example, how *Exile On Main Street*, "the most casually-dis-

---

18   The Saturday edition of *The Daily Courier* with its extended arts/entertainment section explicitly materialises a section of the cinematic order. Its reviewers give each film on release at local theatres a rating out of five stars, and it publishes a weekly consolidated column titled "Movie Review Guide: how the films showing in the city and suburbs have been rated by our critics" with each listed under their rating; five stars, four-and-a-half stars, and so on.

missed of all the Stones albums, is one of the finest". The entry closes with the proposition that:

Though recent albums have disappointed by previous standards, the Stones retain power to be, on their night, the finest rock group in the world. Their imitators are legion; their legend marginally tarnished but they are still the most charismatic (alongside Dylan) in rock (1973: 427).

Their recordings and concerts, according to this view, remain an objective and superior measure against which all other rock recordings must be compared. They remain at the pinnacle of the order of rock and roll things.

The examples offered so far demonstrate explicit examples of the publicity effect created by public goods production. Other semiotic allocations of significance are made implicitly through the internal structures of their commodities. For example, the fact that a particular film or series or item is scheduled by a television channel in prime time signals its obvious worth[19]. A recording gains in significance if a radio station nominates it as 'No 1', or as 'the album of the week', or puts it on its 'hit' playlist; the same for a star if selected as the headline guest in a television chat show or if profiled in the features pages of a newspaper or magazine; or when a book or film is given the lead position in the review pages of a newspaper. In each of these cases, the prominent positioning of the item in the structure of the text attributes reputation, making it appear like an important object in the field – regardless of what else is said about it (perhaps we see here the truth of the adage that 'all publicity is good publicity'). Further, when public goods producers present their commodities to the market, they too package and publicise them. Part of the putative reputation they thereby acquire, flows over to the goods used in their making[20], but this promotion flows in two directions and in an

---

19  The same effect is produced for political events and persons in the operation of news, when items are prioritised in a bulletin or edition.

20  It is also worth noting that the semiotic work of publicity is also done by the retail sector in the merchandising work done immediately prior to exchange. The cultural hierarchy established through publicity is reproduced in modern merchandising techniques. The appearance and layout of shops selling private goods for individual consumption (e.g. books, records, videos) is built out of the existing cultural hierarchy and based upon its terms. Goods are laid out according to stars and styles in a layout which expresses and signifies their recognisable value. They are laid out according to conventional star/style categories: e.g. science fiction, gardening, popular classics; rock, jazz and classical, and marked as stratified variations within each style; e.g. a separate rack for 'this week's top 10 records', 'feminist fiction', 'new releases from Penguin'.

ever-expanding motion. The medium selects significant items to make up its product thus it gains in significance itself. Some of its own significance after creation and marketing flows back the items used, expanding their value, and so on, and so on – as in the case of Channel One and the *Star Wars* films. The publicity effect is not merely a circle of significance but more akin to an upwards-moving spiral of significance, item to content and back again.

In the second phase of the publicity process, the work of the producer/-publicist has the dual effect of creating public goods for consumption. As a consequence, it serves to construct a naturalised order of cultural things and ascribe privileged status to the stars and styles at its pinnacle. This objective hierarchy confronts potential purchasers as if a known value before consumption; this is the taste-mediator effect of the publicity complex. It is part of the industry-wide work performed by the publicity complex for the manufacturing sector as part of their marketing effort, exactly the same effect as that of advertising, but carried out free.

# 7.3 The Institutionalisation of the Publicist and Its Consequences

## 7.3.1 The Manufacturer/Publicist Connection as a Structural Feature of the Culture Industry

The institutionalisation of the publicist has changed the structure of the culture industry since about the last quarter of the 19th century and has proved to be an important element in constituting its corporate form. From beginnings as the provider of a sales service, the publicist in the culture industry has progressively become a fraction of partly productive capital. It is now a position within the corporate structure of cultural relations but operating outside their organisational form, although articulated to it through the corporation's marketing department.

The publicist is a complex unit of capital, operating partly as a commodity producer, partly as a circulator of manufacturers' products. Thus, as the publicist produces cultural and economic value, it simultane-

---

They are surrounded by point of sale material (e.g. posters, signs, display bins, window displays) which support the marketing work already done in the production of the commodity's appearance.

ously distributes it. As discussed in chapter 3, its economic and cultural functioning stems ultimately from its constituent commodity form, the quasi-public good. Because of difficulties selling their products at prices which recover production costs (e.g. rising cover prices for press, political and technical barriers for broadcasting)[21], publicists have found it more profitable to rent their distributive capacity to advertisers[22] and take a share of publicity profits as their primary base for accumulation. They survive on their effectiveness in attracting desired target audiences with their products, manoeuvring individuals into consuming it habitually and for long periods. The large aggregate audience share-of-consumption profile achieved by public goods producers makes them effective and efficient communicators, able to offer advertisers significant efficiencies in the process of publicity. Furthermore, as the media moved away from their own production towards exploitation of consumer goods in making their own products, manufacturers cooperated because of the high-quality publicity such use brings. In short, despite their dependent or secondary position as producers, through their symbiosis with manufacturers, publicists such as the media have been able to force themselves into the core of the culture industry – so to speak, onto its centre-stage.

Their relationship with manufacturers brings benefits to the publicity sector in their role as commodity producers. By using consumer goods as intermediate goods, public goods producers are able to significantly reduce their production costs, especially in the area of labour. Collection and assembly is cheaper and less skilled than creation. The creative staff of commercial radio station FM-RADIO, for example, is comprised almost solely of continuity announcers and programmers, skilled only in programming and presenting playlisted recordings according to the format. The situation is analogous on Channel One[23]. Furthermore, since using the

---

21  It needs to be emphasised again that the press have an ambiguous position in this discussion. As previously pointed out, newspapers, for example, have the technical form of private goods but the cultural form of public goods. I am treating them in this discussion as public goods.

22  Recall the shift to the second model of radio discussed in chapter 3. Note also that with the downturn in box-office receipts, cinema owners have recently moved in the same direction.

23  By way of comparison, state-funded television and radio stations, such as those of the Australian Broadcasting Corporation, engage in much more local and national production. Their creative staffs include significant numbers of writers, researchers and specialist presenters on permanent full-time staff. Their work is organised around principles more like those of a craft workshop (see chapter 4). The conceptual framework and methodology I have used in this

work of significant artists increases the reputation of their own product, publicists profit from easy access to popular stars and styles (which they have helped to create), resulting in long-running battles with manufacturers over use of consumer goods. Over the years they have been forced to pay rights and royalties of various kinds such as mechanical rights, broadcasting rights, copyright fees, licensing and appearance fees, for specific and limited use of manufacturers' cultural commodities. This conflict is currently being re-run in the 'pay for play' debate between television stations and the makers of musical video clips, especially those from recording companies (Stockbridge 1988).

The institutionalisation of the publicist has also changed the shape of the mechanisms whereby reputation is allocated within the culture industry. With the aestheticisation of symbolic interaction, the critic took up this role. With the commercialisation of cultural production, the audience as purchasers and consumers were also accorded the function of assessing value, a judgement which operated through monetary exchange. This function has been pre-empted and changed by the publicist, by virtue of their expertise in communication and their control over the means of public communication[24]. When publicity allocates significance, it does in both aesthetic and commercial terms. Success in the market is risky if the commodity is subject to damaging comments, hence, by virtue of their relationship with manufacturers, 'criticism' in the publicity complex became 'reviewing', where commercial and aesthetic criteria are combined in evaluating the worth of an object.

## 7.3.2 The Battle Over Publicity: Conflicts of Interest in the Allocation of Significance

Competition in the cultural marketplace is fierce, with many competing stars and styles and individual commodities. Accordingly, manufacturers employ large numbers of staff and devote considerable time and expense to capturing the publicity complex. Buddah Record's attempts noted earlier to sell the rock and roll revival in general and Sha Na Na in particular is an excellent illustration. Their rationale reflected the conven-

---

work might be usefully employed in examining state forms of cultural production.

24  Further to footnote 2 above, note how the ontology of communication as an historical category seems to be fundamentally founded on the idea of publicity. In this regard it is interesting to note the preoccupation with persuasion and effects research which is part of the classical models of communication.

tional wisdom in the music business that sales success cannot be achieved without airplay; from the record companies' perspective, "the function of radio is to sell records" (Chapple and Garofalo 1977: 169, also Frith 1978: 89). For the same publicity reasons, recording companies also encourage television stations to telecast the music video clip (Stockbridge 1988), and have their second-level and rising stars booked as support groups for national tours with major artists (e.g. Chapple and Garofalo 1977: 137-154). Similar battles take place in other spheres. At the time when the film *Crocodile Dundee II* was released on Labor Day weekend 1988 in the U.S., film writer Jenny reported that two other potential blockbusters, *Rambo III* (Sylvester Stallone) and George Lucas's *Willow*, were holding off their promotional launches for fear that *"Dundee II* will clean up at the box office and knock their big gun and far more expensive movies right out of the running". Both held off their release dates (*The Sunday Mail*, 8 May 1988: 3-4). Publishers too, attempt to attract attention prior to publication of a title, including the vast publicity and 'hoopla' that accompanies book-club selection, paperback-rights sales, movie or television sales, and excerpts of the book in magazines and newspapers (Coser *et al.* 1982: 316). This not only publicises the particular work or artist. Ongoing publicity also has spinoffs in sales of their earlier works: in particular, it makes possible the success of compilation products such as 'greatest hits' and 'collected works', and the re-release of 'standards' which are important elements of form-based production. The publicity complex, therefore, helps build up immediate and continuing sales and preserve the manufacturer's total invested capital, but the corporations of culture have to work hard to gain its support.

In so far as the media and other publicists are 'opinion-makers' (cf. 'gatekeepers', Hirsch 1970), manufacturers try to influence their judgements, but the publicist's formal independence presents them with certain problems. Personal contacts are one way of overcoming this, by controlling the process of definition through personal influence. Marketing personnel form friendships with publicity agents, invite them to launches, make person-to-person visits with new product, offer 'perks' and gifts of whatever takes the recipient's fancy, in exchange for favoured treatment (Coser *et al.* 1982: 310-312, cf. the media as 'secondary definers', Hall *et al.* 1979: 57-60) – hence the 'payola' scandals which are occasionally uncovered (Chapple and Garofalo 1977: 66-68). Despite this, individuals within the publicity complex not infrequently create their own counter-definitions of artists and works, and in cases of the 'wait and see' attitude to promotion by manufacturers often accompanying releases from second-level stars and in style-based marketing, the media are left to make their own decisions. The corporations of culture, therefore, can be left chasing the tail of the publicity complex as it forges cultural orders which suits theirs or other interests and not those of the manufacturing sector.

Because of the structural position of the publicity complex and the production relations in which they are caught up with manufacturers, stars are forced to work the publicity circuit upon release of their latest work. The logic of their situation makes this necessary. Frith (1978: 111) argues that "The music business...turns musicians into commodities, as stars", although strictly speaking, this is an imprecise formulation. Coser *et al.* (1982: 214-215) are more correct when they say that authors "must be salesmen or saleswomen of their own wares...authors sell books by selling themselves". Artists engaged as contracted artists are positioned in production as (in)dependent intermediate goods producers. To be engaged by manufacturers, they must demonstrate and maintain their commerciality as indexed by their reputation. As independents, they must bear the financial and emotional costs of inflating the market value of their name and talent[25], each becoming their own marketer by presenting themselves in public as an icon of their image via appearances on talk shows, doing interviews, media and in-store appearances, and so on; author Judith Kranz commented to Coser *et al.* (1982: 214-218), "I never realised how much hustling was involved". From the star's perspective, this has a dual purpose. It convinces manufacturers to release their work and familiarises audiences with their name, thereby giving their works commercial potential. Since the media are part of 'show-biz' and tend to select guests with celebrity appearance and entertainment value, artists of quiet demeanour or whose work is outside the public agenda are ignored by the publicity complex. This encourages manufacturers to be partly guided in their creative and employment policies by the publicity potential of an artist. Equally, it encourages artists to put on the popular signs of stardom, to adopt spectacular codes of dress, behaviour and speech in order to make a display of themselves and attract market attention.

The work of the publicity complex has a number of consequences back in production. In chapter 4, I discussed the project team and how both contracted artists and professional creatives can alter their relations with creative management, as can creative management with general management, if they can acquire artistic authority. Significance, in its surface form

---

25  Coser *et al.* (1982: 216) make the tart comment that "Ambition, so it would seem, is a most powerful stimulant". This implies a voluntaristic notion of 'selling out' and is consistent with the whiff of romantic anti-commercialism/elitism which permeates their book. They do not seem to grasp the fact that if contracted artists want to survive in mind and body, they have little option *but* to engage in this publicity work.

as reputation, is allocated by the publicist. Cultural workers collectively and individually can play the publicity game to valorise their name and increase their power in the workplace. Successful contracted artists, for example, can demand a higher rate of royalties from the manufacturer; for example, by 1969, and under the very sharp management of Alan Klein, the Beatles were able to negotiate a rise from 10% to 25% (Frith 1978: 111). Later in his career, by threatening owner Berry Gordy that he would take his talent elsewhere, Stevie Wonder was allowed to move beyond the musical confines of 'the Motown sound' – although he did have to invest his own money in the (1972) album *Talking Book* to make his point (Tucker 1986: 498-499). While initially employed as a professional creative, after major successes, singer Donna Summer was able to force her recording company to give her the artistic and financial conditions of the contracted artist (Tucker 1986: 528-529). In short, publicity can change the balance of power between artists and management and destabilise the order companies impose in the creative stage of production. Moreover, because the publicist is an independent fraction of capital, the corporations can do little about it.

There are other more serious problems for manufacturers. As commodity producers, publicists seek success for their own products, hence they put their own interests first. Radio and television stations, for example, tend towards collecting and scheduling stars and styles which are currently popular with their target audiences. To the manufacturer, this is wasted effort. It is mature product which either tends to sell itself or has ceased selling. They want publicity for their new and rising releases, for the new stars and styles they are trying to market. From the media's angle, new, untested material is culturally and commercially risky. They remain with the tried and tested. Consequently, manufacturers frequently complain of the difficulty in gaining publicity for new works and new acts, complaining bitterly about what they see as the conservatism of the media[26] (e.g. Chapple and Garofalo 1977: 181-183). The cooperation which characterises the manufacturer/publicist relation has to be constantly reforged, and along the way, there are many battles.

---

26  This is more of a problem for the smaller independents. Media prefer to associate with the majors because they have the 'hot' properties, the 'big time' acts. Independents usually operate in the semiperiphery and have difficulty getting media to publicise their product.

### 7.3.3 Stars/Styles, Restructuring the Order of Cultural Things and the Cycles of Fashion

Beginning with the contradictions of the cultural commodity, this analysis has shown how systems have developed to mitigate their effects, including the services rendered by the publicity complex. The contradictions, however, are not resolved but reappear in another form. Marketing strategies adopted by the corporations of culture and supported by the publicity complex, coalesce around stars and styles and an accepted order of cultural things. Paradoxically, while a cultural order promises to stabilise a market, once established, its leadership is challenged – *because of the continued activities of the publicity complex which constructed it in the first place.* There is a constant turnaround of stars and styles; those which are allocated to the position of No 1 this week are dislodged by next week's new releases. This turnover in stars/styles, these *cycles of fashion,* is one of the most important contradictions of the modern culture industry, and needs to be discussed.

To explain: Once stars/styles are made popular and fashionable, other companies exploit them by reproducing their characteristics in formatted production. In the same way as overproduction of the works by an individual artist undermines their popularity, the same thing occurs with stars and styles. Overexposure soon leads to a decline in popularity. As the objects at the top decline, they are replaced by one or another of their competitors. The cyclical collapse and reconstruction of the order of cultural things governing each field of culture flows in part from the market success enjoyed by the market leaders. In its mature form, the culture industry has developed another layer of contradictions over the top of those associated with the cultural commodity and its truncated product cycle. Now there is also a *truncated star/style cycle*; evidence industry puzzlement over the shortening market life span of stars and styles (e.g. Coser *et al.* 1982: 363).

Reordering is also an effect of product differentiation and its promotion. Each corporation publicises its up-and-coming stars and styles by highlighting their stylistic innovation and proclaiming them as the latest fashion. In effect, they are attempting to dislodge those presently in a position of superiority in the cultural order. Competition to the existing order comes not only from the majors. Product specialisation and market segmentation means that with increasingly defined and differentiated tastes, the scale of production needed for local success is sufficiently small to make specialised, boutique production viable. Independents therefore have the opportunity to make inroads into the market. They too can disrupt the order of things: first at a local level, then if the success of their products spreads, perhaps at a regional or national level – if it gets more popular, the majors are likely to step in and take them over or crowd them out of the market.

Perhaps the most decisive impulse behind the constant movement in the hierarchies of value which order corporate cultural production and circulation, flows from the publicity complex itself. The very sector which serves to construct these orders in the first place, plays an powerful role in their undermining and restructuring. Because publicists of all kinds are independent firms outside the direct control of the majors, they determine to a large degree which stars and styles will be publicised. Despite the attempts of manufacturers to influence creative management, the makers of public goods may decide to go their own way; in fact, to compete successfully in their own markets, they *must*. Since they are reliant on advertising, they seek to maximise the extent and habit of audience consumption by using objects with established reputations; but against this, as cultural commodity producers, they too are bound to create commodities which show signs of creativity. In previewing the products of the manufacturing sector they also look for items with relative originality, featuring them in their creation and marketing. These up-and-coming stars and styles, by virtue of the publicity they receive, are turned into powerful competitors for the stars and styles at the top of the cultural hierarchy governing the field of which they are part. Inevitably, each is undermined. It is a systemic necessity that once having played a role in establishing an order of cultural things, the publicist reorders it, and uses the products intended to stabilise the market to do so.

The result is cycles of fashion. Competition in the cultural marketplace leads to its perpetual reordering. With competing publicists seeking to assert new assessments of value, cycles of fashion as a condition of circulation is an institutionalised outcome of the constituent relations between manufacturer and publicist, between the systems of production and circulation which characterises the corporate era of the culture industry. Unpredictability is reintroduced. The conditions in circulation reproduce in more developed form the fundamental contradictions of the art/capital relation.

This has immediate implications for manufacturers. With the constant rise and fall of stars and styles, they have to be replaced. Each company must maintain a catalogue selection of fashionable stars and styles and supplement it with a selection of newcomers. Hence they must constantly scout the periphery for emerging artists and movements[27]. The major

---

27  In fact, it is usually regional offices who do this work, by attending small-time

corporations must invest significantly in an infrastructure for alerting itself to new developments for fear that fashion will take a new direction and leave them unprepared, yet they have no guarantees that the economic or cultural value of this investment will ever be realised. Their business remains a constant game of guesswork which marketing and publicity was supposed to overcome.

## 7.4 Conclusion

As seen in this and the previous chapter, the corporations have developed marketing techniques in an attempt to control the cultural marketplace. They create stars and styles and make them work like brands in an attempt to fix taste communities, whence predictable patterns of sales become more of a possibility. To that extent, the corporate form of cultural production generates tendencies which act to rationalise the conditions of circulation of cultural commodities.

The marketing system, however, cannot work without the public goods producer/publicist. This position in the structure of relations which constitutes the corporate era of the culture industry, plays a crucial role in integrating the circuits of production and circulation, especially in creating cultural orders of things as a pre-requisite of exchange. The publicist-manufacturer relation, however, introduces further tensions into the system. Since publicists are an independent unit of capital and have their own interests, these relations are built upon cooperation and conflict, a product of secondary or higher-level contradictions (see chapter 2) which have developed with the industry. The publicist sets up the objective hierarchy of value which underpins sales across the marketplace, then by the effects of its actions, proceeds to bring it undone. No sooner do manufacturers get their current crop of stars and styles in place than the structure of significance changes underneath them. The normal operations of the publicity machine undoes the potential rationalities to which its systemic relations with manufacturers contributes, and because of which, manufacturers have to cope with a truncated star/style cycle. This endless succession of stars and styles which characterises the industry, represents periodic innovation designed to counteract the contradictions of the cultural commodity. Short term, they might, but over the long term, they

---

venues, reading and listening to unsolicited typescripts or tapes, or poaching stars and styles from their competitors.

exacerbate the industry's instability. These tendencies are more complex expressions in circulation and production of the fundamental art/capital contradiction which underlies the culture industry. The culture industry is caught in a web of its own making.

The paradox of fashion constantly puts corporate investments (artists, back-catalogue) and creative policies (formats) at risk. They must constantly invest in potential talent without any guarantee of return – their caution in signing new artists is a response to these conditions. They lose the benefits of longer-term market control which stars and styles might potentially bring. Instead, consumers are exposed to a series of short-run, intensive overexposures of different stars who disappear as quickly as they surfaced. Instead of reigning for long periods, developing their talents and creating lifetime of work, they are pushed on and off-stage by collection of forces beyond their control, their careers governed not by the depth and development of their talents but by the fashions which flow through the market. Styles remain fashionable for longer – which is partly why the corporations have pushed towards form-based production – but not by much.

This situation provides opportunities for freelancers and independents, both individual artists and companies. Because the market has been heavily segmented, it takes only stylistic innovation or relative originality to seem to be different. Even minor talents with one interesting idea can make it: they too can attract the attention of the majors and see themselves on the way to stardom. However, once their new-found reputation is tarnished by over-exploitation, the publicity machine will just as quickly eliminate them.

The situation also creates opportunities for artists in the project team, especially leading players and creative management. Where stylistic innovation over established form rather than originality is the name of the game, once their name becomes known they can break away from regular employment to become freelancers or independents where they can, if they wish, preserve the creative freedoms of the artist – although financial risk drives some towards an unrelenting commercialism. There is a danger too that they might become the current fad of the publicity complex and just as quickly discarded. The appeal of freelance and independent production creates problems for the corporations who have problems holding their project teams together. Nonetheless, the corporations can live with the system, since it provides a constant flow of innovation and novelty which is the necessary foundation of any cultural commodity, without paying for the cost of gestation.

Do these conditions rationalise the cultural marketplace? The truth is that because it is founded on a contradictory mix of capitalist enterprise and art, the culture industry cannot be made entirely predictable. Immanent tensions play back upon themselves; as quickly as their effects are minimised in one direction, new expressions develop elsewhere. There are limits to rationalisation of the culture industry, limits to the extent to which the systems of production and circulation can be shaped into efficient vehicles of capital accumulation. The structural consequences of the operations of the publicity machine are just one more case and point.

# Chapter 8
# A Postscript

I want to finish by turning briefly to issues outside the concerns of this book but which were touched upon in the first chapter. In so far as it represents a contribution to the political economy of culture, the findings of this study seem to suggest certain immediate directions for a sociology of culture generally, and for those forms of analysis within media/cultural studies centred upon the reading of texts and/or the ideology problematic.

## 8.1 A Sociology of Culture

In identifying and filling out the corporate form of cultural production, this work offers a substantive contribution to the political economy of culture in two particular areas. As indicated earlier, it says something about:

1. the conditions of cultural work in the corporate capitalist context;
2. the mediation of cultural production when it is also capitalist commodity production.

The analytical approach I have taken here would seem to be adaptable to other forms of cultural production in so far as it takes an institutional approach to the objective conditions of production and circulation under which cultural workers are engaged, and focuses upon the specific form of the structure of relations and its constituent positions in which they are caught up.

On that basis, other methodologically-similar investigations could be conducted, for example, of 'pre-corporate' and 'state' forms of cultural production. In state forms, for example, such as government-funded ballet, theatre and opera companies, national and regional orchestras, and national broadcasting systems, the fundamental relation would not be that of capitalist and artist, but of state and artist – where, depending on its precise form, the state might resolve into two core historical positions such as patron/sponsor and manager. Because, when compared to the private sector, institutional goals differ – for example, cost efficiencies and profits have been much less important (although in Australia, New Zealand and Britain this maybe changing), and public interest and aesthetic considerations much more so – and although the organisational form is just as bureaucratised, the relations between managers and the collective artist are likely to be different from those in the corporate model, especially in so far as creative management might have more artistic autonomy. I suspect that the notion of the project team might also be useful in this context to characterise the form of labour organisation, but probably in modified form. There may be less institutionalised separation, for example, between creative management and executants, especially in 'serious' forms of production such as classical music and dance, where executants too may be credited with more artistic authority and hence accorded the right to participate in the planning process. Equally, I suspect that formatting is less likely to be evident and in some cases explicitly rejected. For these reasons, I suspect the state form might sit somewhere between what I have characterised as craft workshop and the craft-based but capitalist workshop, but would be further intersected by specifically bureaucratic dimensions which reshape aspects of its form.

Pre-corporate forms, especially independent commercial production by small-scale firms such as independent publishers and recording companies, might also be investigated using the same approach. Here, the core relation between capitalist and artist is probably much more diffuse and difficult to classify. In some situations, for example, the owner and creative management (producer and director) might be unified in the one position. In others, an artistically passive owner might engage a powerful producer-director-leading artist to take complete control of production from creation through to transcription. Generally, I suspect that the notion of the project team might not be as useful in these cases – or perhaps it could be qualified as a type, such as a petty capitalist project team (cf. craft workshop?), depending on what the evidence suggests.

Returning to production within the corporations of culture, it would be interesting to use my general framework to compare how different aesthetic formations (Williams 1981: 57-86) intersect with the corporate form. I have ignored differences between types of cultural production to build a picture of the general characteristics across all. It is likely, for example, that cultural forms requiring several types of workers (e.g. film-making) fit closely with the model I have proposed. Those where the executant position is filled by a single individual, especially if a star (e.g. a successful novelist), are less likely to do so. In these circumstances, positions in the project team would probably be less defined and would overlap and even perhaps be unified. Another axis which might generate variations may revolve around 'serious' as opposed to 'popular' forms of production. In so far as members of a particular milieu mobilise this aesthetic distinction, those engaged in serious forms such as ballet, opera, classical music, progressive forms of jazz and rock, and so on, are likely to give credence to the idea of the artist as historically constituted, more so, perhaps than those in popular forms. Hence, notions concerning artistic authority and the right of the artist to contribute to the planning process are likely to be much stronger: in other words, one might expect to find differences of degree in the authority relations criss-crossing the project team, which modify its dynamics in production.

The corporate model constructed here is derived from institutional analysis which brackets the issue of agency on the part of the artists involved. In that sense, it represents a cross-sectioning of the specific historical and structural conditions confronting cultural workers when they are brought to the creative stage of production. There seems to be a strong case for using it as a structural basis for conducting historical studies examining how specific artists confront these conditions, the external social, psychological and aesthetic conditions of their agency, and the outcomes generated. Such an approach could be coupled with one which also focuses on formations; it might be interesting, for example, to examine how progressive jazz musicians, or journalists on a quality newspaper or newsmagazine, or novelists belonging to an emerging school of writing, handle their conditions of work – compared to, say, advertising copywriters and layout artists in a mainstream agency, or pop/rock session musicians of no great artistic ambition, or radio announcers on Top 40 radio stations. In other words, my corporate model of the objective conditions under which they can engage their agency would be usefully complimented by specific studies which examined how their artistic agency is realised, and its consequences.

In short, the corporate model provides both a beginning point and a point of comparison for a greater research emphasis in the sociology of culture aimed at examining the conditions of cultural production and the mediation of creativity by the structures in which artists are ensconced.

## 8.2 The Ideology Problematic and Textual Analysis

This political economy suggests that commodities produced under corporate conditions necessarily have certain elements of content; signs of stardom/stylishness are obvious examples. Not that I am suggesting that these imperatives account for all or even most of the signs deployed around an object, but they are certainly elements which must be present, and textual analysis needs to put these on its list of things to look for in contents – they are fundamental elements of the meanings each object is intended to construct. They will, of course, vary in historical and situational ways. Significant signs which might be appropriated in the creation and marketing processes differ across different markets, and even fairly established markets are crosscut by emerging significances. These relations too, might be usefully examined through this approach.

A more important implication is that it raises concerns about what textual analysts take to be their unit of analysis: it seems to me that there is a certain incompleteness about reading single texts. Corporate creation and marketing is geared to creating a whole appearance. The signs made to surround stars/styles, to function around a gamut of objects ranging from contents of the object itself to outside aspects such as the body, live appearances, packaging and publicity objects, and its setting in the publicity arena. To gain an adequate and comprehensive understanding of the meanings being constructed, this range of texts needs to be read and not just a single object, although meanings may certainly be crystalised at certain key points, such as the covers of recordings.

I am more reluctant to comment more generally on the issue of ideology, partly because I have grave doubts about the ontology associated with the term and the functionalist form of theorising it seems to presume, and partly because of the magnitude of the issue it represents. There are, however, two points worth making. One of its aspects relates to the question of ideological effects in production – in that sense, it is part of the class control problematic discussed by Murdock and Golding. This analysis looks at the imperatives flowing from capitalist relations operating in the production of texts, but there is nothing in my analysis which necessitates the production of particular contents. To some extent this is where specific analyses focusing on formations could be important. However, the structure of relations through which these objects are produced, articulates the structures of art with those of capital and makes them the primary forms of lived experience in the cultural workplace. To artists, professionalism and commercialism are made to seem like necessary ways of creative working. This is an ideological effect of the corporate form as it operates in the creative stage of production.

Second, the issue of ideological effects in consumption is complex and needs much more work. The semiotic turn has produced valuable outcomes, especially of a methodological kind. Unlike Garnham, I find their psychoanalytic versions interesting, but would argue that they represent sets of conditional theorisations awaiting an appropriate form of empirical investigation. Consumption practices must be investigated empirically, and not just the consumption of individual works, to see their ideological effects. Corporate production is geared towards the production of a whole appearance which ranges across various objects including the contents of the commodity and engages a particular mode of cultural interaction. Any ideological effects they generate or conditions they generate in the formation of consciousness – and in the absence of appropriate empirical studies these must be taken as conditional – are an effect of all. This connects to the comments I have made at various points throughout this work that the sociology of culture needs an adequate theory of consumption, one based on the idea of consumption as agency, as individual and/or collective appropriation of signs through a particular form of practice in the construction of a life(style). Theoretical and empirical explication of the conditions of consumption, along with further work in the political economy of culture are, to my mind, two of the most urgent tasks confronting a sociology of culture – becoming increasingly so, as more and more, cultural relations in modern society are turned into conditions of capitalist accumulation.

# References

(ABT) Australian Broadcasting Tribunal (1986): *Australian Music On Radio*, Sydney: Australian Government Printing Service.

Abercrombie, N., S. Hill, and B. Turner (1980): *The Dominant Ideology Thesis*, London: Allen and Unwin.

Adorno, T. (1978a): On Popular Music, in P. Davidson, R. Meyersohn, and E. Shils (eds), *Literary Theory, Culture and Mass Communication, Vol. 8, Theatre and Song*, Cambridge: Chadwyck-Healey, 197-230.

Adorno, T. (1978b): On the Fetish-Character in Music and the Regression of Listening, in A. Arato and E. Gebhart (eds), *The Essential Frankfurt School Reader*, London: Blackwell, 270-299.

Adorno, T. and M. Horkheimer (1979): *The Dialectic of Enlightenment*, London: Verso.

Althusser, L. (1979): *For Marx*, trans. by B. Brewster, London: Verso.

Arriaga, P. (1984): On Advertising: A Marxist Critique, *Media, Culture and Society*, 6, 53-64.

Asquith, I. (1978): 1780-1855, in G. Boyce *et al.* (eds), *Newspaper history: from the 17th century to the present day*, London: Constable, 98-116.

Australia Council (1983): *The Artist in Australia Today: Report of the Committee for the Individual Artists Inquiry*, North Sydney: Australia Council.

(B & T) Broadcasting and Television Weekly Editorial Staff (1984): *b & t yearbook*, Sydney: Greater Publications.

Baker, I. (1980a): The Gatekeeper Chain: A Two-Step Analysis of How Journalists Acquire and Apply Organisational News Priorities, in P. Edgar (ed), *The News in Focus: The Journalism of Exception*, South Melbourne: Macmillan, 136-158.

Baker, I. (1980b): Looking Inside the Media as an Institution: Studies on the News-Gathering Process, in P. Edgar (ed), *The News in Focus: The Journalism of Exception*, South Melbourne: Macmillan, 159-182.

Baker, M. (1979): *Marketing: An Introductory Text*, third edition, London: Macmillan.

Baker, M. (1985a): *Marketing: An Introductory Text*, fourth edition, London: Macmillan.

Baker, M. (1985b): *Marketing Strategy and Management*, London: Macmillan.

Baker, M. *et al.* (eds) (1983): *Marketing: Theory and Practice*, second edition, London: Macmillan.

Bannock, G. *et al.* (1984): *The Penguin Dictionary of Economics*, fourth edition, Harmondsworth: Penguin.

Baran, P. and P. Sweezy, (1966): *Monopoly Capital*, Harmondsworth: Penguin.

Barnard, A. (1983): Broadcasting in the 1920s: Government and Private Interest, *Prometheus*, Vol. 1, No. 1, 98-126.

Barnouw, E. (1966-1970): *A History of Broadcasting in the United States*, 3 volumes, New York: Oxford University Press.

Barr, T. (1985): *The Electronic Estate: New Communications Media and Australia*, Harmondsworth: Penguin.

Barthes, R. (1967): *Elements of Semiology*, trans. by A. Lavers and C. Smith, New York: Wang and Hill.

Barthes, R. (1977): *Image, Music, Text*, ed. and trans. by S. Heath, Glasgow: Fontana.

Baudrillard, J. (1975): *The Mirror of Production*, trans. by M. Poster, New York: Telos Press.

Beaud, P. *et al.* (1981): *Television As a Cultural Industry*, Paris: UNESCO.

Becker, H. (1982): *Art Worlds*, Berkeley: University of California Press.

Benjamin, W. (1973): *Illuminations*, Glasgow: Fontana.

Blackburn, R. (1972): The New Capitalism, in R. Blackburn (ed), *Ideology In Social Science: Readings in Critical Social Theory*, Glasgow: Fontana, 164-186.

Bhaskar, R. (1978): *A Realist Theory of Science*, second edition, Sussex: Harvester.

Bhaskar, R. (1979): On the Possibility of Social Scientific Knowledge and the Limits of Naturalism, in J. Mepham and D-H. Rubel (eds), *Issues in Marxist Philosophy: Vol III, Epistemology, Science, Ideology*, Sussex: Harvester, 107-139.

Bluestone, B. *et al.* (1981): *The Retail Revolution: Market Transformation, Investment and Labor in the Modern Department Store*, Boston: Auburn House Publishing.

Bonney, B. and H. Wilson (1983): *Australia's Commercial Media*, Melbourne: Macmillan.

Boreham, P., S. Clegg, and G. Dow (1986): The Institutional Management of Class Politics: Beyond the Labour Process and Corporatist Debates, in D. Knights and H. Willmott (eds), *Managing The Labour Process*, London: Gower, 186-210.

Bottomore, T. (1978): Marxism and Sociology, in T. Bottomore and R. Nisbet (eds), *A History of Sociological Analysis*, London: Heinemann Educational, 118-148.

Bourdieu, P. (1977): *Outline of a Theory of Practice*, trans. by R. Nice, Cambridge: Cambridge University Press.

Bourdieu, P. (1981): The production of belief: contribution to an economy of symbolic goods, *Media, Culture and Society*, 2, 225-254.

Bourdieu, P. (1984): *Distinction: A Social Critique of the Judgement of Taste*, trans. by R. Nice, Cambridge Mass.: Harvard University Press.

Bowman, D. (1988): *The Captive Press*, Ringwood: Penguin.

Boyce, G. *et al.* (eds) (1978): *Newspaper history: from the 17th century to the present day*, London: Constable.

Boyd-Barrett, O. (1977): Media Imperialism: towards an international framework for the analysis of media systems, in J. Curran *et al.* (eds), *Mass Communication and Society*, London: Edward Arnold, 116-135.

Boyd-Barrett, O. (1980): *The international news agencies*, London: Constable.

Bradley, D. (n.d.): The Cultural Study of Music, Occasional Paper No 61, Centre For Contemporary Cultural Studies, University of Birmingham: Birmingham.

Bramble, T. (1988): The Flexibility Debate: Industrial Relations and New Management Production Practices, *Labour and Industry*, Vol. 1, No. 2, 187-209.

Braverman, H. (1974): *Labor and Monopoly Capital: The Degradation of Work in the Twentieth Century*, New York: Monthly Review Press.

Briggs, A. (1961-1970): *The History of Broadcasting in the United Kingdom*, 4 volumes, London: Oxford University Press.

Brown, A. (1986): *Commercial Media in Australia: Economics, Ownership, Technology and Regulation*, St. Lucia: University of Queensland Press.

Burawoy, M. (1978): Toward a Marxist Theory of the Labour Process: Braverman and Beyond, *Politics and Society*, Vol. 8, No. 3-4, 247-312.

Burawoy, M. (1979): *Manufacturing Consent: Changes in the Labor Process Under Monopoly Capitalism*, Chicago: University of Chicago Press.

Burgess, R. (1984): *In the Field: An Introduction to Field Research*, London: George Allen and Unwin.

Burns, T. and G. Stalker (1961): *The Management of Innovation*, London: Tavistock.

Campbell, I. (1986): Workers and Capital: The Development of a Real Subsumption, in R. McQueen (ed), *Work, Technology and the Labour Process*, S.I.A. Working Papers, Vol. 1, No.2, 38-51.

Cassady, R. (1982): Monopoly in Motion Picture Production and Distribution: 1908-1915, in G. Kindem (ed), *The American Movie Industry: The Business of Motion Pictures*, Carbondale and Edwardsville: Southern Illinois University Press, 12-24.

Chapple, S. and R. Garofalo (1977): *Rock 'n' Roll is Here To Pay*, Chicago: Nelson-Hall.

Clegg, S. (1975): *Power, Rule and Domination*, London: Routledge and Kegan Paul.

Clegg, S., P. Boreham, and G. Dow (1986): *Class, Politics and the Economy*, London: Routledge and Kegan Paul.

Clegg, S. and D. Dunkerley (1980): *Organisation, Class and Control*, London: Routledge and Kegan Paul.

Clifford, D. (1981): Managing the Product Life Cycle, in R. Rothberg (ed), *Product Strategy and Product Innovation*, second edition, New York: The Free Press, 26-35.

Colletti, L. (1977): A Political and Philosophical Interview, in New Left Review (ed), *Western Marxism: A Critical Reader*, London: New Left Books, 315-350.

Collins, R., N. Garnham, and G. Locksley (1988): *The Economics of Television: The U.K. Case*, London: Sage Publications.

Connell, R. and T. Irving (1979): *Class Structure In Australian History*, Melbourne: Longman Cheshire.

Corrigan, P. (1983): Film Entertainment as Ideology and Pleasure: A Preliminary Approach to a History of Audiences, in J. Curran and V. Porter (eds), *British Cinema History*, Totowa New Jersey: Barnes and Noble, 24-35.

Coser, L. (1976): Publishers as Gatekeepers of Ideas, in P. Altbach S. and McVey (eds), *Perspectives on Publishing*, Massachusetts: Lexington Books, 17-25.

Coser, L., C. Kadushin, and W. Powell (1982): *Books: The Culture and Commerce of Publishing*, New York: Basic Books.

Cowie, P. (1971): *A Concise History of the Cinema*, 2 volumes, London: A. Zwemmer.

Crompton, R. and J. Gubbay (1977): *Economy and Class Structure*, London: Macmillan.

Cunningham, H. (1980): *Leisure In the Industrial Revolution 1780-1880*, New York: St. Martin's Press.

Curran, J. (1977): Capitalism and Control of the Press, 1800-1975, in J. Curran *et al.* (eds), *Mass Communication and Society*, London: Edward Arnold, 195-230.

Curwen, P. (1981): *The U.K. Publishing Industry*, Oxford: Pergammon House.

Dahrendorf, R. (1959): *Class and Class Conflict in Industrial Society*, Stanford: Stanford University Press.

Davis, D. (1966): *A History of Shopping*, London: Routledge and Kegan Paul.

Davis, H. and P. Walton (eds), (1983): *Language, Image, Media*, London: Blackwell.

Denisoff, S. (1975): *Solid Gold: The Popular Record Industry*, New Brunswick, New Jersey: Transaction Books.

Dermody, S. and E. Jacka (1987): *The Screening of Australia: Anatomy of a Film Industry*, Sydney: Currency Press.

Dessauer, J. (1974): *Book Publishing: What It Is, What It Does*, New York: R.R. Bower.

Dreier, P. (1976): Newsroom democracy and media monopoly: the dilemmas of workplace reform among professional journalists, *The Insurgent Sociologist*, Vol. VIII, No. II and III, 70-86.

Dumazedier, J. (1974): *The Sociology of Leisure*, trans. by M. McKensie, Amsterdam: Elsevier.

Dyer, G. (1982): *Advertising As Communication*, London: Methuen.

Eagleton, T. (1976): *Criticism and Ideology*, London: New Left Books.

Eagleton, T. (1983): *Literary Theory: An Introduction*, London: Basil Blackwell.

Eco, U. (1976): *A Theory of Semiotics*, Bloomington: University of Indiana.

Edwards, R. (1976): The Social Relations of Production At the Point of Production, *The Insurgent Sociologist*, Vol. VIII, No. II and III, 109-125.

Edwards, R. (1979): *Contested Terrain: The Transformation of the Workplace in the Twentieth Century*, London: Heinemann.

Elger, T. (1982): Braverman, capital accumulation and deskilling, in S. Wood (ed), *The Degradation of Work ? Skill, Deskilling and the Labour Process*, London: Hutchinson.

Elliott, P. (1972): *The Making of a Television Series: A Case Study in the Sociology of Culture*, London: Constable.

Elliott, P. (1977): Media Organisations and Occupations: an overview, in J. Curran *et al.* (eds), *Mass Communication and Society*, London: Edward Arnold, 142-173.

Elliott, P. (1978): Professional ideology and organisational change: the journalist since 1800, in G. Boyce *et al.* (eds), *Newspaper history: from the 17th century to the present day*, London: Constable, 172-191.

Erenberg, L. (1981): *Steppin' Out: New York Nightlife and the Transformation of American Culture 1890-1930*, Conneticutt: Greenwood Press.

Escarpit, R. (1966): *The Book Revolution*, London and Paris: Harrap and UN-ESCO.

Ewen, S. (1976): *Captains of Consciousness: Advertising and the Social Roots of the Consumer Culture*, New York: McGraw-Hill.

Featherstone, M. (1987): Lifestyle and Consumer Culture, *Theory, Culture and Society*, Vol. 4, 55-70.

Featherstone, M. (1988): In Pursuit of the Postmodern: An Introduction, *Theory, Culture and Society*, Vol. 5, 195-215.

Febvre, L. and H-J. Martin (1976): *The Coming of the Book: The Impact of Printing 1450-1800*, trans. by D. Gerard, London: New Left Books.

Fiske, J. (1982): *Introduction to Communication Studies*, London: Methuen.

Fowles, K. and N. Mills (eds) (1981): *Understanding Advertising: An Australian Guide*, revised edition, Kensington: NSW University Press.

Fox, S. (1984): *The Mirror-Makers: A History of American Advertising and Its Creators*, New York: Vintage Books.

Freedley, G. and J. Reeves (1968): *A History of the Theatre*, third revised edition, New York: Crown Publishers.

Frith, S. (1978): *The Sociology of Rock*, London: Constable.

Frith, S. (1988): *Music for Pleasure: Essays in the Sociology of Pop*, Cambridge: Polity Press.

Galbraith, J.K. (1970): *The Affluent Society*, second revised edition, Harmondsworth: Penguin.

Gallagher, M. (1982): Negotiation of control in media organisations and occupations, in M. Gurevitch *et al.* (eds), *Culture, Society and the Media*, London: Methuen, 151-173.

Gans, H. (1979): *Deciding What's News: A Study of CBS Evening News, NBC Nightly News, Newsweek and Time*, New York: Vintage Books.

Garnham, N. (1979): Contribution to a political economy of mass communication, *Media, Culture and Society*, 1, 123-146.

Garnham, N. (1987): Concepts of Culture: Public Policy and the Cultural Industries, *Cultural Studies*, 1, (1), 23-37.

Garnham, N. and R. Williams, (1980): Pierre Bourdieu and the sociology of culture: an introduction, *Media, Culture and Society*, 2, 209-223.

Gedin, P. (1977): *Literature in the Marketplace*, trans. by G. Bisset, London: Faber.

Gelmis, J. (1970): *The Film Director As Superstar*, New York: Anchor Press.

Giddens, A. (1979): *Central Problems in Social Theory*, London: Macmillan.

Giddens, A. (1981): *A Contemporary Critique of Historial Materialism, Vol. I, Power, Property and the State*, London: Macmillan.

Giddens, A. (1984): *The Constitution of Society: Outline of the Theory of Structuration*, London: Polity Press.

Gillett, C. (1971): *The Sound of the City*, London: Sphere Books.

Gitlin, T. (1978): Media Sociology: The Dominant Paradigm, *Theory and Society*, 6, 205-253.

Glasgow University Media Group (1976): *Bad News*, London: Routledge and Kegan Paul.

Glasgow University Media Group (1980): *More Bad News*, London: Routledge and Kegan Paul.

Godelier, M. (1972): Structure and Contradiction in *Capital*, in R. Blackburn (ed), *Ideology in Social Science: Readings in Critical Social Theory*, Glasgow: Fontana, 334-368.

Goffman, E. (1971): *Relations In Public*, Harmondsworth: Penguin.

Gombrich, E. (1975): *Art History and the Social Sciences*, London: Oxford University Press.

Gomery, D. (1982a): Hollywood, the National Recovery Administration, and the Question of Monopoly Power, in G. Kindem (ed), *The American Movie Industry: The Business of Motion Pictures*, Carbondale and Edwardsville: Southern Illinois University Press, 205-214.

Gomery, D. (1982b): The Movies Become Big Business: Publix Theatres and the Chain-Store Strategy, in G. Kindem (ed), *The American Movie Industry: The Business of Motion Pictures*, Carbondale and Edwardsville: Southern Illinois University Press, 104-116.

Grannis, C. (ed) (1957): *What Happens in Book Publishing*, New York: Columbia University Press.

Granovetter, M. (1985): Economic Action and Social Structure: The Problem of Embeddedness, *American Journal of Sociology*, Vol. 91, No. 3, 481-510.

Guback, T. (1982): Film As International Business: The Role of American Multinationals, in G. Kindem (ed), *The American Movie Industry: The Business of Motion Pictures*, Southern Illinois University Press: Carbondale and Edwardsville, 336-350.

Hadjinicolaou, N. (1978): *Art History and Class Struggle*, trans. by L. Asmal, London: Pluto.

Hall, S. (1976): *Supertoy: 20 Years of Australian Television*, Melbourne: Sun.

Hall, S. (1977): Culture, the Media and the 'Ideological Effect', in J. Curran *et al.* (eds), *Mass Communication and Society*, London: Edward Arnold, 315-348.

Hall, S. (1981): Notes on Deconstructing the Popular, in R. Samuel (ed), *People's History and Socialist Theory*, London: Routledge and Kegan Paul, 227-240.

Hall, S. *et al.* (1978): *Policing the Crisis: Mugging, the State, and Law and Order*, London: Macmillan

Harris, M. (1978): 1620-1780, in G. Boyce *et al.* (eds), *Newspaper history: from the 17th century to the present day*, London: Constable, 82-97.

Hartley, J. (1982): *Understanding News*, London: Methuen.

Hartnoll, P. (1967): *The Oxford Companion to the Theatre*, third edition, London: Oxford University Press.

Hartnoll, P. (1968): *A Concise History of the Theatre*, London: Thames and Hudson.

Harvey, D. (1982): *The Limits to Capital*, Oxford: Basil Blackwell.

Haug, W. (1986): *Critique of Commodity Aesthetics*, Cambridge: Polity Press.

Hauser, A. (1962a): *The Social History of Art, Vol. III, Rococco, Classicism and Romanticism*, London: Routledge and Kegan Paul.

Hauser, A. (1962b): *The Social History of Art, Vol. IV, Naturalism, The Film Age*, London: Routledge and Kegan Paul.

Hauser, A. (1982): *The Sociology of Art*, Chicago: University of Chicago Press.

Hebdige, D. (1979): *Subculture: The Meaning of Style*, London: Methuen.

Higgins, C. and P. Moss (1982): *Sounds Real: Radio In Everyday Life*, St Lucia: University of Queensland Press.

Hill, D. (1983): *A Writer's Rights*, Sydney: Australia and New Zealand Book Company.

Hirsch, P. (1970): *The Structure of the Popular Music Industry: An Examination of the Filtering Process by which Records are Pre-selected for Public Consumption*, Mimeo, Survey Research Centre, University of Michigan.

Hobsbawm, E. (1962): *The Age of Revolution 1789-1848*, New York: Mentor.

Jameson, F. (1984): Postmodernism, or the Cultural Logic of Late Capitalism, *New Left Review*, No. 146, 53-92.

Jefferies, J. (1954): *Retail Trading in Britain 1850-1950*, London: Cambridge University Press.

Jordan, M. (1983): Carry On...Follow that Stereotype, in J. Curran and V. Porter (eds), *British Cinema History*, Totowa New Jersey: Barnes and Noble, 312-327.

Keat, R, and J. Urry (1975): *Social Theory as Science*, London: Routledge and Kegan Paul.

Kent, J. (1983): *Out of the Bakelite Box: The Heyday of Australian Radio*, Sydney: Angus and Robertson.

Kindem, G. (ed) (1982a): *The American Movie Industry: The Business of of Motion Pictures*, Carbondale and Edwardsville: Southern Illinois University Press.

Kindem, G. (1982b): Hollywood's Movie Star System: A Historical Overview, in G. Kindem (ed), *The American Movie Industry: The Business of Motion Pictures*, Carbondale and Edwardsville: Southern Illinois University Press, 79-93.

Laing, D. (1978): *A Marxist Theory of Art*, Sussex: Harvester.

Laing, D. (1985): *One Chord Wonders: Power and Meaning in Punk Rock*, Milton Keynes: Open University Press.

Lane, M. (1970): Books and Their Publishers, in J. Tunstall (ed), *Media Sociology*, London: Constable, 239-251.

Lane, M. (1980): *Books and Publishers: Commerce Against Culture in Postwar Britain*, Lexington Mass.: Lexington Books.

Lash, S. and J. Urry (1985): *The End of Organised Capitalism*, Cambridge: Polity.

Laurenson, D. (1971): The Writer and Society, in D. Laurenson and A. Swingewood, *The Sociology of Literature*, London: Granada, 91-166.

Laurenson, D. and A. Swingewood (1971): *The Sociology of Literature*, London: Granada.

Layton, R. (ed) (1973): *Australian Marketing Projects*, Sydney: Hoover Awards for Marketing National Committee.

Layton, R. (ed) (1980): *Australian Marketing Projects*, Sydney: Hoover Awards for Marketing National Committee.

Leavis, Q. (1979): *Fiction and the Reading Public*, Harmondsworth: Peregrine.

Lee, A. (1978): 1855-1914, in G. Boyce *et al.* (eds), *Newspaper history: from the 17th century to the present day,* London: Constable, 117-129.

Lefebvre, H. (1971): *Everyday Life in the Modern World,* trans. by S. Rabinovitch, London: Allen Lane Penguin.

Lever-Tracy, C. (1988): The Flexibility Debate: Part Time Work, *Labour and Industry,* Vol. 1, No. 2, 210-241.

Lilien, G. and P. Kotler (1983): *Marketing Decision-Making: A Model-Building Approach,* New York: Harper and Row.

Litman, B. (1982): The Economics of the Television Market for Theatrical Movies, in G. Kindem (ed), *The American Movie Industry: The Business of Motion Pictures,* Carbondale and Edwardsville: Southern Illinois University Press, 308-321.

Littler, C. (1982): *The Development of the Labour Process in Capitalist Societies,* London: Heinemann Educational.

Littler, C. and G. Salaman, (1982): Bravermania and Beyond: Recent Theories of the Labour Process, *British Journal of Sociology,* 16, (2), 251-267.

Lofland, J. (1971): *Analysing Social Settings: A Guide to Qualitative Observations and Analysis,* Belmont Calif.: Wadsworth Publishing.

Logan, N. and B. Woffinden (1973): *The New Musical Express Book of Rock,* London: Star Books.

MacDonald, J. (1979): *Don't Touch That Dial! Radio Programming in American Life, 1920-1960,* Chicago: Nelson-Hall.

Macgowen, K. (1965): *Behind The Screen: The History and Techniques of the Motion Picture,* New York: Delacorte Press.

Madge, J. (1953): *The Tools of Social Science,* London: Longman.

Mandel, E. (1968): *Marxist Economic Theory,* trans. by B. Pierce, London: Merlin Press.

Mandel, E. (1976): Introduction, in K. Marx, *Capital, Vol. III,* trans. by D. Fernbach, Harmondsworth: Penguin, 9-90.

Mandel, E. (1978a): *Late Capitalism,* London: Verso.

Mandel, E. (1978b): Introduction, in K. Marx, *Capital, Vol. II,* trans. by D. Fernbach, Harmondsworth: Penguin, 11-79.

Marcuse, H. (1972): *One Dimensional Man: Studies in the Ideology of Advanced Industrial Society,* London: Abacus.

Marglin, S. (1974): What Do Bosses Do? The Origins and Functions of Hierarchy in Capitalist Production, *Review of Radical Political Economics,* Vol. 6, No. 2, 60-112.

Marshall, A. (1983): *Changing the Word: The Printing Industry In Transition,* London: Comedia Publishing.

Marx, K. (1954): *Capital: A Critique of Political Economy, Vol. I,* Moscow: Progress Publishers.

Marx, K. (1956): *Capital: A Critique of Political Economy, Vol. II,* Moscow: Progress Publishers.

Marx, K. (1959): *Capital: A Critique of Political Economy, Vol. III,* Moscow: Progress Publishers.

Marx, K. (1973): *Grundrisse*, trans. by R. Livingstone and G. Benton, Harmondsworth: Pelican.

Marx, K. (1976): Results of the Immediate Process of Production', *Capital, Vol. I* (Appendix), trans. by D. Fernbach, Harmondsworth: Penguin.

Marx, K. and F. Engels (1976): *The German Ideology*, Moscow: Progress Publishers.

Mattelart, A. (1979): *Multinational Corporations and the Control of Culture*, Sussex: Harvester.

Mayer, H. (1964): *The Press In Australia*, Sydney: Landsdowne Press.

McCarthey, E. *et al.* (eds) (1987): *Readings and Cases in Basic Marketing*, fifth edition, Homewood Illinois: Urwin.

McQuail, D. (1983): *Mass Communication Theory: An Introduction*, London: Sage.

McQueen, H. (1977): *Australia's Media Monopolies*, Melbourne: Widescope.

McQueen, H. (1979): *The Black Swan of Trespass*, Sydney: Alternative Publishing Cooperative.

Melbourne Age, The (1982), *The Age Lifestyle Study*, Melbourne: David Syme and Co.

Mepham, J. (1979): From the *Grundrisse* to *Capital*: The Making of Marx's Method, in J. Mepham and D-H. Rubel (eds), *Issues in Marxist Philosophy, Vol. 1, Dialectics and Method*, Sussex: Harvester Press, 145-173.

Miège, B. (1979): The cultural commodity, *Media, Culture and Society*, 1, 297-311.

Miliband, R. (1973): *The State In Capitalist Society: The Analysis of the Western System of Power*, London: Quartet Books.

Mills, S. (1986): *The New Machine Men*, Ringwood: Penguin.

Moran, A. (1982): *Making a TV Series: The 'Bellamy' Project*, Sydney: Currency Press.

Moran, A. (1985): *Images and Industry: Television Drama Production In Australia*, Sydney: Currency Press.

Morley, D. (1980): *The 'Nationwide' Audience: Structure and Decoding*, London: British Film Institute.

Mundy, G. (1982): 'Free Enterprise' or 'Public Service' ? The Origins of Broadcasting in the U.S., U.K. and Australia, *Australia and New Zealand Journal of Sociology*, Vol. 18, No. 3, 279-301.

Murdock, G. (1978): Blindspots about Western Marxism: a reply to Dallas Smythe, *Canadian Journal of Political and Social Theory*, Vol. 2, No. 2, 109-119.

Murdock, G. (1982): Large corporations and the control of the communications industries, in M. Gurevitch *et al.* (eds), *Culture, Society and the Media*, London: Methuen, 118-150.

Murdock, G. and P. Golding (1974): For A Political Economy of Mass Communication, in R. Miliband and J. Saville (eds), *Socialist Register 1973*, London: Merlin Press, 205-234.

Murdock, G. and P. Golding, (1977): Capitalism, Communication and Class Relations, in J. Curran *et al.* (eds), *Mass Communication and Society*, London: Edward Arnold, 12-43.

Murdock, G. and P. Golding (1978): The structure, ownership and control of the press, 1914-76, in G. Boyce *et al.* (eds), *Newspaper history: from the 17th century to the present day*, London: Constable, 130-148.

Murdock, G. and P. Golding (1979): Ideology and the mass media: the question of determination, in M. Barrett *et al.* (eds), *Ideology and Cultural Production*, New York: St Martin's Press, 198-224.

Murray, R. (1988): Life After Henry (Ford), *Marxism Today*, October, 8-13.

Music Board of the Australia Council, (1987): *The Australian Music Industry: An Economic Evaluation*, Sydney: Australia Council.

Myers, K. (1983): Understanding advertisers, in H. Davis and P. Walton (eds), *Language, Image, Media*, London: Blackwell, 205-223.

Nicholson Broadcasting Services (1975/76): 6PR – Gentle On Your Mind – Marketing Report, in R. Layton (ed), *Australian Marketing Projects*, Sydney: Hoover Awards for Marketing, 234-265.

Nicolaus, M. (1973): Foreword, in K. Marx, *Grundrisse*, Harmondsworth: Pelican, 7-63.

Packard, V. (1957): *The Hidden Persuaders*, Harmondsworth: Penguin.

Pendakur, M. (1982): Cultural Dependency in Canada's Feature Film Industry, in G. Kindem (ed), *The American Movie Industry: The Business of Motion Pictures*, Carbondale and Edwardsville: Southern Illinois University Press, 351-360.

Penn, R. and H. Scattergood (1985): Deskilling or enskilling?: an empirical investigation of recent theories of the labour processs, *British Journal of Sociology*, Vol. 36, No. 4, 611-630.

Perrow, C. (1979): *Complex Organisations: A Critical Essay*, second edition, Glenview Illinois: Scott Foresman.

Pichaske, D. (1979): *A Generation in Motion: Popular Music and Culture in the Sixties*, New York: Schirmer.

Powdermaker, H. (1950): *Hollywood, the Dream Factory: An Anthropologist Looks At the Movie-Makers*, Boston: Little and Brown.

Ravage, J, (1978): *Television: The Director's Viewpoint*, Boulder: Westview Press.

Raynor, H. (1972): *A Social History of Music: From the Middle Ages To Beethoven*, New York: Taplinger Publishing.

Raynor, H. (1976): *Music and Society Since 1815*, New York: Taplinger Publishing.

Rickword, E. (1979): The Social Setting (1780-1839), in B. Ford (ed), *From Blake To Byron: Vol. 5, The Pelican Guide to English Literature*, revised edition, Harmondsworth: Penguin, 11-30.

Rose, H. and S. Rose (1969): *Science and Society*, Harmondsworth: Penguin.

Rossiter, J. and L. Percy (1987): *Advertising and Promotion Management*, New York: McGraw-Hill.

Ryan, B. (1981): Commercial Radio and Public Accountability, in B. Dwyer (ed), *Broadcasting In Australia: Today's Issues and the Future*, Canberra, CCE Australian National University, 145-151.

Saussure, F. de (1974): *Course In General Linguistics*, trans. by W. Baskin, Glasgow: Fontana.

Sayer, A. (1984): *Method in Social Science: A Realist Approach*, London: Hutchinson.

Sayer, D. (1979): Science as Critique: Marx vs Althusser, in J. Mepham and D-H. Rubel (eds), *Issues in Marxist Philosophy, Vol. III, Epistemology, Science, Ideology*, Sussex: Harvester, 27-54.

Sayer, D. (1983): *Marx's Method: Ideology and Critique in Capital*, second edition, Brighton: Harvester Press.

Schicke, C. (1974): *Revolution in Sound*, Boston: Little and Brown.

Schiller, H. (1969): *Mass Communication and the American Empire*, Boston: Boston Press.

Schlesinger, P. (1978): *Putting Reality Together*, London: Constable.

Schmoller, H. (1974): The Paperback Revolution, in A. Briggs (ed), *Essays in the History of Publishing*, London: Longman,

Scholes, P. (1955): *The Oxford Companion To Music*, London: Oxford University Press.

Shepherd, J. (1987): Towards a sociology of musical styles, in L. White (ed), *Lost in Music: Culture, Style and the Musical Event*, Sociological Review Monograph, 34, 56-76.

Smith, A. (1978): The long road to objectivity and back again: the kinds of truth we get in journalism, in G. Boyce, *et al.* (eds), *Newspaper history: from the 17th century to the present day*, London: Constable, 153-171.

Smythe, D. (1977): Communications: Blindspot of Western Marxism, *Canadian Journal of Political and Social Theory*, Vol. 1, No. 3, 1-27.

Sontag, S. (1979): *On Photography*, Harmondsworth: Penguin.

Souther, G. (1981): *Company of Heralds*, Melbourne: Melbourne University Press.

Staiger, J. (1982): Dividing Labour for Production Control: Thomas Ince and the Rise of the Studio System, in G. Kindem (ed), *The American Movie Industry: The Business of Motion Pictures*, Carbondale and Edwardsville: Southern Illinois University Press, 94-103.

Stanislavski, C. (1967): *An Actor Prepares*, trans. by E. Hapgood, Harmondsworth: Penguin.

Stark, D. (1980): Class Struggle and the Transformation of the Labour Process: A Relational Approach, *Theory and Society*, 9, 89-130.

Steinberg, S. (1955): *Five Hundred Years of Printing*, Harmondsworth: Penguin.

Stephen, A. (1981): Agents of Consumerism: The Organisation of the Australian Advertising Industry, 1918-1938, in J. Allen *et al.* (eds), *Media Interventions*, Liechardt: Intervention Publications, 78-96.

Sterling, C. and T. Haight (1978): *The Mass Media: Aspen Guide to Communication Industry Trends*, New York: Praeger Publishers.

Stock Exchange Research, (1983/84): *The Stock Exchange Financial and Profitability Study: Service Sector*, Sydney: Stock Exchange Research Pty Ltd.

Stockbridge, S. (1985): New Representations of Popular Music: Has Video Killed the Radio Star?, paper presented to SAANZ Annual Conference, University of Queensland, Brisbane.

Stockbridge, S. (1988): The Pay-for-Play Debate: Australian Television versus the Record Companies, and the Myth of 'Public Benefit', paper presented at *Rock Music: Politics and Policy*, Public Seminar, 20 August, Griffith University, Brisbane.

Stokes, G. (1986): The Sixties, in E. Ward, G. Stokes and K. Tucker, *Rock Of Ages: The* Rolling Stone *History of Rock and Roll*, New York: Rolling Stone Press/Summit Books, 290-465.

Stuart, F. (1982): The Effects of Television on the Motion Picture Industry: 1948-1960, in G. Kindem (ed), *The American Movie Industry: The Business of Motion Pictures*, Carbondale and Edwardsville: Southern Illinois University Press, 257-307.

Swingewood, A, (1977): *The Myth of Mass Culture*, London: Macmillan.

Tebbel, J. (1981): *A History of Book Publishing in the United States, Volume IV, The Great Change, 1940-1980*, New York: R.R. Bower.

Thompson, E. (1968): *The Making of the English Working Class*, revised edition, Harmondsworth: Penguin.

Thompson, P. (1975): *The Edwardians: The Remaking of British Society*, London: Weidenfeld and Nicolson.

3AK Melbourne Broadcasters, (1973): A New Station Image, in R. Layton (ed), *Australian Marketing Projects*, Sydney: Hoover Awards for Marketing, 179-190.

Throsby, C. and G. Withers (1979): *The Economics of the Performing Arts*, Melbourne: Edward Arnold.

Towers, T. (1976): *Electronics in Music*, London: Butterworths.

Tuchman, G. (1978): *Making News: A Study in the Construction of Reality*, New York: Free Press.

Tucker, K. (1986): The Seventies and Beyond, in E. Ward, G Stokes and K. Tucker, *Rock Of Ages: The* Rolling Stone *History of Rock and Roll*, New York: Rolling Stone Press/Summit Books, 467-621.

Tudor, A. (1974): *Image and Influence: Studies in the Sociology of Film*, London: George Allen and Unwin.

Tulloch, J. (1982): *Australian Cinema: Industry, Narrative and Meaning*, Sydney: George Allen and Unwin.

Tulloch, J. and Moran, A. (1986): *A Country Practice: 'Quality Soap'*, Sydney: Currency Press.

Tunstall, J. (1971): *Journalists At Work: Specialist Correspondents: their news organisations, news sources and competitor-colleagues*, London: Constable.

Tunstall, J. (1977): *The Media Are American: Anglo-American Media in the World*, London: Constable.

Turner, E. (1965): *The Shocking History of Advertising*, revised edition, Harmondsworth: Penguin.

Umiker-Sebeok, J. (ed) (1987): *Marketing and Semiotics: New Directions in the Study of Signs for Sale*, Berlin: Mouton de Gruyter.

Volosinov, V. (1973): *Marxism and the Philosophy of Language*, trans. by L. Matejka and I. Titunik, New York: Seminar Press.

Walker, R. (1973): *The Magic Spark: 50 Years of Radio in Australia*, Melbourne: Hawthorne Press.

Walvin, J. (1978): *Leisure and Society 1830-1950*, London: Longman.

Watt, I. (1972): *The Rise of the Novel*, Harmondsworth: Pelican.

Weber, M. (1970): *From Max Weber: Essays in Sociology*, trans. and ed. by H. Gerth and C. Wright Mills, London: Routledge and Kegan Paul.

Weber, M. (1976): *The Protestant Ethic and the Spirit of Capitalism*, second edition, London: Allen and Unwin.

Weber, W. (1975): *Music and the Middle Class*, New York: Holmes and Meier.

Wellek, R. and A. Warren (1963): *Theory of Literature*, third edition, Harmondsworth: Peregrine.

Wenner, J. (ed) (1987): *20 Years of Rolling Stone: What a Long, Strange Trip It's Been*, Sydney: Fontana.

Whitney, S. (1982): Antitrust Policies and the Motion Picture Industry, in G. Kindem (ed), *The American Movie Industry: The Business of Motion Pictures*, Carbondale and Edwardsville: Southern Illinois University Press, 161-204.

Wild, P. (1979): Recreation in Rochdale, 1900-40, in J. Clarke *et al.* (eds), *Working Class Culture: Studies in history and theory*, London: Hutchinson, 140-160.

Williams, R. (1963): *Culture and Society 1780-1950*, Harmondsworth: Penguin.

Williams, R. (1965): *The Long Revolution*, Harmondsworth: Penguin.

Williams, R. (1976a): *Keywords*, Glasgow: Fontana.

Williams, R. (1976b): *Television: Technology and Cultural Form*, Glasgow: Fontana.

Williams, R. (1977): *Marxism and Literature*, London: Oxford University Press.

Williams, R. (1980): Means of Communication as Means of Production, in *The Problems of Materialism and Culture*, London: New Left Books.

Williams, R. (1981): *Culture*, London: Fontana.

Williamson, J. (1978): *Decoding Advertisements*, London: Marion Boyers.

Willis, P. (1983): *Learning To Labour: How working class kids get working class jobs*, Hampshire: Gower Publishing.

Wilmshurst, J. (1984): *The Fundamentals and Practice of Marketing*, London: Heinemann.

Windschuttle, K. and E. Windschuttle (eds) (1981): *Fixing the News: Critical Perspectives on the Australian Media*, North Ryde: Cassell.

Wolff, J. (1981): *The Social Production of Art*, London: Macmillan.

Wolff, J. (1983): *Aesthetics and the Sociology of Art*, London: Allen and Unwin.

Wright, E. (1979): *Class, Crisis and the State*, London: Verso.

Wright, E. (1985): *Classes*, London: Verso.

Wright, E. (1987): Reflections on *Classes*, *The Berkeley Journal of Sociology*, Vol. 32, 19-49.

Other textual references:
*Australia and New Zealand Journal of Sociology*, Vol. 12, No. 3.
*Australian Society*, September, 1989.
*b&t advertising, marketing and media weekly*, 3 February, 1983.
*Cinema Papers*, March, 1987.
*Marketing*, May, 1989.
*Marxism Today*, October, 1988.
*The Australian*, 6 June, 1984.
*The Australian*, 31 June, 1985.
*The Australian*, 21 May, 1985.
*The Bulletin*, 5 February, 1985.

*The Independent Monthly*, August, 1989.
*The National Times*, 4-10 October, 1985.
*The National Times*, 28 December-4 January, 1985.
*The National Times*, 8-14 March, 1985.
*The National Times*, 21-27 June, 1985.
*The National Times on Sunday*, 7 December, 1986.
*The Sunday Mail*, 1 November, 1985.
*The Sunday Mail*, 7 November, 1987.
*The Sunday Mail*, 29 February, 1988.
*The Sunday Mail*, 13 March, 1988.
*The Sunday Mail*, 8 May, 1988.
*The Sydney Morning Herald*, 19 August, 1989.
*The Weekend Australian*, 25-26 March, 1985.
*The Weekend Australian*, 6-7 July, 1985.
*The Weekend Australian*, 21-22 December, 1985.
*The Weekend Australian*, 22-23 November, 1986.
*The Weekend Australian*, 23-24 January, 1987.
*The Weekend Australian*, 4-5 July, 1987.
*The Weekend Australian*, 25-26 July, 1987.
*The Weekend Australian*, 6-7 February, 1988.
*The Weekend Australian*, 5-6 March, 1988.
*The Weekend Australian*, 12-13 March, 1988.
*The Weekend Australian*, 19-20 March, 1988.
*The Weekend Australian*, 26-27 March, 1988.
*The Weekend Australian*, 2-3 April, 1988.
*The Weekend Australian*, 25-26 July, 1988.
*The Weekend Australian Magazine*, 19-20 March, 1988.
*The Weekend Australian Magazine*, 8-9 July, 1989.
*Time*, 12 February, 1973.
*Time*, 28 September, 1981.
*The Times on Sunday,* 31 January, 1988.

# Index

# de Gruyter Studies in Organization

An international series by internationally known authors presenting current research in organization

Vol. 27
**Witold Kieżun**
## Management in Socialist Countries
**USSR and Central Europe**
1991. 15.5 x 23 cm. XIV, 375 pages. Cloth.   ISBN 3-11-010670-1; 0-89925-166-8 (U.S.)

In his book the author, former chairman of the Praxiology Institute at the Polish Academy of Sciences and Professor at the Universities of Warsaw and Montreal, provides a profound organizational analysis of the sources, development, attempts to improve, and ultimate failure of the Marxist-Leninist management system.

Vol. 28
**Gerald E. Caiden**
## Administrative Reform Comes of Age
1991. XII, 347 pages. Cloth.   ISBN 3-11-012895-0; 0-89925-883-6 (U.S.)
Paperback.   ISBN 3-11-012645-1; 0-89925-743-7 (U.S.)

The book contains case studies of reform campaigns around the world. Special attention is given to current attempts to transform bureaucratic centralism in the East Bloc into market socialism, to overhaul the mixed welfare state in the West, and the seemingly fruitless attempts to invigorate public sector administration in the Third World.

Vol. 29
**Mark Dodgson**
## The Management of Technological Learning
**Lessons from a Biotechnology Company**
1991. XIV, 147 pages. With 24 figures. Cloth.   ISBN 3-11-012706-7; 0-89925-768-2 (U.S.)

This book, based on a study of Europe's leading technology firm, examines why new, smaller firms can act more quickly to commercialise scientific discoveries and thus have competitive advantages over large multi-national companies.

## WALTER DE GRUYTER · BERLIN · NEW YORK

Genthiner Strasse 13, D-1000 Berlin 30, Tel. (0 30) 2 60 05-0, Fax 2 60 05-2 51
200 Saw Mill River Road, Hawthorne, N.Y. 10532, Tel. (914) 747-0110, Fax 747-1326